THAILAND'S TURN

THAILAND'S TURN

Profile of a New Dragon

Elliott Kulick and Dick Wilson

St. Martin's Press
New York

First published in the United States of America 1992
First paperback edition 1994
Printed in the United States of America

ISBN 0-312-07952-4 (cloth)
ISBN 0-312-12188-1 (paper)

Library of Congress Cataloging-in-Publication Data

Kulick, Elliott
    Thailand's turn : profile of a new dragon / by Elliott Kulick and Dick
    Wilson.
        p.   cm.
    Includes index.
    ISBN 0-312-07952-4 (cloth)
    ISBN 0-312-12188-1 (paper)
    1. Thailand.   I. Wilson, Dick, 1928-   . II. Title.
DS563.5.E45   1992
959.3—dc20   91-45049
                                                          CIP

To
Brasenose
place of Anglo-American encounters
and
Thailand
site of Asian collaborations

CONTENTS

Who's Who: The Main Characters ix

Glossary of Thai Words and Names Used in the Book xi

Definitions xii

Acknowledgments xiii

Prologue: The Key Player on the Thai Chessboard xv

Introduction: The Asia That Might Have Been 1

  1. **The Military Mission:** Army Boots on the Brake 7

  2. **Politics the Thai Way:** Zigzag Democracy 27

  3. **The Monarchy:** Royal Rainmaker 53

  4. **The Changing Thai Personality:** Behind the Smile 65

  5. **Those Chinese Genes:** A Triumph of Assimilation 83

  6. **Thai Buddhism:** The Response to Modernity 97

  7. **A Fast Growth Economy:** Consolidating for
      Another Spurt 107

  8. **The Price of Economic Success:** Inequality,
      Pollution and AIDS 121

  9. **Farm and Factory:** A Giant in the Making 131

 10. **Continental Diplomacy:** The Hub of Southeast Asia 149

 11. **Dealing with the Bigger Powers:** The Crocodile
      or the Whale? 163

Conclusion: Alone and Free at Last 175

Epilogue: Yuppies Brave the Bullet 183

Notes 189

Select Bibliography 199

Index 201

WHO'S WHO? THE MAIN CHARACTERS

Anand Panyarachun—Prime Minister from March 1991 to April 1992; and re-appointed June 1992.

King Ananda Mahidol—Rama VIII (reigned 1935-46). Bhumiphol's elder brother.

Arthit Kamlang-ek—Supreme Commander of the Armed Forces 1983-86, Deputy Prime Minister 1990-91.

King Bhumiphol Adulyadej—Rama IX of Chakri dynasty (reigned 1946-).

Chalerm Yubamrung—Police Captain, Minister under Chatichai government 1988-91.

Chamlong Srimuang—Major General, elected Governor of Bangkok 1985-92. Founder of Palang Dharma political party.

Chaovalit Yongchaiyudh—Supreme Commander of Armed Forces 1986-88, Deputy Prime Minister and Defense Minister 1988. Founder of New Aspiration Party.

Chatichai Choonhavan—Prime Minister 1988-91.

King Chulalongkorn—Rama V (reigned 1868-1910).

Dhanin Chearavanont—President of Charoen Pokphand Group.

Kriangsak Chomanan—General. Prime Minister 1977-80.

Kukrit Pramoj—Prime Minister 1975-76. Founder of Social Action Party.

Manoon Rupkachorn—Major General, leader of "Young Turks" army faction. Attempted a coup d'état in 1981.

Mechai Viravaidhya—family planning and AIDS prevention activist. Member of the Prem and Anand governments.

King Mongkut—Rama IV (reigned 1851-68), the first great modernizing King.

Phibul Songkram—Field Marshal and military dictator who dominated Thai politics for a quarter century after 1932 revolution.

King Prajadhipok—Rama VII (reigned 1925-35).

Praphas Charusathien—joint dictator 1963-73. Ousted by 1973 student revolution.

Prasert Sapsunthorn—Communist defector whose socialistic ideas were influential in Thai army in late 1970s.

Prem Tinsulanond—Supreme Commander of Armed Forces, Prime Minister 1980-88.

Pridi Panomyong—left-wing leader of the 1932 revolution, assisted "Free Thai" movement during the Second World War. Prime Minister in 1946.

Puey Ungpakorn—economist, set Thailand's economic course in 1960s.

Sarit Thanarat—Field Marshal and military dictator of Thailand 1957-63.

Seni Pramoj—Prime Minister 1976, leader of pro-Allied "Free Thais" in Second World War.

Queen Sirikit—wife of King Bhumiphol, whom she married in 1950.

Princess Sirindhorn—second daughter of King Bhumiphol.

Sophonpanich—Thai Chinese family controlling the Bangkok Bank.

Suchinda Kraprayoon—General and leader of 1991 coup d'état. Prime Minister April-June 1992.

Sulak Sivaraksa—lawyer, writer and social critic.

Sunthorn Kongsompong—General and leader of 1991 coup d'état.

Thanin Kraivixien—Prime Minister 1976-77.

Thanom Kittikachorn—Military dictator 1963-73, forced out by 1973 student revolution.

Crown Prince Vajiralongkorn—only son and heir of King Bhumiphol.

King Vajiravudh—Rama VI (reigned 1910-25).

GLOSSARY OF THAI WORDS
AND NAMES USED IN THE BOOK

Ayutthaya—old Thai capital destroyed by Burmese in 1767.

baht—basic unit of currency in Thailand. 25 baht = 1 U.S. dollar (1992).

Charoen Pokphand (CP) Group—Thai agro-industrial grouping.

Chart Thai—political party of Chatichai Choonhavan.

Dhammakaya—"Body of Truth" Buddhist sect.

dharma—collective name for the Buddhist teachings.

farang—foreigner.

Isarn—the Northeast of Thailand mostly populated by Lao-speaking peoples.

karma—the Buddhist concept of the consequences of past moral actions becoming manifest in one's present and future circumstances.

Palang Dharma—"force of dharma"—political party founded by Major General Chamlong Srimuang.

Phra—a title commonly used to address a Buddhist monk.

Samakkee Tham—"unity in virtue"—political party founded with military backing in 1991.

sangha—organization of the Buddhist establishment.

Santi Asoke—"Peace and No Sorrow" Buddhist sect, political and strictly vegetarian.

sanuk—loosely translates as "fun."

Suan Mokh—"Garden of Liberation" Buddhist sect.

wat— Buddhist temple.

DEFINITIONS

ASEAN—Association of Southeast Asian Nations (Brunei, Indonesia, Malaysia, Philippines, Singapore and Thailand), founded 1967.

dollar—U.S. dollar in all cases.

Gross Domestic Product (GDP)—the total value of national goods and services produced in one year. It differs from **Gross National Product** in excluding income in the form of repatriated profits from foreign investments.

Indochina—used in this book in its original meaning of the countries between India and China, i.e., Burma, Cambodia, Laos, Vietnam and Thailand.

NIEs—Newly Industrialized Economies, formerly known as Newly Industrialized Countries (NICs)—the four "Little Dragons" or "Asian Tigers": Hong Kong, Singapore, South Korea and Taiwan.

Sino-Thai—people of mixed Chinese and Thai ancestry.

Southeast Asia—used in this book as meaning countries either in Indochina or member nations of ASEAN.

ACKNOWLEDGMENTS

We wrote this book to introduce the new Thailand, where fast economic growth now builds upon ancient tropical charm.

Our debts are numerous. One of us has visited Thailand about seven or eight times, on average, every year since 1978. The other has averaged twice a year, spread over the years since 1958. The numerous professional friendships thus built up gave us the initial confidence for this venture. We spent four months researching and interviewing in Thailand, partly before the February 1991 coup and partly after it. This series of almost a hundred interviews, culminating in a royal audience of almost three hours with His Majesty the King, forms a major basis for our book.

We cannot inflict on our readers the full list of persons whom we interviewed, but very special thanks are due to:

Ajarn Saneh; Amnuay Viravan; Anand Panyarachun; Anek Srisanit; Arsa Sarasin; Bhichai Rattakul; Phra Bodirak; Chai-Anan Samudavanija; Chalerm Yubamrung; Chamlong Srimuang; Charit Tingsabadh; Charn Sophonpanich; Chayachoke Chulasiriwongs; Chirayu Issarangkun na Ayuthaya; Chongsarit Dhanasobhon; Chote Sophonpanich; Chupong Kanchanalak; Dhanin Chearavanont; Direk Patmasiriwat; Kasem Kasemsri; Khien Theeravit; Krirkkiat Phipatseritham; M.R. Kukrit Pramoj; David Lyman; Mechai Viravaidya; Patya Saihoo; Prasit Tansuvan; Prok Amranand; Saeksan Prasertkul; M.R. Seni Pramoj; Snoh Unakul; Somsakdi Xuto; Suchit Bunbongkorn; Sukhumbhand Paribatra; Sulak Sivaraksa; Sumitr Pitiphat; David Tarrant; Thanat Khoman; Theh Chongkhadikij; Thirayuth Boonmee; Tongroj Onchan; Derek Tonkin; Peter Mytri Ungphakorn; Vichit Suraphongchai; Vijit Supanit; and Bob Wallace.

We are also grateful to Yvan Cohen, a Thai speaker, for his assistance in interviewing and research in Bangkok, and Tobias Newland for his patient contribution in processing the information in London.

Spellings of Thai names and words can vary when transliterated into English; we have mostly followed the English spellings preferred by each person and apologize for any lapses in consistency.

Prologue:
The Key Player on the
Thai Chessboard

A lone slight figure stood stiffly in the dim light of the Chitralada Palace receiving room as we stepped in from the double stairway. His left hand was lifted as if to clutch the hilt of a sword. King Bhumiphol Adulyadej, Lord of Life, Master of the Octagonal Throne, Possessor of the Twenty-four Golden Umbrellas, ninth of the kings of the formidable Chakri dynasty and by common consent the most influential figure in Thailand, posed in the attitude of one of his own royal family portraits gazing down from the walls—King Mongkut, who had single-handedly launched the modern Thai state in the nineteenth century, or his son King Chulalongkorn.

The king's red tie and blue lounge suit, roomy around the chest, hardly smacked of royalty. There was no sword. Could this slim, almost boyish figure, ears sticking out from an immobile face, be the strongest political force in the nation? Standing alone so tensely in his receiving room, the king radiated no blaze of power. For that matter, his residence was hardly grand.

The palace lay hidden from the general gaze by vast lawns and shrubberies at the edge of the city of Bangkok. Rounding the trees at the end of a long drive from the road, we came upon a wedding cake in mustard-ochre, a turn-of-the-century Mediterranean confection, an unexpectedly modest house for a monarch, with only 45 rooms.

The entrance was through anterooms with romantic European paintings and giant pairs of ivory tusks. There the Director of the Royal Household, much bemedaled and epauletted over spotless white ducks, entertained us with light conversation. We asked him about the king's white elephants, which are kept in stables behind the palace, to bring good luck despite the colossal feeding bills. White ducks pointed airily over his shoulder through the window behind him.

"We have six of them at the moment," he said, rather in the manner of a New York tycoon admitting to six Cadillacs in the garage. "They are not really white," he went on. "They only have pinky-white patches on their skin."

We stifled the instinct to show off our homework to the effect that white testicles are the sure test for a male.[1]

Shaking hands with King Bhumiphol, we felt momentarily daring. His ancestors used to be regarded as gods whom ordinary mortals would never dare to touch. A queen and two little princes were once allowed to drown in front of retainers, for whom reaching out an arm to save such divinities would have been an unthinkable crime. King Bhumiphol's own father, who wanted to be a doctor, had to practice in America because intimate personal contact with a royal prince was taboo in Thailand.

"We are giving you a *very* warm welcome to Bangkok." The King put us at ease with small talk. We conceded that the April heat was terrific, meanwhile appraising this remarkable monarch, born in Cambridge, Massachussetts, 44 years on the throne and a legend to his people—part Buddhist saint, part social worker, part rural economist, part inventor, part political umpire, part sailor, part painter and a good enough Dixieland saxophonist to be invited to join Benny Goodman's band.

We began by recalling the king's remark that democracy needed to be modified to suit Thai customs and values if it were to succeed in his country. We asked him to elaborate. This is a perennial topic of debate in Thailand.

The king explained how King Mongkut and his successors had gradually introduced democracy in Thailand over the past hundred years or more, but it was an uphill task. He was especially proud of his own part in launching, in 1973, the National Convention representing all walks of life and all parts of the country. *That* was democracy!

"The democratic formula was so popular that the Nurses' Association complained: why had they not been asked to send a representative?"

Everyone wanted to be in this "real" democracy, with 2,346 delegates of farmers' organizations, professional bodies, teachers, trade unions, chambers of commerce, industrial organizations, bankers' associations and the Buddhist monkhood herded together in a stadium to argue out by themselves how to elect a drafting body for a new constitution. Against the advice of the liberal prime minister he himself had picked, the king insisted on convening what international experts hailed as the most representative assembly ever seen on the continent of Asia.

Then in 1991, after the military coup by Generals Sunthorn Kongsompong and Suchinda Kraprayoon, another chance presented itself.

"Why not a convention of ten thousand people?" the king hopefully concluded.

His own authority, he insisted, went beyond the long and tortuous history of his kingdom's written constitutions. He recalled his own accession to the throne, which could not have been in more tragic circumstances, following the violent death of his elder brother. Until then, Bhumiphol had not expected to reign at all.

The succession to the Thai throne has been complicated by the large broods of children sired by the nineteenth-century monarchs. King Mongkut (reigned 1851-68), the first systematically to introduce Western ideas and inventions into the country while simultaneously keeping his realm independent from British and French colonialism, had 82 children. Of these, Chulalongkorn (reigned 1868-1910), succeeded him, continuing and broadening the reforms. He abolished slavery, for example. Already a father at fourteen, Chulalongkorn sired 76 children, of whom Vajiravudh (reigned 1910-25), the first king to have studied at Oxford University and hold the rank of major general in the British army, succeeded to the throne. He brought more of the West into the country, introducing surnames, for example, which had not been known in Thailand before.

All these voluntary political and cultural transplants enabled the Thai kings to parry the fatal blow to tradition and to national self-confidence that so many other Asian states suffered in becoming European colonies. When the new "democrats" staged their coup d'état in 1932, the next king, Prajadhipok (reigned 1925-35), was forced to give up his absolute powers. He soon lost heart and abdicated, opting for a quiet life of exile in England.

His heir was a ten-year-old boy, Ananda Mahidol (reigned 1935-46). When he had completed his education at Lausanne, King Ananda returned to Thailand at the age of 21. He was the only Chakri king to have the bad luck not to own a single white elephant. Six months later he was found dead in his bed in the Grand Palace, a bullet wound in his head. No one has yet discovered the true explanation for his demise.[2]

The throne then passed in 1946 to Bhumiphol, who was Ananda's younger brother. Shattered by the ugly death of a brother he had loved and idolized, he could not check the tears as he walked behind the funeral chariot. Bhumiphol was only eighteen, born in the United States, brought up there and in Europe, and virtually a stranger to his new kingdom. His Harvard-trained father, known as the Father of Thai Medicine, had died when Bhumiphol was a baby. No wonder that loneliness still lived in his face more than forty years later.

Now Bhumiphol confided to us why he had agreed to take the blood-stained and apparently powerless throne, in spite of the fact that his grief-stricken mother pleaded with him to refuse it.

"It was the only way I could be sure of giving my brother a proper funeral. In any case the people asked me to succeed, and there was a vacuum which had to be filled."

Assemblymen representing different regions and levels of Thai society entreated him to take the crown. Their impact on Bhumiphol was traumatic, and from this experience his lifelong bond with "his people" was born.

The magic was renewed at the coronation, where eight National Assemblymen gave the king holy water collected from rivers in the eight directions of the compass. He now enjoys popular authority far exceeding the official powers laid down by successive constitutions, even though he is the first king to have devoted a working lifetime to being a merely constitutional monarch.

"When a constitution is abrogated or a parliament abolished," he explained to us with increasing animation, "the people's mandate reverts to me." There have been all too many instances of that, culminating in the coup of 1991 and the king's appointment of Anand Panyarachun as Premier.

This residual authority was not easily won. When Bhumiphol ascended the throne in 1946 the omens for a royal role were not good. For fourteen years no Thai king had exercised any real power. The generals and the politicians—much older and more experienced than Bhumiphol—were making the most of their new constitutional opportunities, encouraged by the strong international preference for democracy over monarchy.

Bhumiphol responded, shrewdly, by allowing an image of himself to be projected as an amiable and harmless dilettante. He needed frivolous distraction from his royal burden, and a disguise for his real ambitions, to avoid the attention of power-hungry generals and politicians. The world saw him absorbedly playing his saxophone or clarinet, sometimes with Benny Goodman or Louis Armstrong. He led an amateur jazz group that played over the palace radio station every Friday, and his friends noted that he smiled "only on Fridays."

As a boy he used to make model trains out of old coat hangers. When he grew up he adored boats, painstakingly built his own and won many sailing championship trophies. He is a painter and composer whom *Time* once called "the royal jitterbug"; his song "Blue Night," described as a "sensuous beguine," was featured in a Broadway show. He translated *A Man Called Intrepid* into Thai.

He married his teenage sweetheart, his cousin Sirikit, an outstanding beauty in a race famed for its good looks and named one of the ten most beautiful women in the world. The couple were sprinkled at their wedding with holy water that had been blessed by four Buddhist priests every day since the Chakri dynasty had first sat on the throne in 1782. There smoldered beneath the king's merriment an intense seriousness which was only gradually unmasked. It was to make this slight and seemingly diffident young king a player for high political stakes. Once Bhumiphol grew accustomed to the extraordinary impact he made on the ordinary Thai, he realized how that mystique, anachronistically surviving from the days of Mongkut and Chulalongkorn, could be used to serve the country and influence politics to serve the people. He could at one and the same time personify the rich archaic traditions of the monarchy and invest it with an avant-garde nationalistic function.

"First of all, he is god," said the kingdom's leading novelist, when asked what the king stands for. "He is a sacred being. Secondly he is the 'Big Father' or head of the family . . . And he is the godhead of Thai nationalism. He is more than a symbol. He is an actual godhead to Thai pride, nationalism and vanity."

Others do not put it as strongly. Sulak Sivaraksa, the independent lawyer and writer, cites early Buddhist practices to argue that the king was originally elected, and can therefore be unseated: his rule derives from the people, not from gods. Bhumiphol himself agrees. "I am really an elected king. If the people do not want me, they can throw me out . . ." But people instinctively behave as if he were divine, and neither he nor his court seek to disabuse them.

The king's grandfather, King Chulalongkorn, had decreed that his subjects no longer needed to prostrate themselves on the floor when approaching him. That was a hundred years ago, and yet King Bhumiphol still cannot—or will not—stop his courtiers from voluntarily flinging themselves to the ground before him. Ancient magic is still dispensed: at the ceremony of presenting the colors to the regiments the king fixes cuttings of his own hair to each flagstaff, so that each unit can claim to have a physical piece of him in its flag standard.

This semidivine image is a throwback to the character of King Mongkut whom Yul Brynner portrayed so amusingly (though irreverently) in the Hollywood musical *The King and I*. Bhumiphol is the grandson of the Crown Prince portrayed in the movie as a precocious young teenager. Officially the Thais disliked the musical. A *Bangkok Post* editorial in 1972 blasted it as "patronizing, ignorant, stupidly comic and an affront to the Thai people," and it is still banned as historically inaccurate. But King Bhumiphol conceded when he visited Hollywood that it had "done a considerable service to my country" in terms of tourism and public relations. Videos now circulate clandestinely in Bangkok. We asked the king for his considered opinion, and he replied that the musical had good and bad parts. His great-grandfather had never danced with Anna, the English governess, he expostulated, yet the scene where King Mongkut bared his fears about British and French colonialism was true enough.

King Bhumiphol does not reject the mystical, magical side of kingship as practiced by his nineteenth-century forebears. But he also pursues scientific modernity when he travels through the provinces, urging farmers to use chemical fertilizer and other new agricultural techniques to increase their harvests, and to grow alternative crops instead of the opium poppy.

We asked the king about his rural development projects, of which he is so proud, and the criticism sometimes heard that they are not always successful. He defended his rural program vigorously. They are pilot projects, he insisted. If only one succeeded where two or three did not, that was worthwhile.

"There may be more failures than successes, like our experimental rice mill where three different ideas misfired, but the fourth did the trick. It is the successes that count. If a project succeeds, the government takes it over. If not we pay for it and try again later."

The king became eloquent about one of his own inventions, a machine based on the paddle wheel which cleans stagnant water, as an example of "if at first you don't succeed—try again." He painted a positive picture where others carp. His now lively face, spread-eagle ears and scientific enthusiasm recalled Prince Charles, another royal figure looking for a sociopolitical role.

This is a king who, alone in the line of monarchs stretching back, has visited every one of Thailand's 73 provinces. He was the first king in 80 years to enter for a time the Buddhist priesthood, to receive morning food offerings from ordinary people on the streets of Bangkok, shoeless and headshorn, clad only in the saffron robe of the monk, carrying only his metal alms bowl. This is the king who for many years personally handed out diplomas to all the thousands of new graduates of all the state universities.

This is the king who has not left his kingdom to visit other countries for twenty-five years because he dislikes the protocol and tedium of state visits—but also because he believes there is so much that needs to be done in his own kingdom. (Possibly medical factors may also impinge, and he may worry about a military coup happening while he is not there to temper it.) This is the king who has matured over 45 years of rule from the clever playboy to the severe ascetic. "I think the Queen may have told you," he said to a foreign journalist, "we don't have a private life."[3]

Yet his popularity is assured, and will not be lowered by overzealous courtiers. His apogee came in 1987 with his sixtieth birthday, an important event for every Buddhist. A movement was launched to secure signatures for "the Great" to be added after the king's name. Incredibly, almost 40 million were obtained, meaning that virtually every adult male must have signed.

On the day itself most Thais, it was claimed, killed no animals, caught no fish and ate no meat—and the especially virtuous abstained from all food, alcohol and sex as well. Some 20,000 amnesties were issued, and the national family planning campaign notched up a record of 1,202 vasectomies.

Today in the dim light of the Chitralada Palace Receiving Room, King Bhumiphol looked hale enough for 63. His face was unlined, his complexion clear, his hair full and black, his figure spare. Now that he relaxed with us in conversation he became more expressive, gesturing with both hands, reaching for a pocket handkerchief to mop at his face, raising his eyebrows interrogatively. Only his back remained ramrod taut, spurning the support of cushions, and when he turned in his seat there was a hint of stiffness and discomfort. Everyone hopes for a very long reign, but everyone knows that the succession may come sooner rather than later. Can the magic be perpetuated? Can the sometimes intemperate Crown Prince Maha Vajiralongkorn follow his father's act? Who will next ascend the Golden Lotus Throne?

Normally an only son's claim would be unquestioned. But because of questions as to his suitability, and the unprecedented provision in the most recent constitutions for a female succession to the throne, altering the rules of centuries, there is now discussion of the case for Princess Maha Chakri Sirindhorn, whose unique title roughly corresponds with that of the princess royal in Britain, succeeding to the throne. When the king dies, the crown prince will expect his due, but others may weigh the damage he might do to the institution of the monarchy against the imponderable uncertainties of giving the people for the first time a queen in her own right.

With us the king played down the problem.

"The people," he says, "will decide. I do not myself think that gender is so important. But there is a lot of male chauvinism in this country. In any case my son and the princesses are on intimate terms. Whatever happens in the future, they will support each other. Certain people make use of each of them for their own purposes, but my children are well aware of that."

Flying in the face of the popular gossip about bad blood between son and daughter, the king here made a brave show of family harmony. He also indulged in the familiar Thai trait of ambiguity. Public consensus should decide the issue, and gender should be left out of it: that would probably favor Queen Sirindhorn. But the weight of male chauvinism must be acknowledged, and that means King Vajiralongkorn. The king himself professed neutrality. A certain Buddhist fatalism and personal conservatism seemed to incline him toward letting tradition find its own way in the confusing circumstances of today. Meanwhile people recall the prediction that there will be no King Rama X in the Chakri dynasty.

The matter of succession is important because of the political role which any future monarch would be expected to play. The tensions between Thailand's salaried bureaucrats who dream of status and duty and the businessmen-politicians who strive for profit and power are now increasingly self-mediated. Politicians win elections, enjoy their brief power and go a little too far in abusing their office or putting the generals or bureaucrats down. The army then sweeps them out in favor of a caretaker government of bureaucratic talents. Eventually a modified constitution is drafted, new elections are held and the cycle resumes, with minor variations. The army will explain its intervention to the king, even seek his advice, but no difficult royal action or decision is needed unless people behave badly, that is to say unless generals disagree, citizens are killed or the royal authority publicly flouted.

Bhumiphol's worst moment came in 1973 when soldiers were fighting students in the streets. He admitted unarmed demonstrators into the palace for protection. He also ordered his guards to remove the ammunition clips from their rifles so that they could never be accused of shooting anyone or becoming involved in the struggle. Then he worked behind the scenes to stop the carnage. The 1991 coup by General Sunthorn was a much more well-mannered revolution, yet the king remained understandably ambiguous. He delicately indicated to us his concern, shared with the army, about the rising level of corruption in recent democratic governments.

"After Premier Chatichai's last cabinet reshuffle," he said with some indignation, "there were only a few Assemblymen who had never sat in the cabinet. Is that not comic?"

Some might say it was very democratic, but the scramble for ministerial rank has more to do with the vast amounts of money available through holding office than with the mere prestige of office.

The temptation for politicians or officials to accept bribes is magnified, of course, by Thailand's sustained fast economic growth of more than 10 percent a year in the last few years. The king deplored this, preferring a more modest pace which would not hurt the poor so much. Thailand benefited from undergoing Westernization at its own preferred pace over the past 150 years, instead of being subjected to the sudden cultural blanket of Western colonialism which smothered India, Vietnam and Malaysia. In the same way, "slow but sure" growth rates today would be more comfortably digested and benefit more people. That chimes with Buddhism too.

On these issues, the king appeared to approve the 1991 coup—and yet he still only initialed the revolutionary proclamation submitted by the generals, without signing it. Once again he was the man in the middle, which is, of course, the best place from which to influence events, and conforms with the Buddhist ideal of the middle way. In the popular rising against General Suchinda's assumption of the premiership in April 1992, King Bhumiphol stayed his hand for several days before publicly rebuking the General, who by then looked a loser.

If Thai politics do become more self-policing, then Rama X, whoever he or she may be, could become the first figurehead monarch on the British or Japanese model. At this point the king's tone of voice softened. He spoke of Emperor Akihito of Japan asking his advice about monarchhood and his fears of gradually closing in on himself as his father Hirohito had done, confined to purely ceremonial duties and not consulted in the country's political life. How do Elizabeth and Juan Carlos cope with the problem? Bhumiphol speaks of them with the affection of fraternity. They are all in the same small exclusive club, and his children may share their fate—whereas he himself was allowed a more creative political role.

By now the king was so engrossed in our long conversation that we began to perceive the man beneath the crown—a man who has lost more in his family life than any other ruler. As a small child he lost the much-praised father whom he can hardly remember. At eighteen he lost to the bullet his most intimate boyhood companion, his elder brother Ananda. Then his eldest daughter, on whom he doted and whose academic brilliance was acclaimed on two continents, opted out of his kingdom to marry a Westerner (something that no Thai, however enlightened, could really forgive) and live in exile. Finally it turns out that his only son's erratic behavior may not just be a phase of spoiled childhood but could carry over into adulthood and render him, in many people's view, a dangerous candidate for a throne demanding tact, patience, wisdom and good judgment. How many men in public life carry such burdens?

There are other contradictions. Bhumiphol spent most of his childhood and youth outside Thailand, yet in his middle age he turned his back on the West and vowed never to leave the country which he had rediscovered as his own—thus adding more substance to the king's role. He believes passionately in the need for more democracy, yet he does not surrender the privileges of a Thai king in dealing in a highly authoritative manner with his subjects.

He uses his magical authority in order to propel people along a more rational and modern path. His ideal is to preside over a ruggedly independent and self-reliant peasantry—and yet he derives much of the income that he spends on rural programs from the profits of modern steel and cement industries.

Most of all he is the best policeman Thailand could have had. Fortunately for the Thai nation, the first generation of Thai democrats after the coup d'état of 1932 felt that they could use a circumscribed monarchy. They allowed the crown to continue, whereas kings in neighboring countries, like many of those in Europe, were rejected as undesirable anachronisms. Bhumiphol held his ground through successive military dictatorships, gradually gaining popularity through good works. Now he has emerged as the key player on the political chessboard. He is arbitrator, judge and conscience in every national trial or contest. In his mediation of public conflict, Bhumiphol can transmute his private grief while performing an irreplaceable service to his country.

By now the daylight had vanished. Palace retainers were lingering in the open corridors at the edge of the receiving room to gaze from a distance at our long conversation. The aide-de-camp grimaced at them and started to tap his watch. Almost three hours had passed and the king seemed ready for more—or was that just politeness? It seemed better not to outstay our welcome. We shook hands again and left. At the entrance we turned for a last bow of thanks.

He had not moved. His severe, lonely figure seemed consciously to stand between Thailand and disorder—King Bhumiphol Adulyadej, Rama IX, the highest authority for the conciliation of disputes, the sacred symbol of the national qualities that have led his kingdom to such unexpected success.

Introduction:
The Asia That Might Have Been

Thailand is changing fast. It used to be thought of as a gorgeous El Dorado of gilded Buddhas and the chromatic sheen of Thai silk, a paradise of sweet frangipani and tall languid palm trees rippling in the sunshine, a land of graceful people and soft smiles. For many tourists that is still how Thailand appears. This mysterious and charming kingdom has progressed so far, however, in modernizing itself and building an industrial base that its personality has altered. The old glamour is still there, but is increasingly obscured by the overlay of modern economic and international life. As the emerging leader in Southeast Asia, straddling strategic sea-lanes at the point where the interests and security concerns of all the powers of West and East converge, this new Thailand demands the sympathetic attention of the West.

Millions of Americans and Europeans have gone on holiday in Thailand to be charmed by its physically attractive people and their beguiling ambiguity. The Thais missed out on the puritan experience which so inhibited the West. Their attitude toward the natural world, including sex, is spontaneous and guiltless. In Thailand a cabinet minister blows up condoms at family planning rallies and commissions measurements to be taken at massage parlors in order to ensure that condoms are manufactured to fit Thai males. This is the same man who has most recently warned of the grave danger of a large proportion of the Thai people succumbing to AIDS.

Thai society has a distinctive composition. It is hierarchical, with the king at its pinnacle, yet it allows a good measure of personal independence within that hierarchy. The Thais are more individualistic than either the Chinese or the Japanese. On the other hand they do not treat each other as equals; Western egalitarianism means little to them.

The Thai accepts events more philosophically than the Westerner; he does not strive so methodically to control nature and bend it to his will. There is social conformism, which makes it difficult, for example, for homosexuals to "come out," but there is also a tolerance of deviation from the expectations of the majority—so they are not harassed. The contradictions in Thai society are different from those in Western countries, and they affect the new developments in Thailand's politics, economy, foreign relations and social affairs, all of which are examined in this book.

So a new national personality is emerging. Thailand's economic growth has spurted to outpace all the other countries on the Asian mainland except South Korea. Indeed, Thailand has probably been the most rapidly growing economy in the world over the past three or four years. Only five Asian states have succeeded so far in breaking out of the underdevelopment trap, namely Japan and the four Newly Industrialized Economies (NIEs)—the so-called little dragons—of South Korea, Taiwan, Hong Kong and Singapore. All of these are direct beneficiaries of Chinese civilization, which teaches high social discipline and the virtue of hard work.

Thailand is the first of the remaining countries of Asia to arrive at the threshold of economic development and knock on the door of the NIE club. So much so that many Thais, especially devout Buddhists, are alarmed by the greed, pollution and corruption which 10 percent annual growth brings in its wake. They argue for slower growth in the interests of social goals—a debate which few other Asian countries can afford because fast growth eludes them.

One reason for that is that most Asian countries have their economic growth mortgaged to population growth. Thailand, by contrast, was able to popularize condoms and family planning to bring the annual increase in population down to about 1.5 percent, something that can be assimilated in an economy growing at around 10 percent.

In the course of this qualitative leap, Thai agriculture is being transformed into agribusiness, especially mass-scale chicken and hog breeding, and aquaculture. Some leaders talk of Thailand becoming "an agricultural super-power." Yet the country also boasts now of rapidly expanding petrochemical, steel and electronics industries, while its textiles factories supply more than two million garments every day to overseas customers.

These economic achievements rest on private enterprise and a liberalized open economy. An experienced American analyst calls Thailand "one of the half-dozen most diversified, best managed, stablest, most attractive business environments in the Third World."[1] Because they did not hysterically over-react to the ugly or unwanted features of Westernization, the Thais were sometimes scorned by fellow Asians as cultural lackeys. Time has shown that they demonstrated a good sense of proportion, and made a better choice of borrowings from the Western showcase than many other countries. Those who are surprised at the growing number and variety of Thailand-made products on sale in Western high streets, and the modern industries and

diversified agriculture that back them up, must admit to having underestimated "fun-loving" Thailand in the past.

The same goes for politics. When *The Guardian* writes of the "revolving
door" of frequent Thai coups d'état, it pokes fun at a country that seems to
run its government ineptly.[2] Thailand was a late developer in politics. The
king gave up his absolute powers barely 60 years ago, and since then there
have been numerous dictators. Western-style democracy has developed by
fits and starts, if only because an adversarial election system suited to the
autonomous individuals of Western societies does not catch on in a population trained to defer to authority and preserve the self-respect of others.

Several political parties have nevertheless become active, and seventeen
free general elections have been held. That they tend to result sooner or later
in unstable coalitions and become vulnerable to corruption does not impede
the gradual acceptance of democracy. Thailand has the good fortune to have
several centers of political power which can balance each other, so that no
one of them can gain permanent supremacy. There is a kind of moving
equilibrium, involving the political parties on one hand, the army on the other
and the king as the mediating force—with the business world as an increasingly important participant. That makes it difficult for the military to exert
long-term dictatorship.

Thailand is doubly lucky in having not only a constitutional monarchy
(an institution which many other countries have thrown out) to umpire
political disputes, but a king of such character and dedication as Bhumiphol,
who has become the elder statesman of his kingdom, preventing much of the
discord and violence that political conflicts could precipitate. Whether his
successor will be able to play the role with similar finesse is doubtful. King
Bhumiphol is the incarnation of the mystical traditions of Thailand that bind
the people together, yet his political and economic interventions are
quintessentially modern.

The third force in this shifting equation of Thai politics is the army, which
no longer has wars to fight, and therefore has time and talent on its hands.
As the 1991 coup d'état demonstrated, the army believes that it is still obliged
to intervene to throw out elected governments in the interests of political
morality and military honor. Yet the two military coup attempts before that
in the 1980s failed. The last military prime minister, General Prem
Tinsulanond, turned out to be more democratic than some of the civilians,
and the government installed by the 1991 coup leaders was indisputably the
best for decades.

The outside world saw the 1991 coup as bad news for Thailand, but the
makings of a successful and reasonably representative "democratic" system

are there. The soldiers have always returned to their barracks after a time and sometimes leave behind a contribution to the nation's politics. The army generals who seized power in 1991 promptly arranged for a new interim civilian constitution to be introduced and for general elections in March 1992.

Thailand is much in advance of most of its neighbors and of some of the larger countries in Asia. Even its military dictatorships compare very favorably—on human rights issues or economic policy—with those in Burma, Indonesia, or South Asia.

If the old Western image of the lazy, superficial, unserious Thai were true, Thailand would cut little ice in regional or international diplomacy. The facts are different. By virtue of its economic success and underlying sociopolitical stability, Thailand finds itself at the top of the Indochinese tree. The weakling that used to apologize for its capitalism in a region dominated postwar by socialist thinking is now the region's economic leader. The fragile "domino" which the West, in the 1960s, had to prop up in the front line against communist expansion, has become in the 1990s a regional power with the potential to influence its neighbors.

In the postcolonial, postCold War and now postsuperpower Southeast Asia, Thailand will play a major role, possibly in the end *the* major role. Indonesia, its traditional rival in the region before the European conquests, is not in a position to challenge Thai leadership for another decade at least, and Vietnam, the other contender with historical credentials and ambitions, will take another two or three decades. Former Prime Minister Chatichai Choonhavan's initiative in calling for Indochina to become a marketplace instead of a battlefield is the first sign of Thailand's new self-confidence.

On the increasingly serious trade disputes with the West, involving cigarette imports, cassette copyright, tapioca exports and trade liberalization in the GATT, Thailand is taking a stronger stand colored by nationalism. The image of Thailand as gentle and deferential has to be discarded when viewing the current activities and postures of a country bigger, in both land area and population, than, for example, Great Britain.

How was this national transformation achieved? A crucial preliminary was the successful and almost trouble-free assimilation in this century of several million Chinese immigrants, the vast majority of whom have become fully integrated into Thai society and culture through intermarriage and education in Thai schools. This astonishing social transplant, for which there is no parallel anywhere else in the world, injected a dose of Chinese vigor and dynamism, complementing the rather different qualities of the Thai personality. But whereas tens of thousands of immigrant Chinese were killed in Indonesia and similar numbers suffered harsh discrimination in Malaysia in the 1960s, the Thai Chinese were so accepted that most of them now feel more Thai than Chinese.

Another reason for Thai success can be found in Buddhism, with its stress on finding the middle way, its emphasis on the salvation of the individual, and its tolerance. True, Thai Buddhism does not teach people to strive for material improvement. It tells them instead that whatever achievements or setbacks they encounter in their lives are determined more by actions taken in previous incarnations than anything which they may have done in their present lifetime. That encourages a fatalistic and passive view of the world which does not match the modernization fever. On the other hand, Buddhism promotes calmness and compromise, consensus and conciliation, all of which have their place in modern industrial society.

But the primary reason for Thailand to be singled out from many other Asian countries with similar histories and backgrounds is the fact that it escaped the debilitating effects of colonialism. Thailand is unique, not only in Asia but in the Third World as a whole, in never having suffered colonial rule by another country, never having seen violent revolution of the kind that shattered China, for example, and never having been occupied by foreign armies as China, India and Japan were in the 1940s. This has allowed Thai society to undergo the buffeting of Western ideas without interrupting the authority of its own institutions.

Westernization and modernization were taken on board voluntarily, with no loss of self-confidence of the kind that occurred in India, Burma or Indonesia. Those countries swallowed a forced dose of Westernization, then reacted violently against it because it was thrust on them by foreigners at gunpoint. These countries were consequently delayed in being able to import ideas from outside on a calm, pragmatic basis.

There were periods in Thai history when the king had to come very near to taking orders from stronger forces on the Thai borders. Even today there are intellectuals who will tell you that Thailand was, for all intents and purposes, a colony of the United States in the 1960s and is still today undergoing "intellectual colonization" by the West. But these are common experiences in twentieth-century international life that fall short of supplanting indigenous authority. The fact is that the king preserved and continued to exercise his sovereignty, even though he felt his policy choices to be constrained by the actions of the great powers of the day. Thailand was able to take an altogether more objective view of the West.

Some Westerners are amused to learn that in this century King Vajiravudh obliged his subjects to invent surnames for themselves, or that Field Marshal

Phibul, the first of the military dictators, ordered Thai men to kiss their wives in public and Thai women to wear hats like the Europeans because that was being "modern." Thai leaders were not always able to select the most important things to imitate or absorb, but at least they did it on their own initiative—knowing the Thais as no foreigner could and knowing that change would come at the country's own pace.

This does not make Thailand a model, since no country can undo its colonial experience. Rather it stands as a case study of what might have happened without colonialism, a pointer to "the Asia that might have been." Thailand's advantages are not and cannot be shared by other countries. But many Third World states might benefit from observing how Thailand has maximized her independence and used it to safeguard the constructive and enduring parts of her tradition so that they could underpin modernization.

Now it is Thailand's turn to step into the ranks of industrial countries, to become a powerhouse for Southeast Asia and a haven for the industrial and financial investments of the West. It may also be Thailand's destiny to demonstrate to the world that the European tradition is not a necessary foundation for either progress or modernity. In the multicultural world of the twenty-first century, with Asian powers on the ascendant, that will be a welcome and vivifying proof of what others outside Europe only dream of. It would serve as an apt revenge for the insults of *The King and I*.

King Mongkut would have been delighted.

1

The Military Mission: Army Boots on the Brake

Early on the morning of Saturday, 23 February 1991, men of the Anti-Air-craft Division, First Army Division and 11th Army Circle of the Royal Thai Armed Forces left their barracks in Bangkok on secret assignments. At 8:30 A.M. 50 of them took control of Government House from the police security guards. A smaller posse of 25 took over at the Parliament. They were not resisted.

At 10:30 A.M. Chatichai Choonhavan, the seventeenth prime minister of Thailand, left his home in Soi Rajakhru for Don Muang Airport to board a Royal Thai Air Force C-130 transport plane to Chiang Mai in the far north of Thailand. There he was to present his new deputy defense minister, General Arthit Kamlang-ek, to be sworn in by His Majesty the King.

Chatichai entered the plane with Arthit and his aides and the usual gaggle of journalists at 11:10 A.M. The plane taxied toward the runway. But before it could take off, a dozen Air Force commandos in safari suits, who had been mingling with the reporters, stood up and drew their pistols. Telling everyone to stay calm, they removed the guns and mobile telephones of the prime minister's guards. The premier's party was led off the aircraft through the scorching sunshine and detained at Air Force headquarters on the airport. Soldiers looked for a document which the prime minister was said to be intending to present to the king, ordering the dismissals of the Supreme Commander of the Armed Forces, General Sunthorn Kongsompong and the Army Commander, Suchinda Kraprayoon—but they did not find it.

Meanwhile two armored personnel carriers took another 50 soldiers with rifles into Radio Thailand, which dropped its regular program and played martial music instead. Two more armored personnel carriers and troops with M-16 assault rifles assumed control of TV Channel 9. General Sunthorn

Kongsompong, Supreme Commander of the Armed Forces, known for his tight-fitting uniforms and enthusiasm for piloting helicopters, broadcast to the nation at 2:55 P.M. in the name of a new body, the National Peace Keeping Council. He announced the total seizure of power by the armed forces.

In subsequent broadcasts the army leaders cited the government's corruption, political meddling with the civil service, "parliamentary dictatorship," attempts to destroy the military institution and interference with the long-term investigation into an alleged plot to assassinate the queen and others as the rationale of their coup.

At 4:50 P.M. the Constitution, the Senate and the House of Representatives were summarily abolished. Five minutes later martial law was declared. Political gatherings of more than five people were prohibited. At 6:15 P.M. permanent secretaries of government departments were told to assume ministerial authority and report to the coup leaders on the following Monday, along with bank chairmen, editors, newspaper proprietors and trade union leaders.

General Sunthorn and General Suchinda flew north to Chiang Mai for an audience with the king and queen at 7:50 P.M. at the Bhuping Palace. Their explanations to the nationally revered head of state, known as a stickler for legality and protocol, were apparently satisfactory. The king initialed a royal command agreeing that "the government of Chatichai Choonhavan had lost popular support for failing to control the internal situation." He granted the customary royal amnesty to the leaders of the coup. If the king did not cooperate, there was always a risk that rash generals would overthrow the monarchy or put a more amenable member of the royal family on the throne. So he played along enough to make them feel partly dependent on the continuing royal approval, thereby maximizing his chances of influencing them later.

This endorsement, which many expected the king to give in more distant terms without naming Chatichai, enabled the generals to fend off student protest and reassure foreign opinion. Over the next hours the final blessing came from the Supreme Patriarch of the Buddhist *sangha,* after which the generals donned full dress uniform to go to the Grand Palace in Bangkok. Here they paid ceremonial respect to the Emerald Buddha (a sacred and ancient jasper statue), as well as to the eight earlier kings of the Chakri dynasty and the *Phra Siam Thevathiraj* statue, which is Thailand's guardian spirit. They solemnly swore to the Emerald Buddha to administer the nation honestly and justly, for the well-being of the people and their country.

Twenty armed soldiers with two jeeps mounted with machine guns were now stationed round the Chatichai residence in Soi Rajakhru. They had to pee in the street because no house would admit them, but after such an exhibition of bad manners, people inside Chatichai's house relented and allowed them to use its toilets. Not until 8 March, almost two weeks after his detention, was a slumped and pallid Chatichai, casual in slacks and the top half of a track suit, released to go home. "I have washed my hands of politics," he told reporters. "I am no longer the leader of the Chart Thai Party. I have resigned. I am now 71, I should get out of politics."[1] Soon afterward it was arranged for him to leave the country, and he chose to go to London.

There was deep irony in the manner of Chatichai's abrupt removal from power. He had been the hero of the Black September hijack in 1972, also at Don Muang Airport. That was when Arab terrorists marched into the Israeli Embassy in Bangkok, took ten hostages, hustled them on board a hijacked Thai Airways International DC-8 and demanded safe conduct to Cairo. The king's son was about to be ceremonially invested as Crown Prince of Thailand, and everyone shuddered at the possible ill omen of that being interrupted or put off.

Chatichai was then a senior official in the Foreign Ministry, though he retained his earlier military rank of Brigadier General. He arranged for the Arab commandos to visit a massage parlor in Pattaya, the famous former rest and recuperation center for American soldiers fighting in Vietnam. As he afterward put it, "they succumbed to nature's charms" and became more amenable to negotiation. Then Chatichai made a swap. The Arabs released the Israelis, and ten Thai officials took their place. Chatichai led them on the flight to Cairo, hailed on all sides as a courageous and astute man of action who had rescued Thailand's international reputation and preserved the serenity of the monarchy.

Now, eighteen years on, he was arrested on that same airport tarmac by Air Force men young enough to be his grandsons and humiliated by the Armed Forces commanders who were once his juniors. Chatichai had, after all, led Thai units in Burma and Yunnan in the Second World War, and later against the Communists in Korea. He had been an ambassador to Austria and Switzerland and several other European and Latin American countries and had served as an aide-de-camp to the king. Now he stood accused of massive personal corruption, covering up treason and disloyalty to the army of which he had been so gallant an officer in earlier times—a sensational descent from white knight to villain.

Later, as if to apologize for their heavy-handedness, the coup leaders in typical Thai fashion allowed him back to Bangkok to receive a high honor from the king, after which they went to Chatichai's home (it was the time of the Thai New Year festival) to pour holy water over his hands as juniors traditionally do to pay respect to elders.

Flights at Don Muang Airport were never interrupted during the coup, and tourists clambered in or out of their jumbo jets unaware of the drama unfolding in another corner of the airfield. Telephone calls always continued normally, and the clogged commuter road traffic made its smoky stop-start way into the center of town as usual. Only one road intersection was blocked, the one serving the National Peace Keeping Council headquarters: six unmanned tanks barricaded the main road there.

By the third day troops and armor were withdrawn from all public places. This was a coup with a light touch. "It's a very Thai coup," one Bangkokian commented. "Everyone's busy keeping out of the way." There was no blood spilled, no life lost, no violence. Thais digested the news on TV and radio or in newspapers with no more interest than they would normally attach to a football match or one of those lugubrious Thai soap dramas. They showed little sense of involvement. Suthichai Yoon, editor of *The Nation,* the leading English-language paper, bravely led a personal comment on the morning after the coup with the sentence: "Under no circumstances can we condone the toppling of an elected government by force." He reflected the dismay of many political commentators who had confidently predicted the demise of the military coup.

When the army named the civilian diplomat-turned-businessman Anand Panyarachun as interim prime minister, promised early elections and set in motion the writing of a new constitution, there was a sigh of relief all around. This coup did not necessarily set Thailand back in its slow march to democracy, but was presented as a corrective measure after misbehavior by the politicians.

Investors worried about share prices nose-diving. General Suchinda had a cool response. He told a public audience, tongue in cheek, that "we soldiers also invest in stocks. I'm thinking of scooping up some stocks at a bargain price myself on Monday."[2] There was indeed a fall on Monday, but only of 7.3 percent—and that was largely recovered by a 5.7 percent gain on Tuesday. It quickly became clear that the generals did not oppose the basic tenets of Chatichai's economic policies. Economic growth through private enterprise and market forces would still be the recipe.

The coup automatically caused American aid to be suspended, and induced hiccups in other foreign aid handouts, perhaps with a loss of some $20 million. But the kingdom is less dependent on aid nowadays. As Mechai Viravaidhya, the half-Scottish family planning and AIDS activist, once observed, in the unblushing Thai manner, "Foreign assistance is like an erection: you can't keep it there forever."

What was the real reason for the coup? One factor was the general lack of a military agenda. Large and well equipped, the Thai army has not had to fight anyone for a decade. In the 1960s and 1970s it struggled against communist guerrillas often supported from Chinese or Vietnamese territory. At their height the guerrillas numbered about 14,000, controlling hundreds of villages and influencing thousands more in the poor fringes of the kingdom in the north and northeast. They were assisted in various ways by China, usually bent on exporting revolution to nearby countries. To the east, the Vietnam communists were embattled until the early 1970s with the United States in a vicious war which often threatened to spill over into Thailand, and Thai troops were involved in combat in Vietnam under the Southeast Asia Treaty Organization (SEATO). Even with substantial American aid, the Thai army's role was not easy.

Political lectures at U.S. staff colleges left many Thai generals with little understanding of the communism which they were supposed to be fighting. They were more influenced by Prasert Sapsunthorn, a communist defector who was used by the Thai high command to brief officers about the guerrilla bases in the jungle. But his radicalism had not been overturned by his disillusion with the Thai Communist party leaders, and his eloquence made convinced socialists of many junior officers, eager to prevent communism by the introduction of egalitarian welfare programs. Gradually the view emerged that the guerrillas would be defeated not by arms but by civic action, community development and economic projects. King Bhumiphol strongly backed this approach, and so eventually did the Americans.

That stole enough of the terrorists' thunder to help make them lay down their arms in 1984. But then, with no domestic insurgency to repress and no foreign threat to resist, the Thai army lost the purpose in life which had driven it for 40 years. Thailand's generals came to rest on the sidelines of a peaceful society where foreigners, Chinese and multinational corporations had grabbed the limelight, the rewards and the kudos.

Soldiers were already intimately involved in civilian responsibilities. Senior officers led the first coup d'état of 1932 to curb the royal power, and all the dictators since then have been generals. Even under civilian governments, generals do not feel inhibited from openly interfering on such matters as bus fares or the selection of university rectors. The commanders in chief of the three forces expect to sit *ex officio* in the Senate or upper house: one of them invariably heads Thai Airways International, and another the Telephone Organization of Thailand. The army runs its own TV and radio stations as well as the commercially successful Thai Military Bank. Serving officers have held the office not only of prime minister but also of Speaker of the House, governor of a province or municipality, president of a bank and head of a state agency. The army is accepted as a participant in politics.

If the throne is threatened, or the national security jeopardized, the army would certainly step in. As one of its colonels once warned, "We would intervene to save forty million, even if that means killing one hundred or two hundred thousand." The king is the titular head of the armed forces, and could call on them in any emergency.

Even short of such emergencies, the army now shares with the politicians and the king an interest in pursuing economic development, which civilians see as a guarantee of national unity and modernization, and which the generals see as a precondition for national security and defense. It was the controversial General Chaovalit Yongchaiyudh, then Supreme Commander, who crystallized the army's dedication to economic goals in the late 1980s. The fighting had stopped in the rebel areas, but the war for economic uplift was to take its place. "From now on," an army spokesman declared, "it will be a war against poverty."[3] Two new development divisions were created for the Northeast and South. The "Greening of Isarn" in the Northeast, starting in the late 1980s, was the first important collaboration between army and palace. The generals busied themselves with rice distribution questions and grandly predicted that Thailand would become an agricultural superpower.

But sleepy civilian officials sprang to life at the news that the army was taking over their rural work and threw a few bureaucratic obstacles in the way. Tensions on the ground between soldiers and local officials undid some of the intended good. The military officers were untutored in economic development and underestimated its complexity. The end result was less wonderful than Chaovalit had predicted.

A similar standoff had occurred after the 1977 coup d'état, when the army urged leftist redistributive economic policies on the finance minister. Later, after resigning, he lamented:

> They understand business in theory but not in practice. They don't understand the free enterprise system or how to utilise it. They began to have the idea that they must secure control of the country's economy. I have explained to them that they cannot simply go and do it themselves.[4]

The picture this conveys of a bunch of energetic, idealistic and unoccupied men in the prime of life looking for something to do for the public good is a correct one.

There was also a personal motivation for many senior officers who had by this time become involved in business ventures. Field Marshal Phibul Songkram's military dictatorship had set the precedent in the 1930s and 1940s of putting senior officers on the boards of big companies as a means of curbing the growing power of Chinese merchants. New state enterprises (including the lottery and tobacco monopolies) were set up to create a Thai business counterpart to the Chinese, and many directorships went to the armed forces (at that time ethnically "pure Thai"). It was the start, the economist Dr. Puey Ungpakorn complained, "of a pernicious policy which has enhanced the social power of the soldiers and led to massive corruption."[5]

Since then the army has been allowed to regard profitable business activity as an officially approved patriotic gesture. By the 1950s men like Field Marshal Sarit Thanarat or Field Marshal Phin Choonhavan (Premier Chatichai's father) controlled several companies, bringing huge wealth to their families and associates.

By the 1970s Sarit's successors, the linked families of Thanom Kittikachorn and Praphas Charusathien, held 150 company directorships. Phin meanwhile allied with his son-in-law, Police General Phao Siyanond, to form a company to invest in rice trading, and this gained control of the northeast railway freight cars carrying the rice to Bangkok. After being ousted from the government by Sarit in 1957, the Phin-Phao group went into business full-time. Phin's son Chatichai, a former cavalry general, became one of the richest politicians in the Assembly, heading the Chart Thai party, and was elected prime minister in 1988. He now heads the group known as the "Soi Rajakhru clique," after the street where he lives.

In one area of business the army has a built-in opportunity for bribery. Arms procurement is a multimillion-dollar business in Thailand. Past decisions have not always proved wise, and rumors of corruption frequently circulate. Until the 1980s equipment came mostly from the United States, some of it free or subsidized. The diplomatic opening with China, linked with the ending of Chinese support for the Thai communist rebels, provided a splendid opportunity for the army to show initiative by promoting friendship with China and saving money. It bought large quantities of cheap Chinese artillery, antiaircraft guns, tanks, armored personnel carriers, frigates and even fighters (equipped with British engines and avionics).[6] It was fun while it lasted, but realism has now returned. The Chinese tanks break down too often; the users of Chinese equipment find its quality and reliability poor. New orders are going to American and European suppliers again.

An army can be applauded for taking up an economic development role. It can supply the drive, equipment and manpower which the designated civilian authorities often lack, and if its expertise is scanty, that ought to grow with practice. But civilians are understandably less charitable about the army's self-chosen political role. The military believes that this role proceeds logically from the nature of the guerrilla war on which today's generals cut their teeth as field officers. That was as much an ideological war as a military one. The ideological threat of communism persisted even after the fighting stopped, the army argues, only moving into the political arena.

The army slogan is that democracy must be saved from communism. The military definition of that sees corrupt politicians and even the system of general elections that put them in power as enemies of democracy. The parties and elections, Chaovalit argued, had done nothing to expand the sovereignty of the people, and the army was halting the armed struggle against communism at a time when Thailand still lacked a fully democratic political system. The army had a mission, therefore, to develop democracy.[7]

Chaovalit's name means "Brightly Shining." His comrades refer to him as "Big Tjiew" ("Big Little Man"). He plunged, brightly shining, into the debate about the details and definitions of the democracy that his men in khaki would defend. National security, he argued, demanded a wider political participation in politics. That seemed to mean, firstly, the vote at eighteen, to produce a younger electorate; secondly, single-member constituencies, which would load the dice against large political parties and return a more fragmented Assembly, and thirdly, a rigorous separation between executive and legislature. MPs would not be eligible for the cabinet and could not expect to recoup election expenses and the cost of vote-buying from ministerial bribes.[8] Some of these ideas were realized in the new constitution promoted by the army coup leaders in 1991.

In its more extreme utterances, the army argued that free elections were neither suitable nor necessary for true democracy, because they did not guarantee the return of competent, responsible, honest legislators. The Democratic Soldiers faction of middle-ranking officers mocked the old Constitution as an instrument of robbery and exploitation because of the rascals—"liquor merchants," Chaovalit called some politicians—it allowed to sit in the cabinet. It was the sacred duty of the military, therefore, to select suitable prime ministers and protect them, to maintain a strong upper house of appointed members to offset the irresponsible and tainted elected Assemblymen, to keep a military representative in the cabinet and to intervene directly in the economy when development was threatened.

"Big Tjiew" tried to promote this soldiers' use of democracy to fight communism in the 1980s, with the help of his former boss, Prime Minister General Prem Tinsulanond. Politics, as Professor Chai-Anan Samudavanija neatly put it, became a continuation of war by other means—a reversal of Clausewitz. Several of Prime Minister Prem's decrees showed the influence of this radical army line. His famous order No. 66/2523 in 1980 said that people should be made to understand that they owned, ruled and benefited from the land of Thailand. Social injustice and corruption must be eliminated, and exploitation ended. The armed insurgency was blamed squarely on exploitative big capitalists or "dark influences" using fortunes gained from illegal gambling, smuggling and prostitution.

The theme was reiterated in 1982 with an order that monopoly business be strictly punished. The complaint of Boonchu Rojanasathien, who struggled as finance minister during some of this period, that the army did not understand how the economy works, can now be appreciated.

An institutionalization of the army in civilian politics, as happens in Indonesia, does not appeal to Thai opinion. Yet the army now boasts a nationwide corps of civilians ready to carry out its nonmilitary work: it controls a network of 1.5 million national defense volunteers and reservists, many of them involved in the so-called Self-Defense or Self-Development Villages. These were built up in the 1980s by the perspicacious General Chaovalit, and many politicians saw them as a rural population base for military political parties, possibly along the lines, eventually, of the ruling Golkar Party of Indonesia. There are nastier kinds of army supporters too, such as the National Paramilitary Club, which specializes in witch hunts for suspected reds, student radicals, Buddhist students seeking dialogue with Christians, slighters of the royal dignity and similar vermin.

Meanwhile a number of generals, active or retired, founded their own political parties, as a means of furthering their own self-importance and enlarging the military voice in the National Assembly. The pioneer was General Arthit Kamlang-ek, a tough and energetic former Supreme Commander who formed the *Puang Chon Chao Thai* as a loose group of strongly anticommunist officers, said to be favored by the queen.

Arthit clashed with Prime Minister General Prem in the mid-1980s, but won a record majority in the following election (his party won seventeen seats to become the seventh largest party) and he joined the government of General Chatichai Choonhavan. Arthit was by then so unpopular with his successors in the army high command that his presence in the Chatichai cabinet became one of the irritants setting off the army coup of February 1991. Unity eludes the army as much as it does the civilians.

Others had sought a retirement perch in the legislature. General Thienchai Sirisamphan, a former Deputy Army commander in chief who had been instrumental in quelling the attempted coup d'état in 1985, founded the Rassadorn Party (21 seats in the 1988 Assembly) and later became education minister in Chatichai's second cabinet—only to suffer the indignity of being named by the military coup leaders in 1991, for no apparent reason, as a corruption suspect.

More serious is General Chamlong Srimuang's *Palang Dharma,* set up in 1988. For six years General Chamlong was a most popular elected governor of Bangkok, where he sought to reduce the chronic floods which still disrupt the lives of citizens. He once went to work incognito as a road sweeper, and, until he was recognized, was said to have gained insight into the indiscipline and unpleasant work environment of that occupation. Chamlong's upright military bearing belies a strong religious bent: he is a devout Buddhist and a sympathizer with the modernistic "rebel" *Santi Asoke* sect, abjuring superstition, the worship of images and use of amulets. The general drinks only water and uses no soap, and has gone to the extent of giving up meat, alcohol and sex, sleeping alone on the floor rather than in his marital bed. He has a pact with his wife—"no children." He even underwent a fast unto death in 1992—but then gave it up.

For all these reasons Chamlong has become popular, and his proclaimed intention of rooting out corruption from Thai politics arouses a response from the Thai public. Some intellectuals are put off by his dogmatism, however well channeled. One labeled Chamlong a "political Ayatollah," full of fixed extreme beliefs. This unbending but simple general has not, however, made much impact on voters outside Bangkok. His party, lacking funds, experience and organization, won 43 seats in the 1992 elections, to make it the fifth largest party. Of those 43 seats, 32 were in Bangkok under the influence of the general's governorship.

Chamlong's failure to win more of the rural vote is linked with his rejection of vote-buying, among other forms of corruption. Accused of having participated in the military slaughter of students at Thammasat University in 1976, Chamlong replied indignantly that Buddhism did not allow him even to kill an animal—a curious defense for a soldier!9 Across the table this hairshirt governor conveys neither warmth of personality nor depth of intellect. He is not attractive enough to win the political battle, yet he has the steel to succeed in the vital preliminary skirmishes. When the army talks of the need for a "strong executive" it has in mind the presidential U.S. system employed in the Bangkok municipality—and Chamlong sings its praises.

"Big Tjiew" Chaovalit keenly observed all these military forays into the political world and vowed not to make the same mistakes. He surely had the restless energy, drive, organizational ability and wider vision to succeed where others had failed. Joining the army as an electronics instructor, he had been the "clever boy" among his contemporaries. His rationalization of the army structure in the 1980s was much admired. He fell into the teacher's trap, however, of not knowing when to stop expounding. "He talks too much," another political party leader complains, "you've got to pull him away from the microphone." He is not even a good communicator, using a tortuous, wordy style that leaves listeners baffled.

The civilian politicians distrust Chaovalit's pinkish-popularist radicalism. He was the one who articulated those slightly scary army theories about true democracy not needing elections, but something called "pure power" instead.[10] He constantly accused the politicians of being venal. He once suggested that corrupt politicians be beheaded. He demanded a popular government that would give the sovereignty to the people and proposed a People's Council under a presidential system separating the powers of the legislature and administration.

Kukrit Pramoj, the left-of-center elder statesman, said that Chaovalit had been brainwashed by the communists, wanting to have "a Royal Communist Party of Thailand."[11] Angry soldiers promptly besieged the veteran ex-premier's house for several days, revealing what anger and frustration hover near the surface of the military mind and how quickly soldiers will resort to illegal action. Politicians did not always realize how strongly these currents run in the largest organized body of men in the state, when they lack a visible and satisfying role.

When Chaovalit retired from the army in 1990, he had a bruising first experience in politics. Prime Minister Chatichai immediately made him defense minister and deputy prime minister, with a virtual assurance of succeeding Chatichai in the premiership. After one of Chaovalit's frequent tirades against political corruption (delivered now as a civilian, not as a serving officer), a young prime ministerial aide suggested that Chaovalit put his own house in order before criticizing others: army officers also lived on more than their salaries. A thousand angry officers gathered in a Bangkok hotel to register their formal protest, and the aide had to resign. Police Captain Chalerm Yubamrung, apparently close to Premier Chatichai and, in military terms, the "loose cannon" of the government, then serving as a junior minister, piled on the jibes, mocking Chaovalit's wife as "a moving jewellery case." In the end "Big Tjiew" himself resigned from the government after only ten weeks in office. His former colleagues still in the army high command were furious at these successive humiliations of their former chief. They made a laughingstock of the army and demeaned it as an institution. Chaovalit then went about the creation of his own political party, the New Aspiration party, with his customary organizational thoroughness. It claimed a quarter of a million members by 1991, making it the biggest party in the kingdom, though its target was much higher. For the secretary generalship Chaovalit chose Squadron Leader Prasong Soonsiri, who had served as Premier Prem's cabinet secretary, a good thinker as well as organizer, and most vocal against corruption.

How many NAP members came from the militia and defense volunteers, we do not know. But the general certainly capitalized on his popularity in the two economic development areas spearheaded by the army under his leadership, the Northeast and the South. Teachers and Muslims in the South were said to be particularly taken with him, and he donated a hundred motorcycles to them. But he also challenged the other parties on their home ground, winning over a "godfather" of the Social Action party, for example, in Chonburi province.

Somehow he usually failed to hit the right note in political comments. When a Ramkhamhaeng University student burned himself to death in 1990 in protest against the Chatichai government, Chaovalit praised the young man's courage in terms which allowed his critics on the government side to allege that he was instigating the student protests. He is easily worsted in verbal skirmishes, but is not put off his stride by such exchanges.

The army had loudly protested that it would stage a military revolution only if the people wanted it. Intellectuals speculated how the army intended to measure this public opinion. Election results were ruled out because votes, the army insisted, could be bought or unduly swayed by personality. That left the press, especially the letter columns, and personal informal discussions.

Prior to the 1991 coup General Suchinda Kraprayoon, then a supposed acolyte of Chaovalit, had said that receiving a million letters from the public begging the army to act against a corrupt government could be a sufficient signal. Letters to the editor or to the army command, calls to radio stations and chats with the janitor can also, of course, be stage-managed. Was this political naïveté on the army's part, or shrewd political groundwork for a coup?

The pundits had enjoyed themselves before February 1991 explaining why military coups were now passé. Their reasons were most plausible. The army was more professional than it had ever been, especially after General Chaovalit's overhaul, and professional officers do not relish the idea of political involvement, or taking on responsibilities for which they are not trained. By the same token the armed forces had become a more complex organism, more resistant to the efforts of any one leader or group to wind it up in a new direction. Field Marshal Praphas could command the army of the 1960s with a snap of the fingers, playing on the placing of trusted officers at key points. Generals Sunthorn and Suchinda could not do it so easily, needing a substantial education campaign within the army, followed by extreme provocation on the part of the civilian government, to ensure a united stance behind their 1991 coup.

The government should also, in theory at least, have been less vulnerable to army coups d'état. It was more efficient and effective than it had been in the 1960s. It had more persuasive and competent technocrats in its service, capable of explaining to the public why unpopular decisions like price increases must sometimes be taken.

After seventeen coup attempts, politicians should have known the risk of army intervention, and were thought by 1990 to have become more astute and sensitive in dealing with the army. General Prem had shown in the 1980s how a government of elected ministers under an army leader could hold the country together. He faced violent rebellions from some army quarters, but succeeded in defusing them. When another ex-general, Chatichai Choonhavan, succeeded Prem in 1988 as an elected premier and party head, the civilians hoped that would be the penultimate stage leading to an elected civilian prime minister accepted by the army.

By 1990 it was believed a head of the army no longer needed to become head of the government in order to protect the army's corporate interests. Prem had done that in 1980, but was surely the last of that line. Other factors catalogued to show that coups d'état were extinct by 1990 included the growing ties between political parties, businessmen and the professional middle class (meaning that an army coup would upset more people); the spread of the shareholding habit to the army (which would lose financially from any market downturn after a coup): the sheer riskiness of a coup (for which an army commander would not lightly put his career achievements on the line) and the monstrosity of Bangkok's traffic jams (which could quickly grind to a halt the tanks proceeding to Government House and the Assembly).

Some intellectuals still believed in the army's "guiding role" to check political misconduct. Dr. Kanala Sukhabanij-Khantaprab of Chulalongkorn University is a specialist in analyzing military affairs who has done tower jumps, driven tanks and fired rocket grenades as part of getting to know her informants well. She saw the army as engaged in a long-term process of withdrawing from civilian politics and undergoing a "soul-searching exercise" to define how it can defend political security. But it should not be hurried. "Let it pull out with dignity, of its own will," she said, "for the sake of democratic evolution."[12] But most civilians are not as generous or accommodating.

Premier Chatichai and particularly his young council of personal advisors seemed to calculate that the government did not need to keep the army sweet (a strange misapprehension on the part of a man who was for fifteen years a cavalry officer). Alternatively Chatichai may have had to give priority to keeping his troublesome coalition together. Or did he deliberately play with fire, for the sheer excitement of it? In any case, he reckoned without the army's factionalism and its thin-skinned reaction to the swapping of insults which politicians take for granted.

It may sound surprising for an old cavalry officer to want to challenge the army. But Chatichai had been out of army life for most of his working career, and his years in diplomacy and business before going into politics had prepared him to take a decidedly civilian view of public life. In the Thai political arena an elected government always has to defend itself against encroachments from a technically better informed civil service on the one hand, and from a restless armed military on the other.

Many of the coups d'état which had been attempted earlier were by frustrated officers who felt that the army's high position in society was being downgraded by politicians and bureaucrats. The typical pattern was for a military coup to take place, for a military dictatorship to be installed, for certain basic changes and appointments to be made which the army had wanted, and for the army then to hand back gradually to a civilian administration again. Both sides still agree that civilians are better at government, which was one reason for the army's choosing outstanding civilian technocrats to run the government after the 1991 coup.

In the 1980s a general had emerged who was able to head an essentially civilian government for almost ten years to the satisfaction of most parties involved. That was General Prem Tinsulanonda, a natural diplomat and a cautious administrator. He took on the premiership as a serving general, and ended it as a retired general, but under the constitution of that day the prime minister did not have to be elected.

Even Prem was not able to carry the army leadership with him all the time. He had to deal with more than one coup attempt, and even attempts on his life, by disgruntled officers. He had the courage at one point to dismiss the head of the army after they had disagreed about the devaluation of the *baht*. Prem was convinced by the financial technocrats that a devaluation was necessary and beneficial; General Arthit Kamlang-ek, the head of the army at the time, strongly disagreed.

Their dispute came out into the open and Arthit called Prem a liar, so Prem dismissed him, and the king supported Prem. Yet Prem admitted in 1986: "I would like to say that I could maintain my prime ministership only with the active support of the military, and I will always preserve and maintain the prestige and integrity of the military. The military is one of the nation's most important organizations."

If Prem had all these difficulties, how much more careful should his successor have been? When the political party leaders came together after the 1988 elections to ask General Prem to serve again as prime minister, he refused, to their surprise. Possibly he was angry over Police Captain Chalerm's raising Prem's private life in the House of Representatives and threatening to give more details, apparently about his alleged homosexuality. Perhaps Prem was bored after a record run as head of government. Whatever the reason, he stood down, and Chatichai, leading the largest party in the coalition group, was, it is said, in true Thai Buddhist fashion, "persuaded" to succeed him. Once in office Chatichai proceeded to make clear that military sensitivities were only one consideration in his decision making.

He thus allowed Police Captain Chalerm—his "loose cannon"—to vilify General Chaovalit when he joined the cabinet, and did not bother to disassociate himself from his junior minister's attacks. That was later called by others an unforgivable insult. There was another incident involving Chalerm who, as a junior minister in the prime minister's office, was responsible for a mobile communications interception van said to have been "spying" on the military. The van was "captured" by the army and became the focus of hot recrimination. The military was incensed that a minister in the government should be obtaining surreptitious information about the military in this way. There was another standoff when General Suchinda refused—pleading national security—to allow the government Auditor General to inspect Chinese tanks recently bought by the Thai army.

After Chaovalit left the cabinet in a huff, Chatichai used General Arthit as a political ally, bringing his seventeen Assemblymen into the coalition and installing Arthit as deputy prime minister. Arthit was a somewhat blustering officer who had not left many friends behind in the army. As deputy prime minister, a figurehead post, Arthit could do little harm to the army. But Chatichai later appointed him also deputy defense minister with the brief to look after the routine work of that ministry while Chatichai retained the nominal ministerial portfolio himself. This meant that Arthit would make decisions, sign orders and issue instructions about army affairs. That was the straw that broke the military camel's back. It was when Chatichai was taking Arthit to be sworn in by the king that the army pounced.

There is one other strand to this tangled story, and that relates to the mysterious Colonel Manoon Rupkachorn, also a former cavalry officer. He had masterminded an attempted coup d'état in 1981, which the queen, Prem and Arthit had been instrumental in foiling. Manoon was then alleged to have plotted to assassinate Generals Arthit and Prem, as well as Queen Sirikit. Physical attacks on the two generals followed, and Manoon launched a second unsuccessful coup against Prime Minister Prem in 1985.

Manoon was exiled and fled to Germany but was later allowed to return. Thailand is traditionally generous in allowing disgraced citizens to return to their homeland. Chatichai went further: he not only welcomed Manoon back, but had him promoted to the rank of major general and employed him as an advisor. General Suchinda said it was extraordinary that a suspect in a plot to assassinate the queen should be not only alive and well in the country, but influencing the government on policy matters and advising the prime minister himself.

It is not clear why the investigation of this alleged plot had dragged on inconclusively for so many years. The police inquiry was resuscitated during Chatichai's premiership, and just before the 1991 coup Chatichai transferred the police officials in charge. Rumor had it that the investigation was tending to incriminate not only Manoon but also Chatichai's left-wing son, Kraisak Choonhaven, so that Chatichai needed to protect these two people close to him. Further rumor had it that Chatichai had also decided to dismiss Generals Suchinda and Sunthorn in favor of more cooperative generals, and that he carried with him on that fateful day of the coup an order to that effect for the king to sign. Yet no such order was found.

It is in the light of all these incidents that the military claimed to be aggrieved because the civilian government of Chatichai consistently humiliated it and showed disloyalty to it. The armed forces served notice that they would not stand being treated as second-class citizens in the country they had shed blood to defend. Chatichai had apparently misread the strength of factionalism in the army.

Factions are not easy to identify now in a less personalized army, although there is always personal rivalry as well as competition between services—the army is currently resentful of the Air Force's higher profile. In the 1950s there had been three important cabals. The mainstream group, led by that formidable warrior Field Marshal Phibul Songkram, traced its legitimacy to the 1932 coup. He allied with a cluster of cavalry and police commanders led by Field Marshal Phin Choonhavan (Chatichai's father) and his son-in-law, General Phao Sriyanond. But the younger officers chafed under these veteran marshals, and eventually found a more dashing leader in Sarit Thanarat, who deposed Phibul in 1957 and ruled equally despotically—though more sensibly—for seven years.

Those alignments set the main pattern of army groupings for many years. The 1980s saw the extraordinary spectacle of the past army commander—Prem—heading the government, the actual one—Arthit—calling him a liar and being dismissed for his cheek while the future commander—Chaovalit—had to decide which voice to heed. He backed Prem, and the bad blood from the incident still infects the high command.

There are also army circles based on differences of generation, military experience and ideology. Three such "clubs" have become famous. In the 1970s the so-called Young Turks, who graduated from Chulachomklao Military Academy in 1960, led by the radical Colonel (later Major General) Manoon, were prominent. They were perhaps embittered by losing half their numbers in fighting communism. They talked of nationalizing 30 percent of the equity of the commercial banks, taking mines into state ownership and redistributing farm land. They debated in policy terms whether or not to back their individual commanders politically. They pushed the easygoing pipe-smoking General Kriangsak Chomanan into becoming prime minister in the 1977 coup, switching to the bachelor General Prem as premier in 1980, but then turned against him, discovering him to be "a person of low morals and weak as a woman"—a veiled reference to his rumored homosexuality.

Frustrated by being left out of successive promotion rounds, and angry because suspected corruption cases were not being investigated, the Young Turks tried to overthrow Prem in 1981. They failed because they did not carry the whole army with them and because the king openly and effectively protected Prem.

The socialistic economic platform of the Young Turks was largely borrowed from another group called the Democratic Soldiers, led by General Rawee Wanpen. This was the intellectual ginger group in the army, much influenced by Prasert Sapsunthorn, the communist defector who imbued many officers with the necessity of the government's meeting popular needs if the poorer sections of the population were to be decisively weaned away from radical rebellion.

"Treat Communism with Socialism" was Prasert's prescription, and its impact is still to be seen not only on the Young Turks but also on the generation of senior officers who seized civilian power in 1991. An academic said of Prasert, "now he tries not to be a Marxist, but it is not easy."[13] He went on to head a shadowy "Revolutionary Council" or *Sapha Patiwat* movement, sometimes said to instigate student demonstrations. General Chaovalit's opinions bear a certain similarity to those of the Democratic Soldiers, though he later disowned them.

But the new batch of senior generals who dismantled the civilian govern- ment in 1991 has a more important source of cohesion. They were mostly cadets together in Class 5 of the Chulachomklao military academy—a club of exact contemporaries who rose to the top shoulder to shoulder. More unified than other classes before or since, Class 5 has its own economic base in the form of a construction company which undertakes military contracts. The leader of this group, always said to be less political and more profes- sional than its predecessors, is none other than General Suchinda, army commander and deputy leader of the 1991 coup. That is why he and his close colleagues were able to convince the entire armed forces high command to stand united and firm behind that coup. But can the generals keep their arms linked and learn as much about keeping the politicians sweet as the politi- cians were supposed to have learned about keeping the army sweet? Once a senior general leaves his military post for politics, he cannot be sure that his successors will remain fully loyal, and younger aspirants moving up the ladder will seize their own opportunities. Army factionalism may become more dangerous in future.

General Chaovalit's New Aspiration party is capable of playing big-time politics in the constitutional civilian way, although programmed to army targets. Chaovalit's personality does not lend itself to the subtleties of the civilian political arena. But he is a trier, and he has enough pushfulness for ten. With 72 seats, the NAP became the second biggest party in the House of Representatives in 1992. Ambition is a restless bedfellow all the same, and in the end Suchinda assumed the premiership himself despite all his earlier protestations to the contrary. A new party called Samakkee Tham (loosely translated as "Unity in Virtue") was formed with military backing in mid-1991 and won 79 seats in the 1992 election to become the largest party in the new House of Representatives. Meanwhile the Chart Thai party of Chatichai took the wise precaution of selecting a Class 5 Air Chief Marshal for its new party leader—and became the Samakkee Tham's coalition partner in 1992, together nominating Suchinda as Prime Minister.

The army does constitute the most effective brake that can be applied to the unsteady democratic vehicle. Its efficacy was measured in the 1980s by the care politicians took not to drive too fast. In 1991 Premier Chatichai, who loves speeding on motorbikes, did drive too fast, and General Suchinda slammed down the brake. That was a setback for continuity, but not necessarily a big setback for democracy, depending on what use this new generation of generals made of its new political power.

Whether coups will recur in the future depends largely on whether further generations of politicians learn to live with the army. The army's minimum demands are not excessive. Taken as a whole, the contribution of the army to the democratic period since 1980 has been positive. In many other Asian countries—Burma, Indonesia, Bangladesh, Korea—military leaders have taken or retained power and twisted democratic development toward dictatorship and economic ruin, disregarding technocratic advice. The Thai generals have not done that.

In the aftermath of this most recent coup in 1991, the army junta allowed a civilian caretaker premier, Anand Panyarachun, to appoint his own cabinet, pending the writing of a new constitution expected to damp down corruption and lead to a tighter, cleaner elected government with built-in safeguards for the status of the military.

The army had once accused Anand of being a communist because as the senior civil servant in the Foreign Office in the 1970s he had negotiated the closure of American military bases and initiated the rapprochement with China. Anand, as he now pointedly reminded the public, was eventually cleared of the charge, but was sidetracked to an embassy in Europe and soon resigned from the service to become a successful businessman. Clearly the army had not chosen a yes-man. Anand packed his cabinet with technocrats and set about tidying up the many issues left pending by the Chatichai cabinet and initiating reform of outdated legal and economic procedures. Some generals complained that they could not curb Anand's independence without sacrificing their own credibility in having appointed him in the first place.

But the April-May rising after the election in 1992 demonstrated the new strength of the civilians in tempering military ambition. They were able to force Suchinda out of the Premiership.

2

Politics the Thai Way: Zigzag Democracy

The seventeen coups d'état staged during this century may be thought to discredit Thailand's political performance. Actually, eight of those coups failed. Less is heard about Thailand's seventeen general elections, all of which succeeded in producing democratic governments. The first general election in 1933 made Thailand the Asian leader in democratic politics. It was the first country in Asia to implement universal suffrage (women were not given the vote in Japan until 1947). It was less revolutionary than it sounds, because voting was indirect and half of the parliament was appointed. In any case, successive military dictatorships soon put that parliament out of business.

A better approximation to democracy came in the 1950s, under Field Marshal Phibul Songkram, the kingdom's most hard-boiled dictator. Phibul had tried to force-march Thailand into modern times by making the men wear trousers and shirts and carry name cards, and the women wear dresses and hats—and everyone had to eat with spoons and forks. "Hats lead a nation to power" was one of his slogans. When the formidable "Queen Grandmother" of that day was urged to wear a hat, she indignantly replied, "You'll have to cut off my head first and put the hat on yourself."[1]

In 1955 Phibul went on a world tour; he saw how democracy was just as fashionable as wearing hats. On returning home he allowed political parties to be formed. Public meetings were permitted in the manner of Speakers' Corner in London's Hyde Park. Phibul then staged a general election contested by more than twenty parties, some of them Communist-influenced. Even though the balloting was blatantly rigged, the dictator was by then beginning to lose his following in the army. His attempt to modernize from the front by introducing what had all the makings of a chaotic democracy doomed him in the eyes of his fellow commanders. He was forced out by a group of younger officers led by Sarit Thanarat, who ruled as dictator from 1958 to 1963.

Many Thais retain a soft spot for Sarit, the ruthless dictator who would order the summary execution by firing squad of suspected arsonists in the commercial Chinatown sector of Bangkok. Such immediate justice appealed to the man in the street apprehensive about the spread of crime. Sarit had the temperament to act decisively in a country used to the dithering that accompanies consensus. He laid the foundation for fast economic growth, made many badly needed reforms in the administrative structure and helped restore respect for the monarchy and confidence in traditional values.

He was also an unabashed philanderer; when he died in 1963 he was found to have a hundred mistresses, mostly beauty queens and film stars—many living in houses built with government money, driving luxury cars and presiding over lucrative businesses. The money had come from official funds, including government lottery ticket profits. Thais were a little surprised at the extent of Sarit's embezzlements and also at his stable of mistresses and network of procurers, but very few people were shocked or censorious.

Sarit died in 1963 and was succeeded by his deputy, Field Marshal Thanom Kittikachorn, who left routine business to his deputy and co-dictator, the portly General Praphas Charusathien. Early in the Thanom dictatorship, young radical students were angered by the killing of the leftist historian Jit Pumisak, who had written a powerful and influential book, *The Face of Thai Feudalism*. Tension rose between them and an evidently philistine and ruthless regime. In October 1973 police arrested lecturers and undergraduates organizing a meeting to protest about the delays in constitutional reform. This triggered a mass rally at Thammasat University that was joined by other universities. A crowd of 100,000 students then advanced on the police headquarters for a bloody confrontation in which almost 70 lives were lost and the police headquarters was burned down. Marshal Thanom was persuaded to resign, to universal joy.

After decades of military dictatorship, politics was suddenly free and demonopolized. The political parties were by now better organized, and the *phu nooi*—the "little people without power"—made their first real mark on Thai politics. Even in villages and small towns there was a new feeling that if the dictators could be expelled so easily, local bosses and "godfathers" need no longer be feared. Many new pressure groups of monks, students, workers and farmers came out into the open. The student rising in 1973 initiated a new openness in Thai politics. The traditional political system that had served the nation in the past was being eroded. The customary ascertaining of consensus on policy issues had been well suited to a small and intimate group of power-holders and administrators but could not cope with a national electorate.

The radical victory led to the King's National Convention, which in turn produced a new parliament—and from 1975, several shaky elected coalition governments led by one or other of the princely brothers Seni Pramoj (Democrat party) and Kukrit Pramoj (Social Action party). A Center to Promote Knowledge of Democracy, run by one of Chulalongkorn University's best-known political scientists, Somsakdi Xuto, was set up. It trained thousands of student volunteers to go out and work with villagers, investigating their problems and encouraging them to vote.

But the sequel was disappointing. The "student coup" of 1973 might have opened a new chapter in which democracy could flourish and demonstrate its superiority to dictatorship. Instead it brought anarchic chaos. Anybody who had stifled some previous grudge against authority now had his day. Workers, egged on by leftist trade union leaders, struck against their employers. Students disobeyed their professors, children stood up to their parents. Many older Thais saw a communist hand behind it all at a time when the foreign press was speculating how little time it would take for Ho Chi Minh to march to Bangkok.

Since the democratic government could not control these defiers of authority, new right-wing groups emerged to do the dirty work and restrain the victorious students. Navapol, which stood for "king, religion and country," was one of these, and the Red Gaurs, ex-mercenaries who had fought against communists in Laos, were another. They allied with right-wing technical and vocational students who were only too pleased to clobber the supercilious undergraduate elites of Chulalongkorn and Thammasat universities.

These rightist organizations broke strikes at factories, threw bombs at the headquarters of democratic parties, harassed left-wing student leaders and trade unionists and carried out key assassinations. Thirty-five farmers' leaders were murdered, and three academics. One victim was Dr. Boonsanong Punyodyana, a radical Thammasat University sociologist trained in America. A note of racism crept in to the growing tension when it was hinted that Boonsanong had been living clandestinely with an American female student.

The showdown came in October 1976. The dismayed King Bhumiphol agreed to the return of Field Marshal Thanom from exile, expecting that his declared intention to become a Buddhist monk would deflect criticism. This was an obvious put-down to the democratic students, and two student leaders put up posters condemning Thanom's return. To the horror of faculty and students alike, these two were summarily strangled and hanged. Their comrades showed their indignation obliquely by staging a drama at Thammasat University that included a mock hanging.

But the student actor whom they pretended to hang on stage had "thick lips, a long face and white shoes" and was rumored to resemble Prince Vajiralongkorn, the crown prince. True or false, this was enough to attract the right-wing thugs en masse for an orgy of fighting on the Thammasat University campus. They held nothing back. They lynched students, beat them to a pulp, burned them alive with petrol, hacked their heads off and gouged their eyes out. All this was excused by the charge that the monarchy had been insulted. The crown prince himself, who had just returned from military training in Australia, tactlessly appeared on the campus in his army captain's uniform to help disperse the students.

A university lecturer recalled, "It was disgusting—people were hanged and were burned alive. I was very sad. In the morning I saw the lists of the dead and the wounded which made me very emotional. Later in my classroom the atmosphere had changed. The students were so quiet. I asked them to write suggestions on what problems they wanted to study. They sent me an empty paper. I had to cry."[2]

The students who had been so euphorically successful in 1973 now had to concede defeat. The country had been allowed to fall into such political unruliness and industrial unrest that the middle class and shopkeepers who had initially sympathized with the democratic students now backed the army and bureaucracy in checking what they saw as a threatening student-worker-peasant movement.

Some student leaders were arrested, others went into hiding; many were driven to join the Communist party guerrillas in the northern jungles (some even traveling the long way around, via France, China and Vietnam). Communists were then winning battles in Cambodia and Vietnam, and the Thai Communist party may have seemed to be the wave of the future. Saeksan Prasertkul became the leader of the Thai students "in the forest," as the Thais put it. He had been an exchange student in an American high school for a year and spoke good English. His wife, Pitpreecha, was a pharmacy student from a wealthy merchant family; she had been elected University Queen. They had a child in the guerrilla camp. Another leader was Thirayuth Boonmee, whose parents were poor. He had won first place in the nationwide secondary school graduation examinations and was studying engineering at Chulalongkorn University.

These expectant students learned for the first time just how hard a Thai farmer has to work. They also found to their chagrin that the Thai Communist party was hardly Thai at all. "Many of the old cadres were of Chinese origin," Pitpreecha said afterward, "and could not even speak Thai properly. We were annoyed because we were concerned with our own revolution. We did not care whether Jiang Qing or Zhou Enlai were fighting each other in Beijing."[3]

The disillusioned Thai students returned to Bangkok a few years later, confessing their mistake. One was asked by a reporter if he still considered himself a revolutionary; he burst into tears. Saeksan was hospitalized for malaria and then flew to Cornell University for further studies. He is now a subdued lecturer. The others have all been reabsorbed into the mainstream of Thai life. One became an MP with the Chart Thai party.

After the Thammasat massacre the armed forces made a coup d'état—evidently with the king's assent. A right-wing law professor, Thanin Kraivixien, was made prime minister. His repressiveness ran to sending Special Branch policemen to the liberal bookshop to take away 45,000 books to be burned. They included Thomas More's *Utopia,* George Orwell's *The Clergyman's Daughter* and Maxim Gorky's *Memoirs.*

Thanin was an uncompromising ideological right-winger, honest, clever and extreme; his father was Chinese. He had studied at London University and Grays Inn and took a Danish wife. He sought to undo most of the changes that the left-wing democrats had tried to bring in. His manifesto after taking office set out his reasons. "Our culture, upheld by our ancestors and customs, was neglected, considered obsolete, and regarded as a dinosaur. . . . Some had no respect for their parents, and students disparaged their teachers. They espoused a foreign ideology without realizing that such action is dangerous for our culture . . ."[4] Thanin would not even allow Lee Kuan Yew, the premier of Singapore, to make an unofficial visit to see if his democratic politician friends were safe. But soon enough the country and its elite tired of Thanin's inexperienced and provocative handling of affairs. He was one of the king's mistakes. The army obliged with yet another coup, this time bringing policy back from the extreme right to the middle ground.

Thailand had a new military dictator in 1977, an officer who declared that the country should "start learning about democracy by practising it." This was the unorthodox General Kriangsak Chomanan, who invited the students released from detention to his house for breakfast—cooked by himself. He smoked a pipe and was rather sensible and middle-of-the-road in his policies, but the establishment found his informality disturbing. So the army in 1980 wheeled forward another general, Prem Tinsulanond, who provided the calm and steady hand that was needed.

A repentant party leader voiced the general feeling of the 1970s when he observed, "I am beginning to think that democracy is not suitable for this country. Nor is dictatorship, for that matter."[5] This was the Asian dilemma. Thailand's traditional autocracy, however efficient, was losing legitimacy— yet democracy, which seemed the only alternative, and which the 1973 "revolution" had put irreversibly into play, seemed weak, chaotic and corrupt.

After the Thanin crackdown, a vital buttressing of the foundations of democracy began to be made by a small group of self-sacrificing professional men and women who steadily enlarged the rule of law. In an old-fashioned shop-house in one of the busy commercial streets of Thonburi, the city on the other side of the river from Bangkok, is a small dingy office where Thailand's best-known civil rights lawyer works. Tongbai Tongpao, son of a peasant and a man who keeps faith with his origins by refusing to join the well-paid ranks of business lawyers, considers that human rights are at last improving in Thailand. The legal rights of the Thai citizen are now, he says, the best in Southeast Asia. "One can look into any matter, and expose whatever the police or soldiers do. We have the law, even though the enforcement is not good enough."

There are gaps. Thailand has not signed the UN Convention on the Rights of the Child, because it objects to the provision that would qualify refugee children for state education and citizenship. There are over 400,000 Vietnamese, Cambodian and Laotian refugees in Thai camps, a legacy of the Vietnam War.

But helped by the increasing interest in civil rights among Thai lawyers, journalists and politicians, and pressure by such overseas bodies as Amnesty and the UN, Thailand has become a country in which arbitrary actions by those in authority do not have to be swallowed without protest or redress. It requires courage and persistence, but wrongs can be righted. "People like me," says Sulak Sivaraksa, who has suffered for his outspoken published comments, "can exist in this country. People like me cannot exist in Burma or Vietnam."

But democratic reformers run into one major problem. However enthusiastic Thais may sound about democracy, when it comes to putting it into practice they hang back. "Democracy has never been a failure," a party leader complained. "It is the people who have failed democracy." His bitterness matched King Bhumiphol's reproach to youth leaders complaining about the lack of interest by government officials—that such indifference could stem "from absence of co-operation from the people, for whose benefit the work is destined."

Why do the ordinary citizens of Thailand not jump at their new democratic opportunities to elect representatives to speak for them in Bangkok? Sulak Sivaraksa explains it on the basis of the difference in culture:

> When democracy was introduced it was an alien concept entirely outside the Thai culture. Before that, when we had to elect the abbot of the temple or the headman of the village, it was done by consensus. You went to the best persons, and most of them declined. You had to ask them three times before they accepted the position. Many a good monk would leave the village because he was afraid of the responsibility of being elected an abbot. That was the tradition. Now the candidate tells us how good he is, how wonderful he is. That is entirely against our own culture. It does not mean anything to the villagers.

Consensus is an informal process of finding out each other's minds, searching for compromise, seeing where the majority lies, and agreeing to make that the unanimous decision. Afterward no bad feeling need be left because A spoke against B, or voted against C. The outward appearance of harmony and unity is preserved.

Democracy in Thailand today, as in India or the Philippines, means that landlords have a better chance than the tenants of winning seats in parliament because that is the way that power is distributed and exercised in the countryside. Having an election does not by itself change the power structure: that will be modified gradually by education and prosperity. The whole force of *karma,* which is such a strong part of Thai Buddhism, flies against the Western notion of equality between human beings. It acknowledges that some do better than others, are richer or better endowed than others, not primarily because of their own efforts but because of past events in earlier incarnations with which it is futile to argue.

Thai society, stiffened by Buddhism, is built on personal relationships, not on principles or laws. Whether you consider another person's act as wrong or not depends largely on who that person is. If he is a friend, relative or colleague, you would not normally condemn him. But if he is a stranger or opponent, you *would* normally consider his act wrong. Looking after your own is an even stronger maxim than it is in Europe. Thai democracy begins with the family, not, as in the more mobile societies of the West, with the individual, and a village will vote as one through its headman. That is why law enforcement is not always effective in Thailand.

The Thai system thus makes a mockery of the Anglo-Saxon theory of equality before the law. The Thai elite admires the concept of rule of law. But in practice, concessions to its own social traditions result in so many exceptions to the concept that its purpose is defeated. It is not that Thailand is behind the West and needs to catch up. Thais' assumptions about other people are simply different from Westerners'. The motivations for voting and for standing as a candidate, in particular, are worlds (or cultures) apart.

If a Thai wants to get on in life, he does things for important people in the expectation that they will reciprocate. Thai "democracy" has produced a network of *chai por* or "godfathers," who maintain battalions of key individuals to whom they give help or presents, and on whom they call at election time to support a particular party or candidate. The "godfathers" in turn expect a quid pro quo from the party or candidate: a recent Minister of Interior appointed more than a hundred salaried advisors in his office in order to satisfy the "godfathers" who had secured his election.

Just as the personal tie prevails over principles, so flexibility (which helps your friends) is more admired than honesty (which may harm them). Thai electors and legislators are always ready to switch votes and wobble in their decisions. The representativeness of the legislator, and his sense of responsibility to his constituency, are shallow. Thais are also quite individualistic and competitive when dealing with their equals and do not hide their natural desire to be boss, rather than be subservient to others, so the possibilities for party discipline within the parliament are slim.

As for policy debates, whether in party caucuses or in parliament itself, these can be torpedoed by the fact that knowledge and truth are in themselves not high on the list of Thai priorities. Personal relations and personal advancement rank higher. "Impersonal attitude towards serious intellectual discussion," said Dr. Suntaree Komin in her *Psychology of the Thai People,* "is very much a Western mentality, quite alien and unfitted in the Thai cultural context, where relationship secures a much more significant priority. . . ."[6] Debate in parliament is strangled, producing either bland platitudes or shrill insults.

From this, two features of traditional Thai behavior can be picked out as creating special difficulties for the implementing of democracy. One is "face" or self-respect. A Thai always tries to soften a negative answer to a question and to avoid if possible a public confrontation with another person, whether senior or junior to him in the hierarchy. It is the gravest social sin to make somebody "lose face." A sensitive and considerate Westerner might also try to avoid a blunt public denial of another person's wish or request. But in Thailand the courtesy is carried to an extreme and is made systematic. Only a rare individual like Police Captain Chalerm Yubamrung ignores the tradition.

Premier Chatichai Choonhavan made a public promise to the armed forces leaders in 1990 that he would remove Police Captain Chalerm Yubumrai, who had consistently exasperated them, from his government. He failed to keep that promise. The army leaders lost face. Their retaliation was to boycott their weekly breakfast meeting with the prime minister: he lost face. These violations of face were intended and were part of a sophisticated high-risk political game. But they caused sufficient unease all around as to make routine business difficult and culminated in an illegal seizure of power. Some Westerners assume that saving face is one of life's little luxuries—spreading sweetness and light, by all means, but hardly essential where public issues are at stake. The truth could not be more different. The mutual protection of self-respect is a bedrock element in Thai society.

Traditional autocratic government in Thailand saves "face" by not lending itself to open debate, but open confrontation is the whole point of Western democracy. Thai culture cannot easily cope with these new demands that democracy makes on it. If breaches of immemorial social rules become frequent enough, the intricate structure of relationships in Thailand would be damaged, leading to turmoil in which individual egos let rip. Should Thailand tear its whole social fabric apart as the price of introducing democracy?

Take a second example. During the 1980s Thai political scientists like to talk about the country's "semi-democracy," meaning the halfway house that sprang up under the handsome General Prem Tinsulanond. Prem started as a military dictator, but used his powers in a democratic way. On retiring from his position as army commander in chief, he remained as a civilian prime minister, with continuing support from the army. The political parties forming the coalition government under his leadership went on voting for him as prime minister, even though he had never been elected to the parliament.

Prem was a Thai version of President Ronald Reagan, keeping aloof from administrative detail but always acting as the government's avuncular voice. The politicians could play politics, the bureaucrats ran the country and everyone was happy with Prem, except some of the restless generals who succeeded him in the army command—and Chalerm.

Police Captain Chalerm, who often seems to feature in these controversies, declared in parliament that he knew some details of the bachelor premier's "odd" private life that he would share with the House at a later date.[7] The Young Turks in the army had already regretted their backing of Prem for prime minister. Nobody seriously minded whether Prem was homosexual or not, but to have it bandied about in the legislature for everyone to hear and report in the press would be a fearful humiliation. So Prem unexpectedly retired early from politics to save his face.

Second to face as a basic difficulty in transplanting democracy into Thailand is corruption. Presenting gifts to a superior, whether to the king or to your village headman, is the traditional way of inducing a favor in return, so much so that much of the intended egalitarian or equitable purpose of the democratic system is thwarted. Gifts are an intrinsic part of Thai social life. Soon after his coup d'état in 1991 General Suchinda revealed that at the wedding of one of his children he was handed a neatly wrapped package of currency notes with a value of $20,000. That was *not* a bribe, and social custom made it impossible for him to refuse.

Like Westerners, Thais are corrupt in small ways in those humdrum episodes of life such as traffic offenses or getting a job. Unlike Westerners they expect their leaders to be corrupt too, and accept the fact as part of life. Marshal Sarit left an estate of $140 million on his death, and no one pretended that it could have been saved from his salary. Marshal Praphas, himself no saint, once observed that entering politics was like "getting stained with filth."[8] The young King Bhumiphol recalled that his first discovery on taking the throne was to learn that "politics are filthy."

Corruption is disapproved, of course, if it goes beyond a certain limit, and becomes too blatant, too greedy or too open. Phibul executed one of his commerce ministers for taking too many bribes, and a later minister of agriculture was imprisoned for five years (and his wife for ten) for allowing a gold merchant to tap rubber in a reserved forest in return for $120,000. General Chaovalit in 1990 asked for corrupt politicians to be beheaded. King Bhumiphol's view was that "If all corrupt persons were executed, there would not be many people left. I am at my wit's end to know how to remedy it."[9]

A minister, judge or senior official in this hierarchical society is regarded as automatically entitled to the power that he holds, so his actions are rarely questioned or obstructed. It is hard, therefore, for Thai leaders not to be corrupted. Former Premier Kukrit Pramoj puts the problem in strong terms: "We are now living in a sandstorm of corruption . . . the grains of sand get into everything, into the air we breathe, into our hair, into our bed at night, and in the food we eat."

One minister in an earlier government let the cat out of the bag when he was charged with accepting a bribe to amend the safety-control regulations for liquid petroleum gas stations. He explained that his party (the Social Action party) had instructed its ministers in the coalition government to raise $20 million for its funds. The party's Secretary General showed him how to write a figure on a slip of paper, which would afterward be destroyed, and dangle it before the person asking for the favor. Nothing would be taped, and there would be no evidence.

Prime Minister Chatichai, who was a regular target for allegations of corruption, would sometimes reply: "Where is the evidence? Where are the receipts?" These transactions are, by their very nature, almost impossible to prove, and that is why the army after its 1991 coup took the unusual step of reversing the usual judicial burden of proof for the few leading politicians—including Chatichai—whom they suspected of gross corruption. The state had merely to show possession of unusual wealth or property greater than could have been acquired with the person's salary, and then the suspect would have to prove that it was obtained without corruption. Since some politicians like Chatichai have great personal wealth by inheritance or previous bona fide business dealings, such investigations can never be conclusive. The cases of thirteen politicians were ultimately placed under the judicial process with a consequent shift in the burden of proof, and when election time came around again in 1992, military leaders did not hesitate to collaborate with some of these same "shady" politicians and even serve in a new government in coalition with the parties they controlled.

The earlier Commission on Counter-Corruption has had little success, as one might have guessed, in uncovering actual cases. Its director, Suthee Arkasruerk, once estimated that a third of the national budget was being pocketed by corrupt officials. Most bureaucrats cheat on their housing allowance, he said, the main offenders being the already rich and well educated who are clever enough not to get caught. It is a kind of psychological sickness—the more you have, the more you want. The status-conscious, luxury-loving wives of high officials who drove their husbands to greater and greater extremes were, Suthee declared, lamentably to blame.[10]

One man who recently fell into the deep end of the corruption debate is Sukhumbhand Paribatra, the amiable political science lecturer at Chulalongkorn University, who might now be king of Thailand if his conscientious grandfather had not generously waived his claim to the throne. The old Prince Paribatra was considered the likeliest heir when King Prajadhipok abdicated in 1934 without a son to succeed him, but he gallantly bowed the knee to his young half-brother Ananda, apparently in the belief that the younger man could better weather the democratic storms ahead. Paribatra's grandson Sukhumbhand was flung into the hurly-burly of politics in 1988 when he served as an advisor on foreign policy to Prime Minister Chatichai. His closeness to the throne did not save him from paying the penalty for criticizing army corruption. He resigned, sadder and wiser, and composed a set of ten satirical commandments for Thai politics, part of which ran:

Thou shalt have no other god before money.
Thou shalt not steal from the rich, because they are powerful, and shall steal only from the poor, for they are powerless . . .
Thou shalt not steal small money, but only big money . . .
Thou shalt covet thy neighbour's position and his office and his wealth . . .
Thou shalt not touch the military with thy words or thy deeds . . .

Corruption in Thailand is not a side issue, something to be left to anticorruption committees and the courts. It affects the very heart of the democratic process because of the wide extent of vote-buying and vote-selling. A poor northeastern farmer put the matter squarely: "For us a general election is a time for collecting money. Democracy? I must pay off my debts first before thinking about it." One imaginative candidate in Chiang Mai hopefully gave out single shoes to the electorate in his constituency, promising to supply the other ones if they voted him in.

General Kriangsak, trying to come back after his replacement by Premier Prem, spent $600,000 on his by-election—40 times the legal limit. That enabled him to have many more canvassers than his opponents, and to pay out $3 to each voter. Nobody made a fuss, or took him to court, because almost every candidate exceeds the limit, and it is expected on all sides. Another ploy is to pay election officers to follow the "three Nos"—no reading (of the electoral roll), no checking (of the voter's name) and no looking up (to compare face with ID picture), so the moneyed candidate can pack the poll.

Service in the legislature, with the possible bonus of a cabinet seat if you are lucky, is an honor in itself, carrying enormous prestige. Most successful candidates go off to Bangkok with not the slightest intention of interesting themselves in constituency affairs until the next election. Nowadays parties try to play down this feature of the elections. Chamlong's Palang Dharma party and the Democrat party both claim not to buy votes. But what party leaders say is not always done by candidates in the field.

It does not end there. Once a new parliament is sitting, MPs will set financial terms for voting in the government's favor. Kukrit, as prime minister, once spent about $140,000 by way of bribes to MPs in the struggle to keep his administration afloat. He revealed afterward that the prime minister's secret fund had already been used up by his deputy, and the secret military fund was also dry, so he had to borrow the money. It took him four years to pay it back, and his government did not last very long in spite of it.

It is accepted that an MP needs immense sums of money—about $400,000, according to the Bangkok English-language newspaper *The Nation*—to be sure of winning reelection after the parliament is dissolved. The political parties need even larger sums to be sure of a good showing in the next parliament. Where can such funds be found? Some politicians claim that they spend only modestly, from their own pockets and those of their "friends" (i.e., businessmen) and from other legitimate sources. But the great majority of candidates expect to build up their reelection fund from bribes, and in the case of cabinet ministers, particularly those handling large contracts (in the Ministries of Industry, Communications, Commerce and Agriculture), the sums involved are spectacular. One deputy minister was withdrawn from the cabinet by his party because he was not bringing in enough income in bribes for the party funds.

The most recent high point of corruption was said to have been reached when the Chart Thai party was alleged to have spent $120 million on buying votes at the election in 1990. Many blamed this on the large number of businessmen who had won seats, not only in the House of Representatives but also in the cabinet. There was at that time a persistent rumor, as always with big contracts of this kind, that when the last elected government negotiated a $6 billion telecommunications project, for which British Telecom and the local Charoen Pokphand group were the successful partners, it yielded 3 percent of the value to the ministers concerned—to dispose of as they wished, i.e., for party political purposes. The accusation was denied. Though believable, it was never proved. Most people also believed that this was one of the reasons behind the army coup of 1991, and of the king's apparent approval of it. But they were disinclined to blame either Chatichai or the king.

Corruption is also rampant, needless to say, in the civil service. The police operate on scandalously low salaries and expense budgets. Some politicians take pride in the fact that policemen are able to supplement these meager funds by illegal revenues from underground lotteries, gambling, prostitution and bribes from drivers in breach of petty regulations. It would be an enormous setback to the state finances if every policemen, civil servant and soldier were to receive increased wages to substitute for the loss of bribes.

So the Thais practice by fits and starts a kind of halfway democracy. Thailand cannot score high marks for any of the four planks in any democratic system—representation, participation, openness and equity. The way

MPs are elected does not render them genuinely representative; money politics prevails and there are complaints about "too much official guidance" at the polling booths. General Arthit Kamlang-ek justified his call in 1983 for an appointed Senate "proportionally drawn from all social and professional groups" by the fact that "under the present circumstances, we will not be able to have representatives of the poor or the real people's representatives in the House through the general elections no matter how democratic they are."

Participation is not very strong, either. At one election villagers told a visitor who asked what it was all about: "It is the custom of the nation; when we are told to go and vote, we have to do so."[11] That was several years ago and would not be so common today. But as a former prime minister, Seni Pramoj, puts it, "The culture in this country is prone to obeying orders, or letting sleeping dogs lie," which he attributes to the background of economic contentedness in a bountiful land.

Openness is a distant goal for Thai politics, one toward which it is moving only slowly; important public business is still conducted behind the curtains of the cabinet room and government departments and more private places. The media can accelerate the process: a minister may wish not to publicize his action, but if a critic complains on television or in one of the larger-circulation newspapers, it is difficult for the minister not to reply—and divulge more information.

As for equity, it seems a rather hopeless quest in a society of hierarchies infused with Buddhist fatalism. A socialist-minded government once tried to help the rural poor through a subsidy program where the use of the funds would be decided on the spot by each village. It was hoped thereby to encourage both political and economic development. In practice the rural meetings were dominated by the more assertive and self-confident rich farmers, and some critics considered that the program actually encouraged corruption and widened the economic gap within the villages. The head of that government later confessed that this particular welfare-oriented administration of his had been "a luxury my country could ill afford." That was at the peak of the "democratic period" of the mid-1970s.

But in practice the defects of democracy as implemented in Thailand are regulated by a sophisticated indigenous system of checks and balances that is the real strength of Thai politics.

The three major forces in the political arena are the political parties, the army and the king. Each organizes and asserts its power in different ways. The parties have the least cohesion of the three. Many of them are personal factions more than parties, united around a charismatic leader rather than a

principle. Many are short-lived, sometimes disappearing in the space of two
or three parliaments. But there are a few that have a history, and probably a
future.

The parties of the extreme left are now out of the picture. The Communist
party, deprived of Chinese or Vietnamese support, was dissolved in the
mid-1980s. In a Buddhist country where no one starves, it was always
unlikely that Marxism would take any serious hold, though it could possibly
revive in the unlikely event of a serious economic collapse. During the
"democratic period" of the early 1970s, an exhibition was held to celebrate
the success of the People's Republic of China. Maoism came into vogue, and
liberalism was rejected by many idealistic students.

But the story of Boonsong Chalethorn, the "good boy" from a poor family
in Bangkok who became the deputy chairman of the Student Council and
was jailed after the 1973 uprising, is typical. When first approached by the
communists, he resisted; it was the carnage at Thammasat University that
changed his mind. At 24 he sneaked into a guerrilla camp in Laos for training
in the use of bayonets, grenades, N-16s and AK-47s. Like the other students,
he found the discipline difficult to accept. When the Vietnamese army
invaded Cambodia, and China began to fight Vietnam—communist fighting
communist—he lost heart and slipped back to Thailand. His father's comment was that he had always thought him a good boy, because he did not
drink, smoke or carouse.[12]

The 3,000 young activists who headed for the jungle camps of the
communists in the late 1970s could have become the leaders of future
communist drives in Thailand in the 1980s. But their party superiors
squashed their hopes of gaining positions of influence in the party on the
Maoist ground that urbanized intellectuals were unfit. Those superiors were
uncritical followers of the Chinese party line, being themselves mostly of
Chinese origin. Unlike the assimilated majority of those of Chinese extrac-
tion in Thailand—the "Sino-Thai"—they ate rice with chopsticks, liked
noodles, and could not stomach the fiery Thai dish called *namprick paltoo*.
They often spoke Chinese and read Chinese books.

Even when China began to curry favor with the Thai government, selling
petroleum to it during the oil crisis, the guerrilla leaders held to their line.
"We were being bombed by government planes flying with Chinese fuel,"
one student complained, "while Premier Kriangsak was given banquets in
Peking."[13] Only in 1985 did the party "go Thai," indigenizing its structure
and stressing the urban as well as the rural struggle; by then it was too late.
The communist effort in Thailand has been very largely a foreign show. If

it does revive it would have to be as a genuinely Thai party, but where would the party discipline come from?

For the same sort of reasons, the right wing has never won popularity. Some military leaders, like Major General Sudsai Hasdin, the counterinsurgency specialist, tried to organize a political following on an anticommunist platform, and semifascist organizations like his Red Gaurs had their brief period of glory in the 1970s. Since then the furthest right that can be observed in the parliament is Samak Sundaravej, whose Prachakorn Thai party made headlines in the early 1980s. His populist, nationalist, almost Thatcherite message, calling for a reduction of the national debt and privatization of state enterprises, gained some following in Bangkok, aided by his commanding oratory.

The other parties occupy the popular middle ground. The oldest is the Democrat party, founded by Seni Pramoj and others in the 1950s. Its weakness is that it has two wings, one relying on southern Thailand, the other on the Northeast. The Democrats were the largest party in the parliament in the 1970s when Seni became prime minister for the second and third times; he described its program as "soft socialism," a package of cautious economic reform, higher taxes, subsidized crops and land redistribution. A dapper little man, son of a prince, an Oxford-trained lawyer sometimes called "the last Englishman" because of his flawless manners and English accent, he had taken a lead in 1941 in resisting Japanese occupation. He is a *Bunnag,* or descendant of Persian merchants influential in the Thai court since the seventeenth century.

Seni explains his "socialism" in the words "it is better to go along with the left than with the right, because the left are with the poor and the poor are in the majority. . . ."[14] Yet his final government in 1976 was rather conservative and business-oriented. This was confirmed when the leadership passed in 1982 to Bhichai Rattakul, grandson of a Chinese immigrant and one of the "Sino-Thai" business leaders, partly educated in Hong Kong. The Democrats fell to fourth place among the parties elected to parliament in March 1992, with 45 seats.

The two other large parties go back only to the 1970s. Chart Thai was formed by three relatives of Field Marshal Phin Choonhavan, who had been a key supporter of Marshal Phibul. Phin's son, General Chatichai Choonhavan, was the leader until 1991: he was the elected prime minister from 1988 to 1991. Phin's two sons-in-law, Police General Phao Sriyanonda and General Pramarn Adireksarn, were the other co-founders of the Chart Thai party. Chatichai's adventurous career has already been described. He held the party firmly on a pro-business line, while at the same time raising the minimum wage more sharply than previous governments, to the displeasure of industrialists. Chatichai likes a challenge and enjoys swimming against the current.

He reveled in his mission, as foreign minister in 1973, to squeeze oil supplies out of Premier Zhou Enlai. When he became prime minister he set the cat among the pigeons by installing a large group of extremely able young intellectuals, plain-speaking with little respect for age or status, to advise him. His eventual problems with the military may have emanated from the "advice" given by senior members of this group. Chatichai also set some records, beginning as the first elected premier for twelve years and ending as the head of the longest-serving democratically elected government in Thailand's history.

Prem had been almost an absentee prime minister, aloof from the political fray. He passively relied on the bureaucrats to tell him what to do, and allowed the ministers from the various parties in the coalition to have their own satrapies. Chatichai's premiership was highly active, by contrast. He kept the civil servants in their place. But after the 1991 coup Chatichai went into exile in England, where he used to play polo in his younger days and still plays golf at Gleneagles. He declared that he was through with politics, and many of his former ministers were temporarily crippled by the army's corruption investigations. The party astutely chose as its new leader an Air Chief Marshal who belonged to the famous Class 5 of the Chulachomklao military academy and therefore had the ear of the military junta who carried out the 1991 coup. Chart Thai won 73 seats in the March 1992 election, second only to the New Aspiration party, and ironically joined the military-led coalition government.

The third important party of the 1980s is the Social Action party, formed in 1974 under Kukrit Pramoj—another son of the same prince, being Seni's younger brother. At Oxford Kukrit was renowned for his liberality, always keeping a barrel of beer in his rooms. In addition to having been prime minister twice, he is a prolific novelist, commentator and journalist. He founded one of the best Thai-language newspapers, *Siam Rath*, and appeared in *The Ugly American* with Marlon Brando in 1963. Seni calls him a "gadfly" and "mercurial."

Kukrit began as a rural reformer, but the SAP eventually became something of a business party like the others. He preserves his idiosyncratic charm, living alone in a large house in the traditional Thai style with many servants and animals. Of the 2,000 fish in his pond he says proudly: "I know them all personally—and I think I have named them all." He shows visitors two chickens which he personally raised from the egg when their mother died in the laying. "They are part of the family," he declares, "and they have the run of the house."

Now largely confined to a wheelchair, this grand old man of Thai politics has lost none of his gusto. There was one election campaign in which he was accused by General Kriangsak of being homosexual. Kukrit immediately offered to prove otherwise if Kriangsak would send over a close female relative. For good measure he accused Kriangsak of ordering, under the influence of brandy, the release of a dam which had caused destructive floods.[15] Thai political campaigning has that kind of edge. Kukrit's colleagues in the SAP found his act difficult to follow, though Siddhi Savetsila, a capable former Air Chief Marshal and foreign minister, made a good try. It was expected that the SAP would have the same fate as other parties in the past of splitting into fragments after the final departure of the charismatic leader. Montri Pongpanich, whom the army accused of corruption, took the leadership of a reduced SAP after the 1991 coup, and its strength fell to 30 seats in the March 1992 parliament.

The remaining parties in the previous parliament are relatively small. Solidarity, led by Boonchu Rojasathien, the economic wizard of earlier administrations, is one. The others are military creations. Former Governor Chamlong Srimuang's Palang Dharma, only four years old, is a new kind of entrant on the political scene, professing an ascetic Buddhism tinged with popular welfare policies which has gained a following at least in Bangkok. Another general, Arthit Kamlang-ek, leads the Puang Chon Chao Thai, which is a loose association of what used to be called the Democratic Soldiers with a decidedly anticommunist posture. General Thienchai's Rassadorn is another small party based on a military personality.

It is the two newest parties which are currently exciting everyone's interest, the New Aspiration party of General Chaovalit Yongchaiyudh, the former army commander in chief, and the Samakkee Tham, launched in 1991 by friends of General Suchinda Kraprayoon, the former head of the army and leader of the 1991 coup. Both, with their military patronage, have attracted defectors from the older parties.

It is hard to find many people who will say they like or trust Chaovalit, and yet he is such an eager beaver that he may score simply on energy and organization. His party won 72 seats in the March 1992 elections to become the chief opposition party. His credentials are impressive. He successfully negotiated in China, Vietnam, Laos and Burma on various issues on behalf of either the army or the Chatichai government. He mediated a dock strike dispute when the government's plan to privatize future port expansion was under attack, securing a settlement where the prime minister had failed. He also won admiration for his rapid mobilization of military resources to help inhabitants of the southern provinces when they were devastated by a typhoon. But there is a certain bullheadedness and dogmatism about him, which, combined with his poor showing as a public speaker, may make his path to the premiership more difficult.

General Suchinda Kraprayoon is intelligent and good at communicating, but has a hard center. When an MP who had formerly been a Sergeant Major in the army criticized Suchinda in the House, the general commented: "As a general I could not allow Sergeant-Major Songham Panyadee to tell me to do this and that in Parliament. I might kick him in the middle of the floor because of my dignity."[16] That revealed a thin and undemocratic skin. Yet he became prime minister of a democratically elected government.

But Suchinda failed to produce a government stabler or more efficient than the one of Chatichai that he brought down.[17] His Samakkee Tham party lost face when its leader, Narong Wongwan, had to decline the premiership because the United States had refused him entry on the grounds of involvement with heroin trafficking. Suchinda himself then took the premiership but could not cope with mass protests which he allowed his troops to meet with machine-gun fire. A clever general, he betrayed a fatal lack of political sense in a time of crisis. His resignation was unlamented.

Small parties mean coalition governments whose leaders harbor different views and goals. Yet it is rare for one party to control the legislature. Shifting coalitions of the kind that have ruled Thailand in recent years offer little stability of administration or policy making. When they comprise parties that themselves contain different factions whose relative strength varies from election to election, the problem is compounded.

Yet the forces that brought party politics into Thailand in the first place are strengthening, not weakening. Economic growth and the steady enlargement of the middle class mean that more and more people who are better educated and politically aware are taking their places in the electorate, expecting to express their interests through political parties.

As things stand today, the parties are the easiest of the three major political forces to knock aside. The army can simply throw out a civilian elected government, as it did in 1991, or it can insinuate its leaders into controlling positions in politics as it did in 1992. When the army commander, General Chaovalit, retired in 1990, he stepped immediately into the deputy premiership, with the tacit assurance of inheriting the premiership after Chatichai retired. Suthichai Yoon, the outspoken editor of *The Nation,* wrote him an open letter. "Your going straight into the government," he argued, "will imply that either a top army commander can always demand a seat of political power almost at will, or that an elected civilian government cannot survive without the direct support of the military, or both. Neither of these bode well for the political future of Thailand." Suthichai made a similar comment on Suchinda's acceptance of the premiership.

A candid politician would probably retort that an elected civilian government would always, if it wanted to survive with maximum room for maneuver, maintain good relations with the army. Giving the defense ministry seat in the cabinet to an influential retired army general is one easy way of doing this, and most civilian governments (not only in Thailand) have done that. Adding the post of deputy prime minister, as Premier Chatichai did for Chaovalit, is to pay an even higher premium for this insurance policy—although the post carries no power, only prestige. The insurance policy is necessary because an army that is at odds with an elected civilian government is going to cause trouble for it—at first legally, but in the end illegally.

The army has an ally in its efforts to keep politicians on the straight and narrow path—the civil service. Bureaucrats are also salaried servants of the state and are usually as disgusted by the antics of corrupt politicians and businessmen as the soldiers are. They are well placed in their different departments to keep the army informed about what various politicians are up to. After the 1991 military coup, the army chose seasoned civil servants of proven administrative ability for a large number of caretaker cabinet posts, including the new prime minister, Anand Panyarachun. For just over a year the cream of the bureaucrats were able to introduce needed reforms without parliamentary carping and with full military support.

It is natural for a civil servant to feel doubtful about the new politician who comes to take over his department every few months or so. The senior Thai bureaucrat is royalist and conservative, though anxious about the social consequences of unbridled capitalism. He is uncomfortable with the new idea of Chinese businessmen (whom he used to admonish when they were still "outsiders") becoming ministers in control of his promotion. He is above all solicitous of the national traditions and institutions.

He has many ways of obstructing the political intentions of an elected government. When officials cut red tape in Thailand, the complaint goes, they cut it lengthwise. Elected MPs frequently grumble that bureaucrats do not act as public servants but as the servants of the officials above them. Each department is a little empire in itself, loath to collaborate with others. The head of one department may not speak to the head of another for several years. Prime Minister Kriangsak found a place in Thailand where five different agencies requested a budget to build the same bridge.

Arrogant, paternalistic, hierarchy-conscious and personality-oriented—that is the kind of Thai civil servant who filled the power gap after the absolute monarchy was abolished in 1932 and has only recently had to bow to the unfamiliar ways and goals of professional politicians. The army shares these characteristics. General Prem won his reputation as a prime minister who satisfied almost everybody by relying on the characteristic bureaucratic device of getting one hundred percent consensus on every matter—slow though that may be—before acting.

The army can act as a check, therefore, to the political parties and has done so in many of the coups d'état that have been carried out in the past 40 years. It can do so with even more success if it carries the civil service with it—and the bureaucrats would usually prefer to work with the army than with the politicians.

Who can thwart the army, if it grows too greedy and ambitious? This delicate and potentially dangerous role is played by the king. He is the nominal chief and ceremonial figurehead of the armed forces. At first he lacked the years and maturity to give orders to the commanders, but now his age and experience rival theirs. He can try to manipulate the personalities and factions within the army as best he can and bargain with the headstrong when they take such a rash and unconstitutional action as a coup d'état.

The generals need the king's acquiescence, if not full approval, for an intervention, and they are usually willing to take royal advice on a few matters if that will gain them legitimacy. Going against the king would greatly add to the risks of their venture. The king's personal popularity can become a crucial factor in how far a military intervention in politics will go. It does not take much clairvoyance to wonder whether Bhumiphol's successor on the throne would be as effective in keeping the political peace or at least minimizing the political fallout.

And there this remarkable system of checks and balances, the "moving equilibrium" in Thai politics, ends. The checking role is played by the army, which can challenge both the parliament and, if extremely provoked, the king. In some circumstances the king too can check parliament and the army. Parliament's role comes in the balancing part of the system. If another king were to behave arbitrarily or erratically, parliament and army would probably combine to stop him.

For the time being this is a play with three actors. But there are small parts that are enlarging. The businessmen have become more important. The Thai tradition so disparaged commerce that the occupation was specifically allocated to Chinese, no Thais being willing (or able?) to pursue it. It was not unlike the position of the Jews in Europe in the seventeenth and eighteenth centuries. The contempt for the calling was balanced by a determination to keep government as the preserve of "true Thais," and so businessmen were effectively excluded from political power. The 1973 revolution changed that. In the Prem governments of the 1980s, businessmen filled a third or even half of the parliamentary seats, and participated in the leadership of the three largest parties. Unlike Japan or Indonesia, where businessmen merely line themselves up behind professional politicians to make a formidable alliance, in Thailand the businessmen have themselves become politicians. Bhichai Rattakul of the Democrat party is an example. Unfortunately some of the businessmen-turned-politician have given a bad name to politics by escalating the scale of bribery.

The press is also becoming more important. Thai journalism has advanced in recent decades. But investigative reporters are still easily silenced by gifts or threats, and the death rate is high: 47 journalists were murdered over five years in the 1980s, all because of the work in which they were engaged. Pongsak, editor of the Thai-language newspaper *Matichon,* concedes that his colleagues in the press are "not responsible enough to society."[18] The few individuals who reject self-censorship and write their minds are criticized for washing dirty linen in public (the Thai expression is sharper—"pulling out your intestines to let the crows feed on them").

Students were politically important in some earlier periods. As far back as the 1920s a royal prince with the Thai legation in Paris was so strict with the Thai government students under his care that they turned anti-monarchist—and that was said to have been one of the causes of the 1932 revolution, which two of those students, Phibul and Pridi, went on to lead.[19] In 1973, under Thirayuth and Saeksan, the students also took a dramatic political lead, but it was along an ideological cul-de-sac. Then, in 1992, the university students again led angry protests against General Suchinda's assumption of the premiership, protests which led to violent confrontation with police and soldiers, probably a hundred deaths, a royal intervention, and the eventual retirement of Suchinda from the political arena.

Thirayuth himself correctly defined the students body as "an untainted force" in Thai politics that could appeal to the population at large free of the vested interests of the older institutional forces. But now capitalism and economic growth are turning the new generations of students toward consumerism and escapism. In 1990 the president of Chulalongkorn University's student body cut a thoroughly modern figure, holding a part-time job with a business company, collaborating with his professors on research, organizing a team of student tutors to earn pocket money and playing the stock market with some success.

Students still go to rural camps for voluntary social work, but find they are not as much appreciated as before. "We once went to needy villages and built schools," a Ramkhamhaeng University student explains. "Today the government has built schools in all of them. We used to have a simplistic notion about unselfish villagers leading a simple life. We went into a village and there they were—refrigerators and video tape recorders."

Buddhist monks are also beginning to count in politics. The older and more traditionalist priests are mostly wrapped up in their own self-cultivation, though the *sangha,* now losing influence, has always had strong links with the king. There are many younger and more progressive monks whose concern for society leads them to supervise economic development projects, advise politicians, bureaucrats and army leaders and take positions on the political issues of the day. Whereas the *sangha* relates to the monarchy, these modern monks cultivate army and civil service leaders, businessmen and politicians. Although influential, they are by definition a small group and have widely differing political views. In the twenty-first century all three of these groups—businessmen, students and monks—may play more important political roles.

The operation of these checks and balances between different forces dictates a zigzag path for Thai politics, treading into new democratic territory and then retreating for an authoritarian review of the rules. It is a process of two steps forward, one step back, a slow dialectic of democratic advance. The three major instruments in the process, defending different interests in different ways, supply a basis of pluralism to the system. Even the army, which has the most physical force available, would find it difficult to impose its wishes on an unwilling king and parliament. In the periods between military interventions (and these are tending to lengthen) the arguments about democracy can be carried forward and partly realized. Little by little, the kingdom becomes more democratic. The political maturity of the Thai nation was demonstrated by the army's endorsement in 1991 of the most qualified and experienced people to join the interim government as ministers and senior civil servants and by its subsequent staging of a freely competitive general election—though it then spoiled it by grabbing the premiership.

But how should democracy be best fashioned to suit the Thai genius? It is a question that has been posed for more than a hundred years, ever since the absolute monarchy of King Mongkut. Today it is posed with more intensity, more understanding and more knowledge. No one has ever tried to force political change upon the Thai people from the outside; they see it as a purely indigenous progression from autocracy to representative government. They would like their government to represent them more than it has done in the past, and they are beginning to get used to the phenomenon of voting. Gradually they will refine their system to become more democratic, but also more Thai. In the past there were always reasons why democratic experimentation had to be interrupted, the latest being the threat of communist insurgency and the Cold War. But all that has now passed, and the road ahead looks clear.

This step-at-a-time process of political reform is reinforced by the other ways in which Thailand is modernizing. Improved education and growing urbanization will produce more people with a reasoned and informed approach to their problems. When Governor Chamlong is asked how corruption can be reduced, he says, "We have to persuade the people, convince the people to be honest for our country." It is a matter of example, exhortation and education. Novels and movies help. The best-selling novelist Bunchoog Ciamwirija writes powerful books about honest local officials trying to reform the system and achieve justice in the face of vested interests. His novels thunder against corruption and nepotism and other harmful legacies of the past, and they sell in the tens of thousands. Their impact is continuous.

With each election, more voters observe and weigh the results of their previous vote, and have the chance to vote more sensibly, more to their own interest, more intelligently than before. Gradually the Thai voter will become more discriminating. Time is on democracy's side. Suchinda operated through a political party that acts under the same rules as all the other parties. But no one should expect a Western model. In spite of Marshal Phibul's bullheaded imposition of hats and spoons and Speakers' Corner, it is a local model that the Thai people are intuitively groping for.

Thailand has been lucky in its politics. It has been able to control the pace of its modernization and has therefore been able to absorb and adapt Westernization better than other Asian countries succumbing to colonial rule. Its internal disparities have not been exaggerated by colonialism or revolution. Thailand remains a Buddhist country where conciliation is preferred to conflict and where the personal need to preserve "face" is respected.

Thailand's modernization was set in motion by the monarchy. As guardians of Thailand's traditional values, the nineteenth- and early-twentieth-century kings were in the best possible position to mediate between the forces of tradition and modernization—until they lost control of the situation and were challenged by the army in 1932. The military dictatorships during the period of the Second World War and the Cold War preserved the core of the Thai nation through a dangerous era—maintaining independence, periodically introducing short-lived bursts of democracy and concentrating on economic growth.

The generals succeeded in keeping the Thai nation together. But they have so far failed to produce an enduring basis for democracy. To move forward from autocracy Thailand must now reach out in two directions. It must move toward the modern democratic tolerance of pluralism, in which the political parties must play a large role and which the army is supporting by exercising power through the political process. And Thailand must go back to the traditional skills of creative consensus formation, where the monarchy is again beginning to have a unique position, paralleling in some ways the role of the earlier Chakri kings.

The king is a mediator in contemporary Thai politics, but his role also embodies something intangible, but extremely positive, in Thai culture. It shows the handicap that other countries suffered in abolishing their monarchy without providing an alternative source of effective ultimate authority and prestige. India and Singapore have an almost powerless "constitutional presidency," Japan a "constitutional monarchy." The Philippines, Indonesia and Korea have an "executive presidency" that involves responsibility for the government of the country and cannot therefore be an impartial umpire as well. Thailand separates the two distinct functions of head of state and head of government but has not made the mistake of robbing the former of sufficient power and authority to intervene responsibly in the political arena.

On three grounds, therefore, Thailand's political system deserves commendation. It is visibly, though gradually, moving toward a more sophisticated level of party politics and democracy. It operates an effective system of checks and balances that prevents power becoming concentrated in any one quarter, whether military, parliamentary or royal. And it is confronting with reasoned argument and patient experiment the challenge which democratic institutions originating in the West pose for Thai traditional culture and self-respect.

3

The Monarchy:
Royal Rainmaker

The monarchy's balancing function in Thai politics can be discharged even without the absolute power that was surrendered in 1932. His residual constitutional authority provides King Bhumiphol with a platform on which he has been able, through his own character and performance on the throne, to build this indispensable political role. He did not inherit it; he had to earn it. As the years went by he came to know as much about the contemporary politics and economics of Thailand as the politicians with whom he had to deal. After only eleven years on the throne he felt strong enough to back Field Marshal Sarit, the army leader, in his coup against Field Marshal Phibul, the wily old dictator who had been obnoxiously lecturing the young king on what he should and should not do. Yet a few years later Bhumiphol, trained at Lausanne in international law, was firmly overruling Sarit to make him surrender a frontier temple that the International Court of Justice had awarded to Cambodia.

The king's big chance came in 1973, when Sarit's unpopular successors, the military dictators Thanom and Praphas, provoked unstoppable student protest. The king urged these hapless dictators to leave the country while he tried to restore order. He appointed a civilian academic as prime minister and convened the National Assembly of which he was so proud. But student power was not yet dissipated in spite of the democratic regime that followed, and the king was dismayed by the spreading anarchy and advance of Marxism that ensued, especially seen against the background of the growing communist threat from Vietnam. Apparently losing some of his faith in democracy, he began to show a keen interest in some of the new right-wing groups that sprang up in reaction—and that led the "counterrevolution" of 1976.

In the 1980s Bhumiphol learned how to head off unwelcome power-seekers. When the exemplary General Prem's elected government was threatened by dissident officers, the king threw his prestige into the ring. He took Prem under his royal protection and promoted him to the highest rank in all three services as a gesture of support. The coups failed.

There was almost a convention by then that coup leaders should inform His Majesty of their intentions beforehand. In 1977 this courtesy was withheld. General Kriangsak seized power without notice, from a government which the king had himself helped to bring about. Bhumiphol advertised his anger by wearing a business suit instead of traditional court dress at the next royal ceremony. After a later coup in 1991, he refused to sign a royal decree composed by the coup leaders, merely initialing it instead. Furthermore, the king gave the ousted prime minister, Chatichai Choonhavan, a royal honor. To receive this, Chatichai was allowed to return from exile in London—and the coup leaders afterward went to Chatichai's house to pay their respects. There is thus a conciliation role also performed by the monarchy. When Bhumiphol reproached Premier Suchinda before the TV cameras in May 1992, he had Chamlong, Suchinda's fiercest opponent, also on his knees in the Palace. He intervened again later in the year to appoint a Premier of his own choice.

But the king must not overplay his hand. That would risk having his already limited powers further curtailed. If there were a showdown (which Thais will always seek to avoid), the government has the resources and the army has the guns, but the monarchy has only popular goodwill.

This asset will increase in value the longer the king reigns, enabling him more effectively to backstop the nation's destinies whenever the army and political parties fall out. By the same token this royal fail-safe function, the product of age and experience, will fall when Bhumiphol no longer reigns.

The King may not have absolute power to back his political judgment, but he has something else to strengthen his hand—wealth. While developing his political skills, Bhumiphol cannily put his own finances in order. His grandfather, King Chulalongkorn, had founded Thailand's first bank, the Siam Commercial Bank, and King Vajiravudh pioneered the Siam Cement Company in 1913. Siam Cement is now the biggest corporation in Thailand, with a market capitalization of over $3.5 billion, having diversified into steel, shipping, property and papermaking. These two profitable enterprises are still controlled by the king through his Crown Properties Bureau, which has become a professionally managed conglomerate.[1]

This bureau is now an extensive landowner, and has a stake in 40 companies. It is the second-largest asset-holder and fourth-largest investor in the kingdom. Dividends from these royal investments provide a valuable supplement to the government's budget allocation for the royal household and enable the king to compete effectively in the political arena. The impeccably mannered director of the Crown Property Bureau, Dr. Chirayu Issarangkun na Ayuthaya—himself a distant cousin of the king—was considered a possible prime minister after the 1991 coup.

All this income gives the king some clout. In particular it allows him to pursue what he regards as his most important mission in life—economic development projects in the countryside. It may sound unconventional for a modern king to plan and supervise the construction of dams, irrigation canals, roads, fishponds and bridges in the least accessible parts of his realm. But Thailand is a developing country, with backward agriculture and forestry except in the rich central plain, and this king is no conventional monarch.

Bhumiphol's fascination with agronomy began early. "My interest in irrigation and forestry," he once confided, "dates from science lessons at age ten on the importance of soil conservation—how soil on denuded hills is easily eroded by rain. . . ." The king would by choice have pursued higher studies in science in Switzerland if dictator Phibul had not bullied him into taking up international law instead as a supposedly better preparation for monarchy. Bhumiphol's huge science-based development program, equal to that of some Third World governments, was perhaps, alongside its intrinsic worth, also a posthumous revenge on Phibul.

One new technique discussed in the science journals of the West early in his reign caught the king's imagination. Artificial rainmaking, if it really worked, would be most valuable in Thailand where farmers suffered frequently from drought. He calculated fourteen chemical formulae for seeding the clouds, paid for the research out of his privy purse and in 1971 sent up specially equipped light aircraft (ritually anointed by himself) to test his formulations. Now his specialist team induces rain on the fruit orchards, rubber trees, sugarcane and tapioca plantations of the south and east in the early months of the year, switching their attention after April to the paddy farmers of the central provinces. The Royal Rainmaking Research and Development Project has now "graduated" to lodge within the Ministry of Agriculture.

The very first royal development project was a humble fish, the tilapia, which the UN Food and Agriculture Organization suggested introducing into Thailand. The Thais are big fish-eaters. They derive half their animal protein from fish, but the supply had been declining since the 1920s and needed reinvigoration. Bhumiphol at once saw what a difference the tilapia, a hardy, prolific, fast-growing, easy-to-breed winner, could make. Ever the scientist, he first bred it in the palace swimming pool (the comments of his wife and children were not recorded) before dispatching fingerlings to village heads all over the country. Later Emperor Akihito, then Crown Prince of Japan, gave Bhumiphol an even better Egyptian variant of this useful species, the *tilapia nilotica,* which again he raised personally (in a palace pond—this time the swimming pool was voted out) before distributing nationwide. It is an extremely popular fish today.

But most of the king's efforts have gone into irrigation to bring water to parched fields. The initial request usually comes from a village headman. If it sounds worthwhile, the king will study what is known about the topography of the place, its water resources and rural conditions. He makes a preliminary plan, using a large-scale map. Then he goes to the village to see for himself.

The routine is now well established. The king sets off at a smart pace from one of his provincial palaces, camera at the ready round his neck, and compass, grease pencils, tape measure and plastic-covered maps in hand or pocket, followed with varying degrees of enthusiasm by his family and a bevy of doctors, nurses, agriculturalists, foresters, officials, bodyguards and retainers. The queen will show off one of her *haute couture* broad-brimmed straw hats with a colorful silk band, Princess Sirindhorn will write everything down in her notebook with a serious frown and the Crown Prince will try to look interested.

They walk for miles through blistering sun and drenching rain, over muddy paths or dusty tracks, bringing to the lucky far-off village a rare notice of the outside world, a fair hearing for complaints and hopes for a solution of problems. The king asks questions, puts his maps and instruments to good use, makes his own on-the-spot survey for the proposed dam site and gets opinions from his own experts and the government engineers accompanying him.

When all the data are assembled, the king decides what kind of dam should be built. He settles such details as the crest elevation and full supply level and issues instructions about spillways and canal alignments. These are received as guidelines for government action, not royal commands. He does not seek to compete with government agencies, but rather to provoke them into being more active, and his pressure is usually effective.[2]

Bacho, for example, a village in the south, had its crops ravaged every year by monsoon floods. The king explored the area and suggested to officials that they should build a three-and-a-half-mile canal by the sea to regulate the swamp water level and reduce flooding. It was built and it worked, and Bhumiphol reckoned it the happiest day of his life when he was told. Personal problems are also brought to him. A hill tribesman complained to the king that he had paid two pigs and a lot of money for his wife, yet she had gone off with another man. Bhumiphol ruled that the woman should go free but the man should be compensated. "The trouble was," the king laughingly explained afterward, "I gave the money, so the woman belonged to me!"[3]

Hiking one day in the forests around his hill palace of Bhuping in the north, the king came upon a tribal village of the Hmong, one of the poorest communities in the kingdom. Seeing how scraggly their pigs were, he showed them how to breed stronger ones and feed them better. This started a dialogue that was to embrace dams, fruit trees, the replanting of hillsides and a unique war on the opium poppy, their chief cash crop and source of income. In 1968 Bhumiphol donated his own money for an experimental orchard at Kasetsart University where other crops could be identified for them to cultivate. "If the hilltribes people can be encouraged to grow substituted cash crops," the king told agriculture students, "then opium cultivation will certainly diminish."

The Royal Hilltribe Development Project was therefore launched in 1969, and hundreds of researchers, extension workers and key farmers now participate in a network of research stations and crop replacement centers in this Thai section of the infamous "Golden Triangle." Apples, peaches, strawberries, roses, lilies, chrysanthemums, brussels sprouts, turnips and cabbage (of which more later) are among the crops introduced as substitutes for the poppy in this temperate hilly region.

Doubtful at first, the Hmong gradually took up the new crops. They found that strawberries, mushrooms and coffee in particular yield a return two or three times bigger than opium. The fresh flowers at the restaurant tables of Bangkok come from these former opium fields. Relapse to opium growing is now a problem. But the king never pretended that a solution would be quick and easy. At least he has made the effort where his government hung back.

Aside from the tilapia breeding in their swimming pool and a plant in the compound transforming animal droppings into bio-gas, the royal mother and children also put up with a full-scale dairy farm and modern milk plant in their palace grounds. Pasteurized, powdered and condensed milk are produced there. The king even established a demonstration forest in those accommodating palace grounds, having started many important reforestation programs around the country.

The six Royal Development Study Centers bring all these threads together. The king once explained his vision for these centers: "Personnel from all agencies concerned with agricultural or social development are assembled together in one place . . . People who need their services or wish to observe various techniques also gather at the same location . . . This means that those at the giving end and those at the receiving end are brought together at one place . . ." Bridging these gaps between humans in such a hierarchical society as Thailand is just as important, the king now believes, as building bridges across rivers. It also supplies the missing bricks on which democracy must build if it is to mean anything. And it strengthens the king's popular base.

It was always a feature of Bhumiphol's projects that they are formulated not from the air-conditioned comfort of national or provincial offices but after intimate contact and consultation with the future beneficiaries on the spot. "In working out a programme to help people," he argued, "It is necessary that you know the people you intend to help. . . . One does not know a people by merely memorising some research papers. . . . You must meet them and like them." When he is sloshing about in the rice fields, this farmer-king gets nearer to the paddy-roots than the thousands of buttoned-up bureaucrats in his government.

Common-sense humanity of this kind is rare in the development business. When the Food and Agriculture Organization in Rome published a book, *The King and Agriculture in Thailand,* for his sixtieth birthday, it paid tribute to his projects. Many of them "had a pioneering character and have served as path-breakers in agricultural development." The FAO singled out for praise the king's insistence on moderation of costs, use of natural energy, participation of beneficiary farmers in construction and maintenance work, encouragement of cooperatives and the education of farmers to enable them to gain the maximum benefit from projects.

It seems that the king instinctively knew how development questions ought to be tackled long before these lessons had percolated through the ranks of the officials. Of course he is able to act as an individual, however exalted, by, for instance, donating prime crown estate to landless farmers or paying for urgent needs out of his own pocket.

For the "Greening of Isarn"—the irrigation and reforestation of the arid infertile provinces of Northeast Thailand—the king acquired a military ally. The army needed a new challenge after the disappearance of the communist threat in the 1980s, and so it took up economic development in the areas previously vulnerable to subversion. The Northeast was a priority zone, and soldiers implemented the royal blueprints for the area, to the satisfaction of both sides. This gave the king a new point of contact with the generals he so often had to restrain from coups.

These days Bhumiphol sees himself as a "consultant" or "Royal Advisor," passing on to each village his rich experience of 40 years in the development business. Long before it became internationally fashionable, he lectured his peasants about the need to avoid pollution and sustain the environment. Like any good United Nations expert, he wants farmers to "make themselves self-supporting, to stand on their own feet. That is why it is important not to give too much. . . . You must give the minimum. The minimum amount."[4]

The king's rural peregrinations fuse together the two contradictory halves of his personality: the magical-archaic from the past, which guarantees him an audience, and the rational-improving of the present and future, which assuages his guilt at holding such inherited power and prepares the ground for a future Thailand with more equality. That is why he spends more than half the year on his rural rounds. Being a king does not always mix well with being a development economist-agronomist, however. A peasant may turn down the advice of Mr. Smith, the foreign expert sent by the United Nations, but can hardly spurn the improvement recipes of his own god and king. By once proving fallible, the king who tells his subjects where best to align their irrigation ditches or which new crops to grow might stand to lose not only popularity but godhead, too.

There is also a problem of feedback. No Thai likes to tell his king that a royal project has collapsed, or that his recommendations do not work. When he realized that money and resources were being used to make the projects he wanted to visit look good, Bhumiphol started refusing to tell his aides where he intended to go. The unwieldy retinue would assemble without the least idea where it would be heading. That way the wily monarch ensured that he came upon a village or a project without advance warning and could get a realistic picture of its condition. But this approach caused such inconvenience and inefficiency along the way that he now compromises. Half the visits are surprise visits, half are planned ahead—a very Thai solution!

The thousand development projects of King Bhumiphol could fill a book, and do. His admirers have produced just such a volume, a coffee table production packed with photographs and with many technical details.[5] But considering the king's intelligence and drive, and the means at his disposal, it is a little surprising that some observers in Thailand find the results of his development program disappointing.

To some extent the king is a victim of his own pioneering instinct. He was the first to do something, as we have seen, about the cultivation of opium by the Hmong hill people, persuading them to grow cabbages, among other crops, instead of poppies. Now there is some wringing of hands because the cabbages erode the soil faster than the poppies did, and the entire hill economy is threatened.

The king has managed to surround himself with advisors, mostly unpaid volunteers, some of whom may not be up to professional standards. His Director of Royal Development Projects is a cousin and long-time associate, Prince Bhisadej Rajani, who taught the King dinghy sailing and helps him build boats. Bhumiphol, as a Thai, feels the tug of social tradition which puts personal relationships before principles, friendship before material achievement. He instinctively stands by his old friends and long-serving associates. To replace them with unknown young technocrats, however bright, would be a betrayal, a loss of "face." Here is a royal dilemma.

The royal contribution is thus home-grown rural development with all its faults, on a modest scale. That reflects the king's ideal for Thailand—meaning fewer achievements, perhaps, than the World Bank would chalk up, but fewer losses, human or financial, too. Luckily for Bhumiphol, Thai farmers rank the royal good intentions, visible accomplishments and transparent concern for the people's welfare above questions of his actual rate of effectiveness. These farmers are not always very efficient themselves, so perhaps they understand the phenomenon.

Meanwhile who would not be stirred to see his sovereign striding down the valley mudpath to one's humble village—not to levy tax or conscript men, not to gulp the seasonal delicacies without payment, but to offer practical help to augment the income of farmers? Who would not be won over by royal talk of a superior new rice or tapioca hybrid with which the king himself has experimented on his own grounds and of which he has thoughtfully brought samples to distribute? Who would not be impressed by the king's promise to put up a cannery or a food-processing plant to enable farmers to make more from their crops?

So the king leads his cavalcade triumphantly on to the next village, leaving behind another priceless piece in a unique legend. Successful or not, the development projects have created a political following that, however intangible and scattered, allows the king quietly to defy outrageous demands from ambitious generals or political party leaders.

The applause is not quite unanimous. Younger educated people are not so easily mesmerized by the mystique and can be quite dismissive of palace protocol. "The monarchy is an out-of-date institution," declared Thirayuth Boonmee, the left-wing student leader, over the Communist party jungle radio in 1977. "If the people want to destroy it, they will not lose anything."[6]

When he afterward turned his back on the communists and left the jungle for Bangkok again, Thirayuth was not penalized for his incipient republicanism. Some public figures have been punished, however, for criticism of the king considered by officials to constitute *lèse-majesté*. The king is protected by jealous courtiers against comment that most monarchies might shrug off. A Deputy Minister of Interior had to resign in 1986 because he made an election speech in the poverty-stricken Northeast comparing the meager lot of the local peasant with the luxury of the royal family in Bangkok: if he could have chosen where to be born, he would have opted for the Grand Palace. That was portrayed as a violation of the king's dignity, though most people saw the *lèse-majesté* charge as being used for partisan political purposes.[7]

One critic fought back. In a magazine interview, Sulak Sivaraksa declared that the king might think he understood the Thai people, but was actually surrounded by courtiers. "Especially when he goes up-country, a lot of people come to see him, he thinks he understands." Sulak deepened the wound with the remark that "Personally, he is a good man but a weak man. To be quite blunt, he does not know what his present role is in the present society."[8] A right-wing group, the National Paramilitary Club, demanded his prosecution for *lèse-majesté*. But very few Thais are willing to criticize their hero, the only permanent star on a public stage where other actors come and go with bewildering rapidity.

There is one heavy cross which the hard-working king bears. His family does not share his ideals or his outstanding popularity. Queen Sirikit has charm but is said on occasion to lack her husband's political finesse. According to rumors, she was the only member of the royal family singled out as a target for assassination in an unsuccessful dissidents' plot in the early 1980s.

Queen Sirikit promotes rural literacy programs, helps orphans and disad-vantaged children, patronizes handicrafts and heads the Thai Red Cross, but makes no secret of her distaste for the endless traipsing around the rude countryside in Bhumiphol's wake. "I sometimes long to be the wife of a rich man," she told a reporter in 1980, "going abroad shopping or buying beautiful clothes or jewellery. But instead I have to go to a remote area. . . ."[9]

The king's children have also, with one exception, failed to fulfill his high hopes. The eldest of the four, the extremely gifted Princess Ubol Ratana, so distinguished herself in nuclear physics at the Massachusetts Institute of Technology that she abdicated her royal rank and title, turning her back on Thailand to remain in America and marry an American engineer, Peter Jensen. It took nine years and the birth of a grandchild to reconcile King Bhumiphol with his eldest daughter.

The only boy is the crown prince, Vajiralongkorn, whose strained appear-ance, imperious manner and short span of attention make some thoughtful Thais view with concern the prospect of his becoming the ruler of the kingdom. When the prince went to prep school at Seaford in England it was found that he could not tie his own shoelaces. Such things had been done by the palace servants. He went on to Millfield School, also in England, with other princes of small countries and the sons of rich movie actors. There he got his first taste of paramilitary assault, which he loved, and which prepared him for a military career as an Air Force officer flying jets.

Vajiralongkorn married early—perhaps too early—to a childhood friend and cousin, Soamsawali Kittiyakra. But he is, as his mother engagingly admitted, "a little bit of a Don Juan . . . women find him interesting and he finds women even more interesting."[10] Soamsawali bore him a daughter by cesarean birth, and it looked as if he would be denied the son that Thai families, especially royalty, expect. He took a second wife, an actress, who gave him four sons, the eldest called Chudhawatchara. The crown prince is separated from his first wife and insists that others regard his second wife and family as having full status and precedence.

These royal arrangements pose acute problems of protocol, especially when Vajiralongkorn pays official visits to countries with monarchies. In Japan, for example, in 1987, Thai correspondents reported that the Japanese resented being asked to treat wife number two, whom the prince took along, as his consort and "official" wife. The Japanese palace refused to include her in the combined royal party. Afterward some Thai groups hung black wreaths on the gate of the Japanese embassy in Bangkok, and some Thais called for a boycott of Japanese goods.[11]

At one point the crown prince became the target of defamatory leaflets, something without precedent in the monarchy. "If the people of Thailand," his mother said firmly, "did not approve of the behaviour of my son, then he would either have to change his behaviour or resign from the royal family." Many Thais hope that his ways may settle down with the years.

The king's favorite is said to be his second daughter, Princess Sirindhorn. She appears to be capable, sensible, loyal, patient and personable, is unmarried and acts increasingly as her father's right hand. She undertakes a grueling daily round of openings, visits, presentations, ceremonies, celebrations and receptions—all well covered by the media. A natural speaker, she puts people at their ease, and has the inestimable gift of looking interested on all public occasions. She lectures on Thai history and performs traditional Thai music. Many Thais wish that she would succeed her father. But a woman has never ruled this kingdom, and it is the immemorial Thai tradition that a boy inherits.

The third daughter, Princess Chulabhorn, is a biochemist married to an Air Force group captain. She prefers the academic life, but has sold a million copies of her popular songs. Occasionally she speaks in public on scientific subjects, including the question of AIDS, a potential disaster in Thailand.

So the royals, pursuing their official duties, largely go their separate ways, assembling only for those important occasions when the monarchy as an institution would otherwise suffer. Meanwhile the king's health is not first-rate. Never a truly healthy man, he drives himself harder than most other Thais. In the early 1980s he was struck down with pneumonia and myco-plasma—a heart and lung complaint—and suffered a relapse. Since then he has reshouldered his burden of rural treks and drawn-out palace duties where he is on show for hours on end.

If Bhumiphol's successor were to overreact to political events and take sides in partisan contests, that might fuel a cry to pension the Chakris off to their beloved Switzerland and leave Thailand as a republic. But it would not be heeded. The Thais love their traditions and court ceremonial. The warm feelings that King Bhumiphol and Princess Sirindhorn have aroused will not be quickly dissipated. The political and military leaders still prefer a neutral and independent umpire for their squabbling, one far above the smoke of the battlefield, and with a centuries-old mystique that makes it easier for a loser to accept his fate.

The king himself has defined his role as trying to "keep a middle, peaceful and neutral co-existence with all the pressure groups in the country," explaining that "ordinary people who cannot make their views known must look up to someone who is impartial." And if that is not accepted? "If one wants to destroy someone who is impartial," he told us, "one destroys oneself." The ultimate weapon is a moral one, and a very Buddhist one.

Rama X will not need to perform quite as adroitly—or dangerously—as Bhumiphol has done. If only a suitable royal replacement capable of personal growth and self-improvement can be produced, the kingdom should be safe from civil discord and the indispensable royal function of boosting public morale and promoting national unity will go on.

4

The Changing Thai Personality:
Behind the Smile

Just as the personalities of monarchs differ, and the character of the army and parliament changes over the decades, so the personality of the Thai nation itself, and of Thai individuals, is altering. These changes need to be comprehended by those who wish to fathom the modern social superstructure that is being built upon the old foundations.

The Thai cultural tradition continues to perplex foreigners. Stanley Karnow, the *Washington Post* journalist, was banned from Thailand for writing, among other things, that the Thais "smile like Cheshire cats."[1] He may have meant it kindly; in Lewis Carroll's story, the constant smile of the Cheshire cat could still be seen hovering in the air, long after the rest of the creature had disappeared. The impression of the Thai smile remains similarly vivid even after the smiler has gone. Yet a Western professor of Thai studies openly rejoiced on leaving Thailand for the last time, knowing that he would never again be irritated by that unfailing simper. The Thai smile is not just for good news or delight; it comes into play when anger, doubt, anxiety or grief are the underlying emotions, and a foreigner can easily misinterpret it.

Smiling is an integral part of the Thai personality—part of the old traditional culture which is gradually altering, but is still significant in Thai life. It is, of course, presumptuous to talk about a country's personality. Western writers can describe Thai social culture only from a Western viewpoint, and if that is taken to mean regarding Western behavior as the norm, it risks a biased conclusion and bolstered stereotypes. But there is no superculture up in the sky to which we can appeal to describe Thai culture, so cross-cultural reference is natural and unavoidable. Some kind of map of the world of Thai people, however partial and abbreviated, is needed.

There were always exceptions and variations to the traditional Thai mode of behavior. Now modernization is changing the picture in a broadly more Western direction. In the traditional system a poor farmer's work and service obligation to his landlord was matched by reciprocal responsibilities on the latter's part to look after him. But when the peasant moves to the city to work in a factory, he becomes more dependent on his employer, receives less expression of social concern from him, and has fewer alternative options. That is how traditions change.

The best way to look at it is to say that there are three layers of Thai behavior. The traditional "bottom" layer is what outsiders find most difficult to know and understand; it is found mainly in the rural areas, but it also underlies the other levels of behavior in the towns. The second, "middle," layer, smaller than the first, is the modernized urban Thai's behavior, where the traditional system is modified in the light of the increasingly modern demands and opportunities of urban life as it is found worldwide. This is the kind of contrast that the peasant finds when he moves to Bangkok to work in a textile mill. A *farang* would find much of that urban lifestyle familiar, being shared with almost every large town or city across the world, but there is an important part of it that will still baffle him, and that is the traditional underlay.

Finally there is a third and most recent layer of Westernized behavior at the top of society, practiced by well-educated middle- or upper-class people who have adopted some Western customs. With dictator Phibul it used to be compulsory hats and marital kisses on the porch. Today it is a whole range of adaptations from the West including suits and dresses, classical music and pop songs, political parties and vasectomy. Some of the Thais in this thin crust at the top are so Westernized, typically after several years at Harvard or Oxford University, that they speak idiomatic English and are thoroughly familiar with the "international" culture. The *farang* who meets only this favored elite may well leave Thailand feeling that he really understands the place—except, maybe, for one or two surprising incidents where the Thai stuffing pops out from beneath the Westernized crust in moments of stress, forgetfulness or fatigue.

The Thai people never fell for the Confucianist collectivities of China and Japan to the east, or the universal ethic of Christian Europe in the West. The Thai starts by seeing the human world as a world of particular individual persons—not at all sentimentally, but rather in a wholly practical down-to-earth sense. As a Buddhist, he does not see them as a totality, but is aware of them individually, one by one, as they impinge on his consciousness and enter his life, each in a different way with a different purpose and attributes.

Policemen will not stop a minister's car, social superiors are given overtly favorable treatment and Thais do not often play the "good Samaritan" with strangers.

A Thai develops mutual obligations and relationships with the persons he encounters in life, but is not driven as members of many other societies are to bundle them into groups, which can then be labeled for ease of deciding how to treat them—and the labels may then become inflexible. There is vertical hierarchy, but not horizontal grouping. An outsider can walk into a Thai's world without the burden of preconceived ideas or prejudices.

British prisoners of war in a Japanese camp in Thailand during the Pacific War were heartened when local villagers surreptitiously brought them food. After the Japanese surrender the British changed roles with their guards, upon which the Thai villagers fed the Japanese prisoners with the same solicitude. They had no concept of nationality or military alliances, but Buddhism led them to care for persons in need as long as there was no danger of their becoming committed to any long-term obligation. This is the reason why Thailand is so receptive to foreign influences. The family is for the same reason looser in Thailand than in China or Japan.

How a Thai behaves to another person depends on the previous history of mutual services or obligations between them. This gives Thai social intercourse much variety and choice of relationship. It encourages—or perhaps it springs from—a strong individualistic streak. But that can become hidden behind a social disguise of smiles, gentleness and sycophancy.

Buddhism teaches the Thai to concentrate on self-cultivation more than social works. Without the spur of a universal ethic, therefore, and without benefit of labels, the Thai needs to ensure for himself that his social relationships are going to be as smooth and pleasant as possible. *Farangs* sometimes take this as a cover for insincerity and opportunism, and there are occasions when it is. But it is much more than that: it is an insurance against the potential vulnerability of not having either a universal morality or a tightly knit structure of social groups within which to act.

The smile as defense mechanism is one tactic in the general Thai strategy for avoiding conflict. The concept of "face" is another. Thais find it difficult to oppose another person in his or her presence—unless it is a kind of ritualized game such as national politics, where character assassination is acceptable and is enjoyed. Ex-Premier Kriangsak's calling Kukrit a homosexual and Ex-Premier Kukrit's calling Kriangsak a drunkard did not harm either of them during the election campaign.[2] But when Thailand in the 1980s had an elected cabinet under a nonelected prime minister (General Prem), it was praised by an academic commentator as allowing the prime minister to escape the *humiliation* of political campaigning.[3] This kind of concern can be taken to an extreme, as when a Thai teaching the Thai language to a *farang* may not presume to correct the foreigner's mistakes, even though that is the whole point of the exercise and what he is paid for.

Thai people have more than the average human share of pride and sense of independence and dignity. They cannot easily tolerate the violation of their ego—or that of anyone close to them, such as their father or mother. For this reason they go to some lengths not to cause another person discomfort or inconvenience, that being the basis on which they can expect similar treatment from him in return. Without any established network of universal ethic or collective obligations, security and reciprocity have to be established independently within each individual relationship. In this sense social life in Thailand is more fun, but also more tricky, than life in Western countries.

The smile and saving of face do not arise from fear, diffidence or deference. They are part of a more positive and much richer system of relationships. The positive side is that Thais have much choice in their relationships and can be most intense in each one when they feel so inclined, certainly in the short-term, and even in the long. The wasteful side of it is an excessive concentration on outward appearances. Not long ago a number of MPs organized an impressive ceremony at the parliament building to receive honorary degrees from a private university in the Philippines that was actually defunct. Their sole aim was to get the prestige of the initials after their names.[4] Another massive scandal was the forging of thousands of donation certificates by Bangkok businessmen, with the connivance of senior monks and government officials, in order to support requests for royal honors. The cachet of the empty label is so highly valued that little attention is paid to the content. Even individual Thais who do work hard for social goals, like the slum clearance hero Pratheep Ungsongthon or the reformist monk *Phra* Buddhadasa, win little recognition at home until they first attract some international honor.

It follows that if persons are the key, then the system or ideology necessarily takes second place. It is difficult for a Thai to accept the concept of the equality of individuals; the Buddhist teaching that men are unequal in the spiritual stage they have reached in life reinforces his empirical knowledge that in the real world individuals are far from equal, whether in physique, gifts, skill, power or wealth.

Another corollary of being in a world of individual persons is that Thais are themselves very individualistic, enjoying a strong sense of individual autonomy, and liable to stray into eccentricity. Their dislike of group discipline makes them, for example, less than ideal soldiers or, as the student leaders demonstrated in the 1970s, communist guerrillas. The social system is a loose one, tolerating a variety of individual behavior and even the flaunting of nonconformist manners if they harm nobody. The facade of the smile can mask a strong individual ego and hide a tension, competitiveness and determination that a *farang* might never recognize because of the placid exterior.

The apparent gentleness has to be reconciled with the extraordinary violence which does sometimes break out. The horrifying carnage by outside thugs at Thammasat University in 1976 was one example. A water polo match between engineering and science students once erupted into a full-scale battle involving a thousand people wielding sticks, stones and knives. Thailand is said to have one of the highest murder rates in the world, dominated by *crimes passionelles*. A British engineer, David Law, learned about this aspect of the Thai personality too late. When he publicly accused his Thai wife of infidelity in 1987, the humiliated menfolk in her family beat him to death and dumped his corpse in a well.[5] There are often cases of servants who endure an employer's harsh treatment for years and years without complaint, and then their patience suddenly snaps and they attack and even kill their persecutor.

Modernization increases the tensions in the Thai psyche, leading to a surprisingly high incidence of neurosis as well as murder. Their strong sense of individuality makes the Thais yearn for self-expression and open communication, but this is stifled in a society which insists on identifying them by their outward appearance rather than their inner qualities, so psychological tension is generated. The consequence is that they avoid becoming involved in other people's problems. A good rule in Thai life is to keep away from conflict and to restrict contacts with other people to the superficial level.

To escape from all these problems, Thais have a legitimate outlet of relaxation in what is called *sanuk* or "fun." *Sanuk* is a very old part of Thai life that makes life enjoyable. Having fun and deriving pleasure from carefree amusement with congenial friends or companions has a positive value in the code of behavior: no one indulging in *sanuk* would expect to be blamed or criticized. This is when the smile becomes genuine. A Thai author defines the Thai way of life as "an elegant sort of life, surrounded by benevolent and exuberantly plentiful Nature, with adaptable morals and a serene detachment to the more serious problems of life. . . . To a Thai, life itself is one long relaxation."[6] Here we come to the essence of the Thai ideal. Spontaneity is valued in itself: Thais dislike planning ahead, and the best interviews can be when you call without appointment, yet the mood is right. The impromptu encounter is always more fruitful.

The festival of *Loi Krathong,* at the end of the rainy season in October and November, is a good source of *sanuk.* When all the hard work of ploughing and planting rice has been done, leaves molded into the shape of birds or boats are floated down the nearest river. Each one contains a lighted candle, incense and sometimes a small coin or betel nut. Thais come down to the river bank in the evening to socialize and admire the flickering procession of lights on the water, letting off their own water-fireworks for good measure. Downstream, children plunge into the river and scramble for the most beautiful of the boats as trophies. The origins of this, the most important Thai holiday, are now obscure. Perhaps the toy boats carry offerings to the Goddess Me Khongkha, Mother of Water, but the essence of the festival is a joyous celebration of *sanuk.*

The *Songkran* festival at the traditional Thai New Year in mid-April is another highlight in the Thai calendar. It begins sedately enough with Buddhistic merit-making ceremonies and offerings to priests and elders, but culminates in beauty contests, the tippling of rice whisky and a riotous orgy of water-splashing. In Chiang Mai the fun centers around water-splashing on a circuit around the old town moat. All kinds of vehicle—cars, motorcycles with side-cars converted into water tanks and public buses—cruise around with horns, hooters, drums and sirens blaring, while the occupants gleefully volley buckets of iced water at pedestrians and passersby (who retaliate in good-humored kind). Everyone joins in and *farangs* are a prime target—all in good *sanuk.*

Eating is traditionally a sociable activity, and Thai food is most distinctive—quite different from either of the two main families of Asian cuisine, Indian and Chinese. Usually it is eaten with a spoon and not with a bowl of rice using chopsticks. The Thais never acquired the chopstick habit from the Chinese, and the mandatory use of spoons and forks decreed by Field Marshal Phibul 50 years ago has endured.

A Thai meal will characteristically start from the premise of the five flavors which lie at the root of the Chinese cuisine, namely bitter, salt, sour, hot and sweet. But the dishes are made with a subtle opposition of flavors—lime with sweet potato, chili with coconut or lemongrass with ginger. Above all there is *nam prick,* the extremely spicy sauce which many foreigners cannot stomach but the Thais love, and *tom yam,* a spicy soup containing shrimp, chicken or pork. A typical dinner might start with boned chicken wings stuffed with minced pork and spices and then steamed and subsequently fried, served with a sweet-sour plum sauce. As Buddhists, the Thais do not eat much meat, but the main dish could be shellfish, game or fish, perhaps cooked whole with a sauce of galingale, tamarind, lemongrass and chili.

What *farangs* usually remember are the curries, which, unlike the Indian versions, use coconut milk or cream to thicken the stock at the end, thus softening the fierceness of the chili, ginger, coriander, garlic and black pepper that are put in. The green curries are special favorites.

Just as the Thais judge people from their outward appearance more than their inward reality, so they serve meals often with fruits or vegetables carved into blossoms and leaves, or they may garnish puddings and salads with roses or orchids. The quest for harmony is satisfied when each dish has several flavor accents, one of which is predominant—sour or spicy, for example. Nowhere else in the world is this particular culinary concatenation found: Thai cuisine is as unique as the Thai personality, and is enjoyed as such.

What may surprise a foreigner most in all this about Thai characteristics is the length to which a Thai will go to protect the self-respect of other persons, knowing that they will protect his. At a faculty meeting junior lecturers will voluntarily abstain from opposing the department head's proposals, however silly—though if it seems important enough, they might later beard him privately to argue with him. It is not that they are timid or frightened, but rather that damaging his self-respect in front of the others would harm him and the department, as well as opening themselves to his retaliation and the others' condemnation for what would be considered insolent bad manners. There was an element of this when the 1991 coup leaders went to pay their respects to Chatichai, the prime minister whom they had brusquely toppled.

"Face" can hinder public business. If you want to discuss with your colleagues when to harvest the rice or whether to introduce a new tax, the efficient way is surely to hear all the different points of view and ideas and to have them criticized. Thai society denies itself this useful function as the price of protecting the self-respect of the individuals concerned.

In this world of persons, a Thai deals with other individuals in all their different shapes and sizes, with all their different interests and attributes, on the basis of their varying baskets of mutual obligations with himself—not on any preconceived blanket concept of equality. Every relationship is tailor-made, instead of being taken off the shelf. Each individual is *different,* and has room to pursue his own will or destiny —supported by Buddhism. Every relationship has to be separately and individually reconnoitered. The smile and gentleness are there to promote an outward pleasantness of encounter, protecting the smiler against the possible bad intentions of strangers.

This brief sketch of the significant elements that compose the contemporary Thai personality makes it possible to see where Thai behavior sometimes differs from that in other countries. There are many things taken for granted in the West which the Thai "world of persons" neglects. For one thing, most Thais are not so conscious of their race. They may be vaguely aware of being a part of a very large family of peoples speaking languages akin to Thai, or dialects of Thai (including the Karen in Burma, the Lao in Laos and the Tai minorities in southern China, all of whom share similarities of speech and culture with the Thais). But most Thais in Thailand do not think of themselves as members of an exclusive Thai race as such, not in the way that the English or Anglo-Saxon race is sometimes (or used to be) talked about. Race is a collectivity that does not concern them much. In the past six centuries or so the Thais have mixed irretrievably with Mons, Khmers, Burmese, Vietnamese, Malays and Chinese.

"To be a Thai today," says Kukrit Pramoj, "one is not qualified by colour, race or blood but by a certain way of life and . . . respect towards certain institutions. . . . There are Thais with fair hair and blue eyes." He refers to the children of mixed marriages with Westerners. Kukrit's views on this are interesting, and very few other Thais are able to articulate them as he does:

> A Thai can be black or white or yellow and from different ancestry—Indian, Chinese, *farang*, anything—but they are all accepted. There are no half-castes in this country. You may have an English father and a Thai mother, but . . . if you accept Thai values, Thai ideals, then you become a Thai. . . . A Thai . . . knows whether or not another person is a Thai or not, regardless of his skin or his religious belief.[7]

The main criterion for accepting another person as Thai is whether he or she speaks a Thai dialect without accent and lives in a Thai style. Physical features are not important, perhaps inevitably when there has been so much intermixture all round the edges of the kingdom with neighboring peoples.

There are cases of racial discrimination, to be sure. Under the strongly nationalistic Phibul dictatorship, Mechai Viravaidhya's father was passed over in promotion at the Chulalongkorn University medical faculty because he had a Scottish wife. A little earlier, Prince Chula, that lion of London society in the 1930s, may have been barred from the throne, to which he had some claim of succession, because he had a Russian mother (he went on to spoil what little chance he had left by marrying a British girl). But such acts of discrimination are less frequent now and were rarely accompanied by general protestations about the "purity" of the Thai race. They do not upset the definition given by Kukrit.

When American forces were based in Thailand in the 1960s and 1970s, many so-called Amerasian children resulted, and homes had to be found for those who were effectively fatherless. The Pearl Buck Foundation helped many of them, and the Thai government also assisted generously.[8] But a trade grew up in young European-looking girls whose services were sought by rich residents of Bangkok, both Thai and *farang*. These young people, betrayed by their fair features as having Caucasian blood, are found particularly attractive by the Thai middle class. In the pop world, too, models, dancers and singers with a hint of European looks are often more successful with young Thai audiences than fully Thai performers.

The lighter skin color of the Chinese compared with the Thai endows the children of "Sino-Thai" unions with a slightly lighter complexion than most Thais, and that is considered a great advantage in society. "It is well known that mixed-race children are good-looking," writes Uncle Go, author of a famous Thai advice column—meaning Thai-European or "Sino-Thai" children.[9] Filipinos are also lighter-skinned than Thais, so it is no surprise to find pop stars and models carrying Philippine names. One of the most successful singers in Bangkok, Billy Ogan, has a Philippine father.

But Watcharee Chanmansin, the sixteen-year-old child of an unknown black GI, illustrates the other extreme. Her father went back to the United States when she was still a baby. Her mother did not register the birth, and without a birth certificate the girl was entitled to only one year of schooling. By the age of fifteen she had become a solvents addict, marijuana smoker and mother of a baby whose father also walked off into the blue. Her half-black features distinguish her physically in the crowd, the neighbors call her "negro," and young people in the slum area where she lives ply her with insults because of her appearance.[10] The tolerance of Thai society extends to lighter coloring but not so readily to darker.

Many members of the Thai aristocracy and elite have married into the white races. Prince Chula's father was not the only prince to marry a Russian or German girl, and Kukrit's wife is half Russian. Prime Minister Thanin's son married a British girl, and there are many examples of Thais in the professional and middle classes, like Mechai Viravaidhya or Air Chief Marshal Siddhi Savetsila, who show by their features that they have some Caucasian ancestry. They are not noticeably discriminated against. The few cases of race-consciousness do not detract from the proposition that racial identity is not important in Thailand. A Thai is almost always more concerned with Thai culture than with the physical appearance of the person practicing it.

That goes a long way to explain the capacity of Thailand to absorb cultural features from other countries. At the mundane level, one has only to look at the bank balance of Bill Heinecke, who lived in Thailand as a child and returned to enter business life. He shrewdly predicted the swift conversion of Thai taste to fast foods ten years ago, and has now made a fortune out of doughnuts, hamburgers and pizzas. Thais do not look down on other human beings, seeing them as individual persons. Migrants to Thailand are thus made to feel at home. Their apprehensions are disarmed and they are literally charmed into the Thai way of behavior and ultimately assimilated into the Thai identity. Only the Chinese with their large-scale immigration in the past one hundred years placed any strain on that Thai toleration.

Thailand's modernization was stimulated by the import of technology, ideas and values from the West. That process was not handicapped by negative associations of the kind that have sometimes held back similar developments in countries that were colonized. In Burma or India the prospective importer from England had to fight against his nationalistic aversion to England as long as memories of the independence struggle lasted. Machinery or ideas were often deliberately brought from other sources than Britain even if they contributed less to local modernization. Industrial modernization itself could be questioned by Gandhi partly because of anti-Britishism. Thailand suffered from none of these emotional confusions or crossed wires.

Inevitably there is some inverted snobbery, or what Sulak Sivaraksa calls "worship of the white man." He once had a dramatic encounter with this phenomenon when he went to the Oriental Hotel dressed in his usual traditional Thai costume—collarless shirt, loose pantaloons and sandals—to meet the German foreign minister. He was turned back at the entrance, and had to appeal to the hotel manager before being allowed in. "If you want to be somebody in this country," he acidly commented, "you have to dress like a European." It has to be said that there are not many Thais who go out in this kind of dress anymore. Interestingly, the Thai phrase for the Western suit is "international dress."

A striking case of dependence on a foreign culture was the work of Prince Wan, the Thai language expert who coined many new Thai words for concepts coming from abroad. He did this by going back to Pali, the archaic root language from which Thai developed. But his method of entry was Childers's *English-Pali Dictionary,* so he was reexploring Pali via English.[11]

The oddest example of incorporating foreign words is the name of the country itself, Thailand. The old name was Siam, probably derived from the indigenous inhabitants before the Thai arrived in their present kingdom. The Thais themselves also used the phrase *Muang Thai,* meaning "country of the free." But since the 1940s the name Thailand has been officially adopted, in spite of its ugly hybrid nature—one syllable being Thai, the other English. Some Thai writers warn that the new name implies a certain chauvinism and even irredentism, since it could be taken to justify inclusion of Thai or Tai-speaking areas across the border in neighboring countries.[12]

The world of persons is thus more important than any system, group, race or nationality which the Thai may feel himself thrust into. Those groupings have some meaning, but take second place to the intricate arrangement of individual persons within his ken. Thais relish their freedom, and are disinclined to place their lives in the hands of a group. It is a society where an individual tries to build for himself a unique network of personal relations, finding security if necessary by opting for dependence upon a chosen patron, but not in organized groups whose members he does not know, and who might urge him to conform. In resisting strong affiliations to groups in society, unlike the Chinese or Japanese, the Thai can become lonely and isolated. That is his secret sorrow.

In the case of the political parties this results in lack of discipline. The sketch shows the authority relationship between a typical party leader and second- and third-level members of his party.

A has to rely on personal contact with each individual to maintain party solidarity. He may have a strong direct rapport with people at the B level but his connections with the C level are indirect and weak. The Cs joined the party mainly because of their friendship with the Bs. There is neither an ideology nor strict organization to generate consistent horizontal and vertical linkages. Party affiliations and unity shift continuously as the political interests of individuals change. Parliament can assume a chameleonlike appearance.[13]

Living in Thai society is not as easy as the description of looseness and the appeal of *sanuk* might suggest. The language, for example, contains an elaborate system of pronouns requiring the speaker to judge the relative status of another person vis-à-vis himself before even opening his mouth. Strictly speaking you should use one pronoun when talking to the king, another to a senior prince, a third to a junior prince, a fourth to senior officials, a fifth to junior officials, and various others to senior monks, junior monks, senior relatives, junior relatives, close friends, acquaintances, business acquaintances, servants and shopkeepers. Merely to speak in Thailand is to be a prisoner of the hierarchical nature of the society.

Even the absence of hierarchy can cause problems, as in the factory where mechanics refused to take their foreman's orders because he was their social equal—so the boss had to hire graduates of sufficient social superiority to carry the messages to the men. But hierarchy does not mean group; you do not necessarily have to make horizontal common cause with all the others at the same level of the hierarchy as yourself. The lament of the trade union leader Wattana Iambamroong is his members' indiscipline: "The problem boils down to Thai culture, with workers preferring to do things on their own rather than going for collective bargaining."[14] It is not one hierarchy, but many: you may be inferior to one person, but superior to another—and the roles may change over time. Your role remains unique in the total society. You retain your primary quality as an individual person, thus facilitating social mobility.

Further evidence of this singular individuality of the Thai comes in the structure of the family, that most intimate and formative of human groups. In this "loose structure" society (as the anthropologist John Embree has called it), the sense of obligation to the family is not deep. There is nothing like the extended kinship system of China, where you can trace your ancestors back for centuries and continue to worship them. Until the Royal Decree of 1913 very few Thais had surnames; that part of a child's identity that inheres in his name used to be fully independent from the beginning. It is not uncommon for children to change families—a poor family or a family in difficulty arranging for children to be taken care of in a richer family, or children being exchanged. Emotional independence from parental bonds is thus promoted. Love matches à la Hollywood are beginning to replace family-arranged marriages.

Professor Herbert Phillips of the University of California found that families in the village of Bang Chan, where he made a detailed study, were held together more by a practical reciprocity of benefits than by an overriding ethic of family solidarity.[15] A young adult may feel gratitude to his mother for having taken the trouble to bring him up, but it can be a relatively material and pragmatic appreciativeness and little more. One's parents are also "persons" in this voyage through a world of persons.

The position of women is low in theory but not so bad in practice. In the old farming communities there was still to be found recently the superstition that a woman's clothes should not hang on the same line as a man's, in case they pollute them. Even in urban communities there are many inequalities suffered by women with regard to divorce and marriage. If a man's fiancée has sexual relations with another man, the first man can claim compensation from both the others. But the woman cannot claim compensation if her fiancé is unfaithful. Similarly, if a man's wife commits adultery, he can divorce her, but if she wants to divorce him, she must first prove that he has maintained or treated another women as his wife.

Many wives, especially those financially dependent on their husbands or afraid of the social consequences of divorce, accept their husband's minor wives, who have recognized rights of inheritance, as a *fait accompli*. Many Thai women and children suffer from their husband's or father's wayward-ness, in a land where polygamy used to be a way of life. It is a male chauvinist society: the crown prince himself, the pop singer Suthep and the Supreme Commander, General Sunthorn, all have second wives. Sunthorn's first wife embarrassed him mightily by suing the second to stop her using his name. A former prime minister once publicly regretted the old days (in this century) when a man could have as many wives as he liked—and mistresses too.[16]

Yet there are outstanding women who have shouldered their way to the top, or almost to the top. There are businesswomen like Lersak Sombatsiri, owner of the Hilton Hotel, or Sirilak Patanakorn (a London School of Economics graduate), who is president of the Bangkok Stock Exchange. The vice president of Siam Motors, the president of Toshiba's joint venture in Thailand, the head of the powerful Dusit Thani group, the chairman of the wealthy Lamsam family holding and many other leading executives are women. A woman presides over the port and transport trade unions. The former World Bank president, Robert McNamara, once praised the late Suparb Yossondara of the Bank of Thailand for her outstanding competence in a male-dominated world of finance.

The woman of the house usually manages its finances—more astutely, men confess, than the man. A recent proposal by a woman minister to give Thai men paternity leave was withdrawn, because it was feared the privilege would be abused. Saisuree Chutikul, the minister concerned, explained:

"Instead of staying home to help take care of the baby or help wash diapers, the men admit to me that they would probably just go out and enjoy the holiday." Child care and housework are still clearly defined as women's work. Thai women who break out of this stereotype and are successful in public life tend, however, to be either single or widowed, and therefore do not damage a husband's "face" by conspicuously outshining him.

The royals have contributed greatly to the advance of women. King Chulalongkorn's Queen Saowabha was made regent when he visited Europe for many months, an unprecedented appointment which greatly furthered the feminist cause. It was she who pioneered modern childbirth and midwifery in Thailand. A royal of another generation, Princess Poon Pisamai Diskul, was four times elected president of the World Fellowship of Buddhists. The most recent Thai constitution allows for a female succession to the throne, and yet Thai opinion could, it is acknowledged, be upset if the popular Princess Sirindhorn were to be chosen instead of her less appealing brother. Thai women were the first in Asia to win the vote, and have been active in parliament since 1948. Yet the first Thai woman Buddhist priest had to be ordained abroad because it was felt Thai opinion would not approve.

The advances by Thai women in public life may be understood alongside the healthily natural attitude to sex in Thailand, quite free from the puritanism of Europe. A party leader was once asked by a teenager for advice about masturbation. "For heaven's sake, boy," he replied. "I started when I was thirteen and nothing is wrong with me. Look how clever I am. It doesn't affect the brain or anything!"[17] There are not many senior politicians who would speak so frankly—for publication. A woman owner of several bars and massage parlors, and a millionairess in consequence, when asked why her establishments were so successful, replied as if she thought the question silly, "Because everybody likes sex."

The former dictator Field Marshal Sarit is to some extent a role model still for Thai men. What one Thai writer called Sarit's "insatiable appetite for sex" was an open secret at the time, but it did not emerge until after his death just how extensive his established harem was. Thais admired him "for having the effrontery to acquire mistresses on such a grand scale."[18] No one was immune to his overtures—beauty queens, students and schoolgirls, film stars and night club hostesses, young and not so young.

Only the AIDS scare intrudes on this jolly male-oriented picture. The Thais are natural about the phenomenon of sex, but are not permissive about who may openly participate. Men still patronize prostitutes, but such transactions are treated unsentimentally as a matter of business, not in the least personal. No loss of "face" is involved with the passage of money. The authorities do not normally harass the brothels: the cartoonist Prayoon Chanyawongse advocated legalizing prostitution and making it government-controlled—with reduced prices for students and high school boys. AIDS may hasten the day of controls. Under the Thanin government in the late 1970s prostitutes were made to wear number tags—and one columnist gained readers by recommending which numbers to ask for!

Only recently have the Thai leaders begun to regret the popularity of prostitution—which Mechai Viravaidhya, the pioneer in warning of the full dimension of the AIDS problem, now calls the "industry of death." There are said to be 800,000 prostitutes in a population of 58 million, or almost 1 in 70. That is more than there are teachers or monks. Inevitably, it has become a big business, with gangsters exploiting young women from rural areas. There was recently a parliamentary inquiry into the allegation that thirteen-year-olds were being forced into prostitution as if they were slaves.

Trying to galvanize politicians who were dragging their feet in case foreign tourists were scared away, Dr. Praves Wasi, a spokesman for those in the medical profession concerned about AIDS, advised his fellow countrymen to "stop thinking that men must visit brothels, give up such traditions as taking university freshmen to brothels to learn their 'first lesson' in sex, and stop the practice of procuring women for senior government officials during their visits to the provinces." But when Mechai tried to ram home to brothels the message about AIDS he was threatened with violence.

The rector of Thammasat University complained, "There are prostitutes in every country but not to this degree. Not to the extent that men come from all over the world looking for women. Do we want to be a world power in this respect?"[19] Thailand has not become a world sex power, but it has certainly become a world sex magnet. That seemed amusing, profitable and even flattering at first, but now, given the onslaught of AIDS, it is seen as precipitating a major calamity that will ultimately affect all aspects of society.

The blame is usually laid on the American GIs. An ex-premier admonished the Americans in the 1960s at the height of their presence in Thailand for "making countless of our women peddle their bodies; their brazen acts such as kissing and necking in public were beastly behavior which influenced Thailand's young people; they taught the Thai boys homosexuality . . ."[20] Actually, homosexuality was not at all unknown. King Vajiravudh's ambition of going to an English public school had been frustrated, so when he became king he insisted on setting up a public school in Thailand exactly following the English tradition—including, a writer claims, "the homosexual system in which men have one another, for which Vajiravudh's School is famous up to this day and not for anything else . . ."[21]

Not belonging to the Judeo-Christian tradition, the Thais do not regard homosexuality as sinful, morally perverse or criminal. At the most it may be distasteful or inappropriate. A former Deputy Minister of Education described it as a "mental abnormality that two men should have sex together. But nevertheless we should not blame or accuse them if their behavior causes no problems for society."[22] However it is not regarded as good manners to speak openly about one's private sexual concerns, so there is as much ignorance and misunderstanding about homosexuality as there used to be in Western countries. The pressures to conform are powerful, and this alone makes it difficult for homosexuals to "come out."

There were gay bars in Thailand for *farangs* going back many years, but only in the 1970s did gay clubs or bars catering for Thais make their appearance, along with gay magazines in Thai, soon to be followed by gay discos, gay radio programs and professional people openly admitting their homosexual preference. A leading novelist gave this advice to gay Thais: "Do whatever you wish, but don't make it too blatant. The Thai people will accept. They don't really mind. It's an open society."[23] In the 1970s transvestites formed their own association to protect their interests, and Pan Bunnag, a hairdresser and fashion model, led a campaign for the legalization of homosexuality.

This loosely structured society is thus practical and without sentimentality in its treatment of sex and the family. In the West there is another fundamental traditional social grouping, that of religion. But Buddhism in Thailand is essentially a loner's religion which does not depend on communal acts of worship or joint expressions of belief. It is a private solitary faith to which the adherent gives expression as and when he needs to, rather than at frequent regular meetings with co-believers. Birth, puberty, marriage, certain birthdays and death are the most significant events in a Thai's life, and these are all observed with Buddhist ritual.

Buddhism does not operate, in the way that Christianity does in the West, as a channel for social organization. It is a much more individual phenomenon. Islam, of course, is different, but less than a twentieth of the population subscribes to it, and they are concentrated in the extreme south of Thailand.

Where does that leave Thai morality? In the past Buddhist teaching was enough to maintain moral awareness in the population. But now with modernization the *wats* and monks are gradually losing influence, and schools are devoting less time to Buddhism. A recent survey of ethical behavior revealed that most Thais regard personal and professional success as their ultimate goal. Doing good or bad deeds in one's life does not substantially affect that goal. The new middle class is less ethical than its predecessors.

Modernization is sapping the old morality, and not all Thais like it. Somsak T. recently wrote in his popular newspaper column:

> Elements of the old Thai culture and tradition are becoming obsolete. . . . Mutual respect among individuals is not conducive to quick profits. . . . Such cultural frivolities as honesty and concern . . . must be discarded for a slicker image. . . . The culture is undergoing an expedient westernisation.

The modern layers of the Thai personality are thickening, at the expense of the traditional layer. But such changes take generations to complete, and the traditional layer is still the largest, for all of Somsak's sarcasm.

The Thai world outlook thus centers on specific persons rather than generalized groups or systems. When a Thai looks outside himself, what he sees, apart from animals, plants and the world of nature, are individual human beings. He sees a microworld where Westerners strain to perceive a macroworld. A Thai does not commonly reckon himself as part of a racial grouping with other Thais. Individual persons within his ambit are more important than school classes, industrial work forces, farm cooperatives, religious sects, the army, trade unions or any other group in which he may find himself.

This limited world of individual persons also takes precedence over one's family. A Thai is, of course, close to his parents, brothers, sisters and children. But the intensity of that relationship derives from physical closeness and specific mutual experiences rather than from any mystique about the family social unit as such. Family relations are "loosely structured."

The result of this person-based outlook on life, taken to some extreme in Thailand, is that social relationships are rather different than in, for example, a Western country. "Face" becomes an almost overriding factor in social encounters. The Thai system allows a good measure of individuality and variation in behavior, but is not much interested in equality of status or treatment.

One comes back to that Thai smile, the blinking yellow traffic light which is the advance warning of the system, advertising a desire for gentle and peaceful relationships. The smile is not always a defense mechanism or a muscle-straining ritual. Quite often it is simply an expression of pleasure and delight in Thailand's bountiful natural environment. Thailand may be making its way into the club of modern industrialized democratic countries, but it is not going to allow that smile to be wiped off its face.

5

Those Chinese Genes:
A Triumph of Assimilation

"**A** great number of us, myself included," says Kukrit Pramoj, Thailand's genial elder statesmen "have a Chinese ancestor hanging on our family tree."[1] In his case it was great-grandmother Ampha, royal consort of King Rama II in the early nineteenth century, and the Pramoj family's attitude to her illustrates the Thai acceptance of the Chinese, who are notoriously difficult immigrants to assimilate.

Both of Ampha's parents were Chinese, born in China. Her father, a successful trader in Thailand, introduced her to the Thai court as an entertainer; the king was captivated, took her into the palace, and had six children by her. One of those founded the royal family of Pramoj, which still flourishes and boasts the two ex-premier brothers, Seni and Kukrit, at its head. So Kukrit observes the Chinese New Year ritual of setting out dainty little porcelain bowls of rice, vegetables and fruit as a sacrifice to his ancestors, honoring the Chinese girl who launched his family.

Kukrit's annual act of piety is not uncommon. It is doubtless influenced by the belief that the Thai people originated in China. New research by People's Republic of China scholars argues that Thai settlement in present-day Thailand goes back as far as the first century,[2] though the present Kingdom of Siam dates back only 750 years.

In the course of exchanging the southern provinces of China for their present home, the Thais subjugated various Hinduized previous occupants and absorbed some Indian influences from them, especially affecting their kings, courts and temples. Even so, when they came overland to reach the Gulf of Siam in the thirteenth century they found Chinese sea traders already living there. There was no escaping the ubiquitous Chinese. In the seventeenth century there were 10,000 Chinese living in Ayutthya, then the Thai capital.

Acknowledgment of a Chinese forebear is shared by most Thais, some would say 90 percent of them. It is certainly true of 90 percent of the elite, though less so of the peasantry. Bhichai Rattakul, former leader of the Democrat party, belongs to the sixth generation of a Chinese family, but it is more common for a Thai Chinese to be born of recent immigrants, arriving in the past hundred years to find a better life than they could expect in a China ravaged first by war and then by communism. Their motives were economic. "I'd like to have a piece of pork in my mouth *every* day," was the considered rationale of one of them in the novel *Letters from Thailand,* which brilliantly evokes the tribulations of a 1940s immigrant.[3]

The monarchy was also "sinified" by blood. The most illustrious of modern wearers of the crown was King Taksin (1767-82), whose spectacular defeats of the Burmese armies are still remembered. His father was Chinese, his mother Thai. "Wasn't it the son of a Chinaman, Phra Chao Taksin Maharaja," a modern Buddhist medium recently expostulated in defense of his own Chinese descent, "who retrieved our independence?"[4] The Teh clan of Thai Chinese, believing Taksin to have been a member, sacrifices bowls of food and drink in his memory to this day. The Chakri dynasty which followed Taksin absorbed Chinese blood through the women of the court— like Ampha.

Thailand's most famous symbols are sometimes found to owe their existence to the Chinese, like Bangkok's Patpong Road, whose notoriety as a street of ill-repute has spread all over the world. A penniless Chinese called Poon Pat arrived from Hainan Island, off the China coast, around 1900. Only twelve, he took up work with a rice merchant and became such an excellent judge of the rice trade that his employer sent him into the countryside, on the new railway, to buy from the farmers. Puzzled by the white soil in one locality, he brought a pocketful back for analysis. It was calcium carbonate, exactly what the king needed for his new cement plant. The king rewarded him with a title and he took the name Patpong. When his fortune grew, he bought the land where Patpong Road now stands.[5]

It is sometimes said that there are 9 million Chinese in Thailand in a population of 58 million, constituting the largest Chinese population outside China itself—China's number-one colony, in fact. But that kind of figure is dangerous. The cumulative number of Chinese who have immigrated to Thailand from the beginning until now may very roughly be as many as 9 million (mostly Teochew, with some Hakka and Hainanese, all from the south China coast). But their descendants have been undergoing a continual process of assimilation through intermarriage and the adoption of Thai culture.

This has gone so far that today there is only a relatively small number, the so-called *Thai Chinese,* who are completely Chinese in ancestry. Almost all the Chinese immigrants married Thai wives, and several generations of offspring of those unions have so intermarried—with the Chinese, with the Thais and with each other—that Chinese blood has percolated into the veins of most of the Thais in Thailand. The result has been the creation of a large group of people of mixed Chinese and Thai descent, the so-called *Sino-Thais.*

It is not easy to define exactly where the boundary between this group and the "true" Thais lies. Whatever the proportion of Chinese blood in an individual, there is always an element of flexibility in choosing one's identity. For instance, a Thai with one Chinese grandparent may or may not identity himself as Chinese. His choice is determined by a complex web of psychological, social and economic circumstances. The sum result of all these individual choices is in the end just as important in its effects on Thai society as the actual proportion of one's Chinese ancestry.

The genes have become hopelessly jumbled. We want to know not only how people behave but what they feel themselves to be—and that is impossible to measure nationwide. One well-conducted survey in the 1970s suggested that almost half the urban population identifies itself as Chinese.[6] Since the gate for immigration was virtually closed in the late 1940s, the number of fully ethnic Thai Chinese is falling.

The racial integration of the Chinese in Thailand was interrupted by the improved shipping services that, combined with the new wealth of the Thai Chinese, enabled them in the 1920s and 1930s to bring wives out from China. They no longer needed to marry Thais. They began to open Chinese schools for their children in Thailand and became less apologetic about speaking Chinese in public. Some even began to cultivate paddyfields in southern Thailand. The Thais then began to feel imposed upon. *Jek,* the insulting word for Chinese, was heard more frequently.

King Vajiravudh (1910-25) preached Siamese nationalism and called the Chinese the Jews of Asia. He launched a hate campaign against the Chinese, with a semifascist "Wild Tiger" organization to back it up. Thai chauvinism was continued under the dictatorship of Field Marshal Phibul. The fact that he had a Cantonese grandmother and a partly Chinese wife did not at all inhibit Phibul from repressing the Chinese community. He arranged for their passports to draw attention to their "Chinese race." Immigration began to be heavily taxed. Learning the Thai language was made compulsory, and shop signs had to be in Thai as well as Chinese.

The Chinese bore these annoyances uncomplainingly until 1945, when China suddenly emerged as one of the victorious allies that defeated Japan. It had irked the Thai Chinese that, in trying to keep Thailand out of the Pacific War, Phibul had had to make concessions to the Japanese, whose threat to invade Thailand was all too real, rather than to the Allies, who were too far away and preoccupied to come to Thailand's aid. For China to be the winner in the East Asian War and become one of the five allies to set the new world order with a permanent seat (and veto) in the United Nations Security Council was exhilarating, releasing Chinese patriotic feeling which had long been suppressed. The Chinese burst out in celebration, and the Thai nationalists reacted by burning and looting in Chinatown.

That set relations back. But Phibul was succeeded in 1957 by Field Marshal Sarit, whose connoisseurship of Chinese beauty had won him many Chinese mistresses. Sarit allowed the Chinese to stage their Miss China beauty contests and then seduced the winners. He also benefited from the business alliances which Chinese traders had been driven (by Phibul's repression) to forge with respectable but impecunious Thai families. Under Sarit the Chinese regained self-respect and were allowed to express themselves once more as a distinct community, though he made them accept Thai headmasters in their Chinese schools and suspended Chinese language and literature studies in the universities. Since then the economy has prospered to the advantage of both, drawing the Thais and Chinese together again.

The only subsequent contretemps was the rioting for three nights in the Chinese district of Plabplachai in 1974. But that was sparked by police anger over a taxi driver's refusal to hand over the customary bribe to escape a fine.[7] Two rival Chinese teenage gangs, the Eagles and the Dragons, took advantage of this to have another scrap. It was fighting within the Chinese community rather than between Thais and Chinese. There is no comparison with the Chinese who died in race riots in Malaysia in 1969 or the hundreds of thousands of Chinese who were slaughtered and mutilated in Indonesia in 1965.

These few comparatively minor outbursts of violence in Thailand are the exceptions which prove the rule, namely that the Thais are an accepting race. They accepted Southeast Asian Hinduization before the fifteenth century, they accepted Westernization in the late 1800s and they have accepted Chinese immigration in this century. Never has assimilation been so thorough and so nonviolent. Initially it was a physical assimilation through intermarriage (or concubinage). When Chinese wives began to arrive in Thailand in the 1920s, there was less intermarriage. Chinese men still say they prefer to marry Chinese girls (for their honesty, industry and fidelity, they explain).[8] Intermarriage is no longer needed. But it has already produced a vast class of "Sino-Thais" who occupy a large middle ground between the two races, including most of the middle-class, ruling elite and royal family—most of whom would consider themselves culturally Thai.

The common origins of the two races make them sufficiently alike in looks and build to allow one often to pass for the other. The Chinese are not as conspicuous in Thailand as they are in England or America, or even in Malaysia and Indonesia. Their skin is normally a tone lighter, and their eyes a little narrower than the Thais. But the two can be readily confused. Sulak, the nationalist writer and lawyer, reckons he can distinguish correctly by sight and sound only six times out of ten. This goes a long way to explaining the smooth assimilation.

The Chinese were thus not only absorbed into the Thai nation's bloodstream, they were culturally assimilated as well. Since the 1950s the "Sino-Thais" have been forced to go to schools teaching only in the Thai language. They could learn Chinese as a second language, but the effort of mastering thousands of characters is too much for most boys and girls on top of a normal curriculum. Besides, the ambition of most Chinese youngsters living in a Thai city is to become accepted by the Thais of their own age in their neighborhood, and for that a Chinese education is actually a handicap. So they became illiterate in the Chinese language.

Recent immigrants can speak Chinese. Dhanin Chearavanont, the "Sino-Thai" agribusiness king, speaks three Chinese languages—Teochew, Cantonese and Mandarin—as well as Thai, and so does his son. But the trend is toward Thai and English. There are eight Chinese-language newspapers, but only 70,000 people buy them. The Sapin Luang Presbyterian Chinese Church noticed a thinning of its younger congregation in the early 1970s, so it switched from Chinese to Thai language services—and drew them back.[9]

Similarly, Inchcape, the British-owned conglomerate, used salesmen bilingual in Thai and Chinese until the 1980s. Nowadays recruits are expected to know Thai and English. There is, a manager explains, "a falling graph line of who speaks Chinese." Some regret the loss of their ancestors' language, but once neglected in youth it is notoriously difficult to master, especially for reading and writing, in later life.

Those sons of immigrants who attend Thai schools emerge with a perfect Thai accent. Today it is only a few in the older generation, or those who for some reason were sent outside Thailand for early schooling, who speak Thai with a Chinese accent.

Assimilation is eased by the belief of both Thais and Chinese in astrology and Buddhism. This contrasts with Indonesian or Malaysian Islam, which the southern Chinese find almost impossible to accept—if only because it means giving up pork, the staple Chinese food, and legalizing multiple marriage, which no modern Chinese woman will stomach. True, the Chinese followed Mahayana Buddhism, Thais the older Theravada school, but the fundamental beliefs are the same. Skeptical Chinese do not share the Thais' implicit belief in reincarnation or in the effect of merit on future lives. A Thai makes a gift to a monk as a kind of moral deposit in order to store up merit for his next life; a Chinese will do the same with a different motive—that of piety or gratitude, to please the gods of his ancestors.

There are other differences: the Thais wear black to cremate their dead, while the Chinese wear white to bury them. The Chinese are generally more open-minded on religious matters. In particular they have not taken seriously to the excellent Thai custom of men spending some time in the monkhood, democratically living the simple life of the temple. If they do this at all they do it halfheartedly for a few days instead of the traditional weeks or months. To the Chinese it seems an anachronism.

A Chinese in Thailand needs a Thai name. Sometimes he runs his Chinese name together to form a Thai surname. Mr. Chow Kwanyun, the Chinese economics professor, thus became Chow Chowkwanyun, the Thai million-aire entrepreneur. That looks better but is still conspicuous. Johnny Ma, the Chinese businessman, becomes Wallop Tarnvanichkul, chairman of the Asia Trust Bank. That scores higher marks in the assimilation test.

The great majority of "Sino-Thais" see themselves as faithful Thai citizens, justly engaged in the development of their country of birth and residence. Some "Sino-Thais" even excel the "true" Thais in their command of Thai language, culture and history. Phya Anuman Rajadhon, a scholar of the 1950s, is an example, and Suchaat, the Buddhist medium, could claim: "Even though I am only a Chinaman's son, I still dare to say that I love Thailand . . . more than the Thais who are now selling their nation."[10] No wonder Premier Lee Kuan Yew of Singapore denounced Thai policy toward the "Sino-Thais" as a "deculturation" which would rob them of creativity and personality.[11] Now sociologists worry about the discovery that some Chinese at the bottom of the economic ladder (they are not all millionaires) seem to be losing their sense of "Chineseness" without having become fully Thai, a recipe for alienation.

Old-time first-generation immigrants do not like being absorbed into Thai society. "Nobody is going to assimilate me," the fictional hero of *Letters from Thailand* angrily exclaims when his daughter—the first generation of his family to be born in Thailand—tells him how Chinese emigrants are being gradually assimilated into all their host societies. "Papa," she says, "its not something you decide to do. It happens in the normal course of things." Later, brooding on the consequences of his migration for his children, the old man reflects: "I could not shelter them from the thousands of experiences which made them another people, another race. There are so many of us here, yet the Thais have won."[12] "The Chinese have turned into Thais," as many Thai intellectuals would put it—and the Thais accept them as such.

A few are able to resist assimilation. There are still clan associations in Bangkok for the most common surnames. Five Chinese dialects are still spoken and some traditional customs are still observed. A few younger "assimilated" Chinese are even rediscovering their cultural past, becoming receptive to the argument that rather than lose their cultural identity entirely through assimilation, the "Sino-Thais" should have integrated into a multicultural Thailand as the Muslim Malays did in the southern provinces of the kingdom.

But it is too late for that. The Chinese are mostly assimilated already and must live with the consequences of that. For a generation or two they have to grapple with their double identity. Assuming a Thai name does not necessarily mean forgetting your Chinese name, or your Chinese culture, language and tradition. Three in four "Sino-Thais" say that among themselves they hang on to the former culture and speech. Half of them continue to worship their ancestors. A Thai Chinese student in Australia made friends with a Thai fellow student. Months later he found him performing the ritual of a Chinese festival. "I didn't know you were Chinese," said the first student in surprise. "I am not Chinese," came the reply. "But I had a Chinese grandfather to whom I pay respect as he would have wished." Social pressure can erase the outward signs of Chinese culture, but does not automatically modify the fundamentals within. The "Sino-Thai" may still be partly Chinese beneath the skin.

This duality of being Chinese in private, Thai in public—Chinese with elders, Thai with contemporaries—could be distressing. Yet some "Sino-Thais" seem to enjoy it without suffering psychological disorientation. They can choose which side of the line to occupy at any moment. They can move on both sides of the racial-cultural divide, something that is denied to the Chinese in Malaysia or Indonesia. The immigrant hero in *Letters from Thailand* wants his Thailand-born son "to be able to move easily in both worlds, Thai and Chinese, *but as a Chinese.*"[13]

Some discrimination persists. Parliamentarians tried to unseat an unpopular agriculture minister in 1981 because he was, among other things, the "son of an alien"—meaning a second-generation Chinese. It is only twenty years since Chinese were barred from certain occupations or from buying land in their own name and had to report their race on official forms. But none of that crude discrimination survives, and the remarkable thing is how successful the "Sino-Thais" are in public life.

One of the arguments used many years ago against proposals to institute a parliament was that pushy Chinese would dominate it, and sure enough, the parliament of 1991 was "almost Chinese," in a senior politician's words. Now politicians compete openly for the "Chinese vote." In a recent by-election in a Bangkok constituency with many Chinese voters, a right-wing candidate, Samak Sundaravej, was accused of being anti-Chinese, upon which he revealed that his family descended from a Chinese who had come to Thailand in 1791. His opponent, General Chamlong Srimuang, then governor of Bangkok, promptly disclosed that he, too, was Chinese. His father had emigrated from China, his brother died in one of China's communist upheavals and he gets letters from his relatives in China. His mother is also Chinese, but Chamlong was adopted in childhood by a Thai family and thus enabled to enlist in the army, which at that time did not admit Chinese. "Coming out" is becoming fashionable, and this kind of social pressure works now where it would not work before. Some Thais even hint that the Chinese embassy might soon be "telling everyone which candidate to vote for."

Actually some senior officers of the armed forces are now "Sino-Thai," as are very many cabinet ministers. Some "Sino-Thai" youths join the army only for long enough to gain a rank which they can retain after resigning and then use that rank to protect their families against petty official harassment. Almost all of Thailand's prime ministers—including Phibul and Pridi—were part Chinese.

The Chinese had already, of course, scored their greatest successes in the economic field, like Poon, the pioneer of Patpong Road. All but 2 of the 25 top businessmen are Chinese, and two in three of the largest manufacturing companies are controlled by Chinese. The "Sino-Thais" are the country's undisputed entrepreneurial class, and nowadays their younger generation is grasping business opportunities with Harvard MBAs or engineering and science degrees from Stanford and MIT. They look outward, not inward. The Thai Chinese were saved from the unpopularity trap of visibly milking their host country of capital and sending it "home" to invest in China. Nobody wanted to invest in communism. There were modest family remittances sent via Hong Kong, but the real money was invested in Thailand.

One early postwar success among the Chinese businessmen was Chow Chowkwanyun, the Beijing University economics professor, who became a millionaire quite by accident. When the communists seized power in China he was on a sabbatical year in Thailand. Simultaneously cut off from job, income and friends, he had to make some money instead of just lecturing about it. Chow decided to think big. "If you want to borrow a million dollars," he explains, "you go to the bank. If you want to borrow a hundred million, the bank comes to you." He proved to be a shrewd operator, trading in plywood and wheat, becoming an important steel and oil-refining tycoon and attracting international interest as the advocate of a canal across the Kra Isthmus in southern Thailand to shorten the sailing distance between Suez and Far Eastern ports. That never materialized because the saving on mileage did not match the cost, but he never lost his enthusiasm for the scheme.

Next came Tan Piak Chin (1910-1988), better known later by his Thai name Chin Sophonpanich. After school in China, he worked in the Thai construction industry. By 1935 he had his own company and went into rice trading, sawmilling and foreign exchange. After the war friends persuaded him to become a founder-shareholder of the Bangkok Bank. In 1951 the bank ran into trouble, and Chin was asked to rescue it. So he bought a controlling share, sacked the old managers and put in a bright young accountant, Boonchu Rojanasathien, later to become finance minister, who was able to turn the bank around. Chin forged political alliances that served him well under the stern Phibul's dictatorship, but cost him dear under that of Sarit which followed it. Chin had to sit out Sarit's dictatorship in Hong Kong, but the bank itself survived.

After Chin's death, six sons—two from his first Chinese wife, four from his second "Sino-Thai" wife—jostled for the succession of his huge business empire. After some skirmishing a division of responsibility was agreed, and Chatri, the younger of the two Hong Kong boys, became president of the bank. Today the Sophonpanich family owns a third of the bank, but only Chatri is involved in running it, and he has several major outside interests as well. Robin, Chin's eldest son, born like Chatri in Shantou, China, runs the family business in Hong Kong.

Of the Thai-born children, Charn, technically-minded and Australian educated, is the eldest. He has a computer business. Chote uses Capital Finance and Securities as the anchor for a wide range of business interests, though he would have preferred to run the bank instead of Chatri. Chai has insurance companies and Choedchu a smaller bank. Chin's only daughter, Chodchoy, has become a philanthropist and environmentalist. Now the third generation is making its mark, with Chatri's first son, Chatsiri (or Tony), getting an MIT degree in chemical engineering and managing the bank's giant polyethylene plant. A second son, Chali, and daughter, Savitri, are both in securities houses. The Anand Panyarachun caretaker government in 1991 appointed one of the young Sophonpaniches to a senior financial post in one of the state organizations.

A different case is the Sarasin family. Their Thai history began with a Chinese Christian from Hainan island named Tien Hee, who trained to be a doctor at New York University before coming to Thailand and marrying a Thai.[14] His son Pote became prime minister and the first secretary general of SEATO, the Southeast Asian Treaty Organization, one of the most able and distinguished Thais of his generation. Pote's sons all now occupy important positions, one as a political party leader and others in the army, banking, brewing and manufacturing industries, and so on. One, Arsa, became foreign minister after the 1991 coup and another, Pow, joined him in the Cabinet in 1992.

Other important Chinese business families are Lamsam, founded by the Hakka pioneer, Ng Yuk Long (it controls the Thai Farmers Bank), and Ratanarak (Bank of Ayudhya). The late Thiam Chokwatana encapsulates the "rags to riches" story of many of these Chinese pioneers. At sixteen he was a laborer toting sacks of sugar and rice, but eventually opened up his own trading business and then a shop which grew into a giant $1 billion-a-year manufacturing and retailing group of 60 companies with many Japanese joint ventures, run by Thiam's eight children.[15]

Another legend is Pey, who arrived from China before the First World War and started a drugstore patronized by the king, who gave him the surname Osathanagrah. When imports of Chinese drugs were restricted, Pey started manufacturing pharmaceuticals himself and made more money than ever. His children and grandchildren have distinguished themselves in many areas of life, including the civil service, universities, police and political parties: one became Minister of Commerce.*

The Thais were an easy target for all this Chinese hustle and bustle. "New blood and energy were pouring into the Siamese life stream," was Kenneth Landon's 1941 comment on the ethnic intermarriage. "The race was kept fresh and vigorous." The Chinese "bee" overpowered the Thai "butterfly" to create a new race or subrace combining the purposefulness of the former with the political skills and sensitivity of the latter. "Children of the Sino-Thai marriages are good citizens . . . ," Landon concluded. "They have energy, drive and intelligence. They get things done."[16]

---

* There are several Indian case histories, too. Sura Chansrichawla, for example, one of the biggest landowners in Bangkok and worth around $650 million, is a second-generation Punjabi Sikh whose family fortune has been gradually built up over 100 years.

Some Thai feel that a "new race," neither Thai nor Chinese, has been formed in Thailand. Ethnic mingling on this scale is necessarily part of "Thainess," asserts Professor Chai-Anan Samudhavanij, the country's leading political scientist. The economist Dr. Puey Ungpakorn commented that "Chinese-Thai assimilation is a two-way process which in the long run will leave Thailand with something Chinese, and Chinese with something Thai."[17] Nobody knows how to put it precisely, but Thailand has been changed in some way by the Chinese.

The Chinese with their intense clan loyalties and group-oriented behavior are only gradually absorbed into the looser and more individualistic Thai social fabric. The Chinese Confucian-based respect for authority puts starch into the more informal Thai social hierarchy. The drive of the "Confucian work ethic," on the other hand, is modified by the Thai's sense of fun and relaxation. The two philosophies may be moderating each other.

Many "Sino-Thais" are proud of their Chinese blood and grateful for its genes, which produce a vigor lacking in the "pure" Thai. Their contribution to Thai life itself is total and uninhibited. The Thais gain from that infusion and do not appear to lose by it. The younger pacesetters of each side seem in any case to be reaching out now toward globalized Western values. Both the constituent sets of values in Thailand may be significantly refueled by Western material values, and some think they might even find a form of final reconciliation in that "triangular" culture. The outcome of that will not, however, be known for a very long time.

Although the earlier histories of Thailand and China were very much bound up with each other, they have had only minimal contacts in living memory. Thai artists and intellectuals knew about Chinese civilization and culture, but very few artists or intellectuals from either country visited the other. In the present century, China was wrapped in her own domestic struggles, resisting Japanese invasion and undergoing communist revolution. Thailand, too, was undergoing rapid change, particularly with the coup of 1932 and the diplomatic struggle to keep out of the Pacific War as far as possible. It was mostly unskilled laborers and farmers, with a few entrepreneurial traders, who immigrated from China, not the educated professional and intellectual classes.

The new factor in the Thailand-China equation is that over the last ten years "Sino-Thais" have been able to visit China. A few come back from their ancestral villages starry-eyed, their Chinese values reinforced. But the majority are sobered and shocked to see how far China lags behind Thailand. "For me," says Chote Sophonpanich, of the Bangkok Bank family, "returning to China is a bit like an American returning to his country of origin in

Europe. Though my father came from China, I was born and brought up here. I have no close friends there. I am interested in China, but no more than that." These days most "Sino-Thais" would rather visit the United States or Japan. China is a distant phenomenon which cannot yet affect them, even though it may have the potential capacity to tug at their heartstrings.

That tug could perhaps come for some "Sino-Thais" when they watch an international sports event and silently cheer the Chinese team—or when they feel a lack of sympathy with countries normally at odds with China, like Vietnam or Japan. When China became a relatively "respectable" player on the world stage in the 1970s, some "Sino-Thais" felt more self-confident about their Chineseness: it is legitimate now for them to admire Chinese culture and achievements, and they respond. That temptation will increase in the future if China succeeds in her economic reforms and becomes a more active player on the Asian scene. Whether that resurgence of "Sino-Thai" interest in China results in love, contempt or indifference will affect the position of the "Sino-Thai" in Thailand.

There are some signs of Chinese "chauvinism" creeping in again. Some "true Thais" working for "Sino-Thai" enterprises say the atmosphere has gradually changed from exaggerated obsequiousness regarding things Thai twenty years ago to a cruder assertion of Chinese superiority today. No doubt the pendulum had to swing back, but if it now lurches too far toward Chinese chauvinism, or fails to settle in the acceptable middle space, then the "Sino-Thai" assimilation experiment will face a challenge.

The Thais accept Chinese immigration. "This is a land of plenty," a high official explains. "We can afford to be generous." If there was some early jealousy when the Chinese grabbed all the profitable contracts and concessions, it was tempered because the benefits from strong economic development were trickling down to the lower levels, and the great majority of Thais were better off than they were before. Buddhism tells the Thais that if someone else is more successful, it must be the reward for having acquired merit in an earlier life. It is in any case gratifying to the Thais to know that the Chinese, who used to talk of their homeland as the center of world civilization, find Thailand a better place in which to live.

As long as economic development continues, and a world slump is avoided, the race-mingling experiment in Thailand should be maintained. Thailand is not immune from the problems which Chinese immigration has caused in Malaysia or Indonesia, but it does have an infinitely better machinery for dealing with those problems through social absorption. The full success of the Thai assimilation will depend on Thai Chinese and "Sino-Thai" sensitivity and self-restraint. The signs are that this relatively happy marriage of communities will endure to see Thailand into the twenty-first century as a sophisticated modern nation. Most importantly, this ethnic infusion equips Thailand to perform better in regional and world affairs than its competitors and neighbors who still find it difficult to fully accept their Chinese immigrant community.

The Chinese assimilation into the Thai kingdom is a triumph of sociocultural adaptation, an extraordinary accomplishment that, like Thailand's economic policy, initially ran against the current of policy in the other Southeast Asian states and is only today seen as having been the more successful. It is an exemplar to all other countries embroiled in racial or ethnic problems. It is the keystone to Thailand's social dynamism.

6

Thai Buddhism: The Response to Modernity

Buddhism was one of the bonds bringing Chinese immigrants together with Thais, but it is also an important constituent in the general success story of Thai modernization. Thailand is the second-largest Buddhist state after Japan, and the precepts of the Theravada Buddhism that Thais profess explain much about their personality, old and new. Thailand's royal ceremonies, its thousands of high-roofed temples, its gaggles of monks in their orange robes and begging bowls going out for alms in the light of every dawn, the constant citation of Buddhist aphorisms by public figures all point to a national religion that runs deep—deeper, perhaps, even than Christianity in some Western countries.

The influences of the past are various. Herbert Phillips, the American sociologist, found that the spiritual life of a Thai village is actually an amalgam of four separate and distinct systems.[1] Buddhism is the most important, and from it the Thai learns that *karma,* or the result of his lives in earlier incarnations, will dictate whether he is to enjoy long life and good fortune this time around. Rather surprisingly, Brahmanism, the Indian cosmology prevalent in Southeast Asia before the arrival of Buddhism, still retains some vestigial influence, for example in the celebrated Hindu shrine at the corner of the Grand Hyatt Erawan Hotel in Bangkok and the four Brahman priests who officiate at the king's coronation. Both the Buddhist and the Brahman views of life are fatalistic, reinforcing the passive attitudes that many Thais exhibit. But Buddhism at least encourages a Thai to do good, as in the Christian ethic, if only for the "selfish" motive of upgrading his own next life.

Alongside these exotic imports from India stand two further belief systems of a more general kind. Animism was the common credo of rural people before they became exposed to great religions. It diagnosed setbacks in life as the work of bad spirits who may be propitiated by ritual magic or sacrifices. Traces of that can still be detected, some of them carried over into Buddhist practice. In one village an ant hill was worshiped because it housed a ghost who could supposedly tell which lottery numbers were about to win prizes. How these things start can be seen in the story of the statue of Queen Victoria in the British consul's garden in Chiang Mai. A woman unable to conceive had invoked all kinds of gods and spirits to gain fertility. Nothing worked. One day she worshiped in front of Victoria's statue, and lo! she became pregnant. Within days a crowd of worshipers gathered and the statue's fame spread far and wide. The cult then extended to the statue of Victoria in the British embassy grounds in Bangkok, seen as conferring not only fertility but also success in lotteries and affairs of the heart.

Astrology appeals to many educated Thais as a respectable means of keeping on the good side of whatever spirits surround us. When Thanin Kraivixien was prime minister in 1977 he called on fortune-tellers to help him stay in power—in vain! He read the palm of the visiting Japanese prime minister, Fukuda Takeo, but it could not have been encouraging, because Fukuda too fell from power soon afterward. A later premier, Chatichai Choonhavan, was told by his astrologer to announce his new cabinet on a Friday. The Social Action party, a member of the coalition led by Chatichai, had arranged to meet on the Saturday to decide what names to present for ministerial posts, so Chatichai appointed his new team without the SAP. "It is frightening," the SAP leader commented, "that a person at the country's helm believes in using an auspicious time to do things."[2]

The Thai village today treads a twisting way through all these rival systems. The way it often works is for spiritism to be invoked for the practical daily problems of life, Brahmanism when some heightened sense of dignity is needed, and Buddhism whenever people feel able to look forward to the superior good life they would like to lead in the future. Now the great new god Reason has made its appearance in Thai villages to say that a long life is better ensured by giving up whisky and opium, and avoiding venereal disease, than by consulting religious charts, wearing amulets, or putting food in front of the statues of gods. The slow march of scientific reason will no doubt gradually occupy the ground vacated by the three other systems.

Buddhism has no god, or gods, strictly speaking. But the polytheistic superstitions prevailing in Indian society at the time the Buddha lived could not all be stifled by the cleanly rationalized cosmology of his mind. By the time Buddhism reached Thailand it was already wrapped in the packaging of superstition and only too open to attracting indigenous gloss in order to prosper in its new home.

So today the conscientious Buddhist votary ascertains what particular kinds of offerings his neighborhood Buddhist image likes to be given. The Phra Phuttha Chinnarat in Phitsanulok likes pig's heads, while the Emerald Buddha prefers hard-boiled eggs. Many Buddhists take such beliefs at their face value.

The conscientious Thai Buddhist believes that the demerit of drinking beer or, worse, local Mekhong whisky, can be neutralized by first pouring it over an amulet of Buddha. A literal view of reincarnation can spawn a new line of invective. Two scientists were locked in bitter public argument a few years ago over which of two models of Thai language typewriter to adopt officially. One of them, Dr. Utis Narksavat, deputy secretary general of the National Research Council, formally challenged his opponent "to pledge in front of the Buddha image that if either of us is insincere in his motives, he is condemned to hell and be born a dog in his next 500 years."[3]

A monk is accorded great respect by the public. Not only does he get free food in the morning, but he pays no fare on the buses and will usually be given a seat at the back—from which women passengers will retreat to avoid his being defiled by bodily contact with them. But there is a general complaint that monks are charging more for their services at ceremonies, telling more fortunes and perpetuating more mindless superstitions. One, Acharn Suan, made a tidy sum selling phallic symbols. Others were accused of riding motorbikes and having sex with girls. A complaint by the organized church—the *sangha*—revealed that monks had been writing to the Stock Exchange about shares. There was a row within the *sangha* over two monks said to have been wrongly accused of sodomy and communism (the *sangha* did not seem to know which was the worse sin).

For sheer insolence to the modern mind Suchaat Kosonkittiwong must win the prize. Though not a monk himself, he claimed to be the medium for the spirits of three famous departed monks, and in their names he grandly foretold the future. He launched a national crusade against communism and predicted that the Third World War would start in 1982. He urged the king to abdicate and become prime minister (as Norodom Sihanouk of Cambodia had done). The highest in the land, notably General Praphas Charusathien, dictator extraordinary, came to admire him and listen. Suchaat unerringly caught the mood of a generation of old-fashioned military officers who really did feel, especially from the late 1970s onward, that the kingdom was being betrayed to creeping socialism and losing its true values. Suchaat was imprisoned in 1987 for illegally occupying state land, but hundreds of hoodwinked gentry continued to believe in him.[4]

The one extravagance that every Thai indulges is to treat images of Buddha with the reverence owed to the man himself. Hundreds of thousands of Buddha statues are ceremonially clothed, garlanded, washed, fed and festooned with presents by Thais knowing no other way of communication with their deity. More personalized than the rituals of Jesus or Mary figures in Christendom, the Thai style of worship proliferates the realistic, durable three-dimensional figure more than the picture image. There are huge numbers of such statues left abandoned, because bronze outlasts human settlements.

The worst thing a visitor can do is to have himself photographed sitting on the head of a statue of Buddha, as two Mormons did in the 1970s, to a storm of protest. The *New Yorker* magazine published an advertisement in which jewelry was displayed against the background of various props including a Buddha head, and another wave of anger swept over Bangkok's establishment.[5] Over the years hundreds of decaying old temples have been relieved of their bronze figures of Buddha, especially the heads, and you can see them on sale in every antique shop on Silom or Sukhumvit Roads—although a Bangkok newspaper has said that those who cut the heads off deserve to be executed.

Recently their export was forbidden. Customs officers have been told to look out for Buddha heads or figures, and even if it is a new product worth only a dollar or two you will have to take it to the Fine Arts department for permission to carry it out of the country. The same Fine Arts department confiscated Buddha figures which "Silk King" Jim Thompson had bought, and that arbitrary experience soured his love affair with Thailand.[6] When cultural nationalism, stirred by decades of unregulated systematic shipment of national treasures to the United States or Europe, gets mixed up with religious observances and the old Thai trait of taking the appearance for the reality—the statue *is* the Buddha—then the smile stops and the suppressed xenophobia comes out.

There are now about 250,000 monks in Thailand (only a third of the number of prostitutes, Buddhist intellectuals complain). With novices included, the figure might be more than 300,000. But it is declining slowly, and in the next century there might be only pockets of the old monkhood left in different parts of the country, with empty *wats* (temples) left to the mercy of the elements, the villagers and the conservationists. The noble custom of laymen becoming monks for a short time during their early manhood is becoming less popular for the same sort of reason. Boys these days do not see the usefulness of it and resist family pressure to undertake it.

When he was crown prince in 1824, and twenty years old, the man who later became King Mongkut entered the monkhood. Two weeks later his father died, but instead of succeeding to the throne Mongkut stayed in the monkhood and allowed his brother to reign instead. By the time that brother died and Mongkut became king (in 1851), he had worn the saffron robe for 27 years—traveling up and down the kingdom, sharing and intimately observing the condition of its populace as no prince at court could have done, meeting all kinds of foreigners and learning from them. No king ever had a better training, and it is no wonder Mongkut went on to be the great modernizing monarch of Thailand. The present king, Bhumiphol, became a monk at the Wat Borvornnives in Bangkok when he was 28 years old and ten years on the throne. For two weeks he received the alms of the people like any other monk. This is a constructive, educational and democratic institution which contributes greatly to the social and political well-being of the nation.

Personal Buddhism will not necessarily suffer from this decline in the monkhood, and that is just as well, because it is the root of the Thai nation's social, cultural and political identity. Buddhism occupies more than the narrow area allocated to religion in other societies and is constantly involved in economic, business, political, diplomatic, intellectual and scientific contexts as the basic belief on which all human activity in Thailand rests.

The monks themselves are not supposed to enter politics, the *sangha* has ruled, or stand as candidates in elections. At times of great political turmoil, as in the early 1970s, that rule tends to be broken and is challenged still by some rebels. (During the Vietnam War, Vietnamese Buddhist monks fought and incited others to take up arms.) Buddhism is highly individual. It shows a person how to save himself, not how to mobilize society for collective improvement. For that reason it is not an appropriate ideology, either for political campaigns or economic development—those two central quests of modern life. When the *sangha* does get involved in the material affairs of the nation, and it cannot always escape from them, it courts criticism. A few years ago the Supreme Patriarch, who heads the *sangha* and ranks almost as a king in the Buddhist world, blessed a new aircraft. A regional newspaper mildly suggested this was not a very Buddhist act, and narrowly escaped being banned.[7]

Yet monks are asked to bless new shops, factories, vehicles, businesses, roads and canals every day of the week. It is one of their important sources of income. And some monks can be extremely practical, like Phrakru Sakorn, who organized the people in his village to build dikes against flood, and canals against drought. Next he showed them how to switch from rice cultivation to the safer and more profitable crop of coconuts. After that he found out, on their behalf, how to extract sugar from the coconuts in order to retain the most value and earn the most money from them. Now he is studying the agronomy of palm trees, which might do even better for his community. If only there were more like him.[8]

Thais sometimes deprecate their religion in discussions with foreigners, until they discover so many Westerners taking Thai Buddhism seriously, to the point of being "converted." Actually, proselytizing abroad is spasmodic. In 1934 Phra Lokanat, an Italian convert to Buddhism, received much publicity for leading a mission of a hundred Thai monks to convert Christians in Rome. But that was not the best time for such efforts. A little wave of missionaries appeared in the 1960s, when the Americans funded 50 or 60 priests at a time to visit the northern hill tribes and bring them into the Buddhist fold—and thereby into the national political and security system.

The Ministry of Education, which has a department for religious affairs, launched a program to train 25 English, sociology and psychology graduates for two years to prepare for "spreading Buddha's teachings" in such benighted parts as England, Malaysia, Singapore and India—not, as it hastened to add, with the aim of overthrowing other religions. But the missionary role jars with Thai passivity and fatalism and is not sustained.

Politically minded Buddhists are sensitive all the same to the fancied encroachments of other religions, so Christians and other foreign missionaries do not have it all their own way. The existence of a small Thai Christian minority is accepted: Was it not King Mongkut who expansively donated land to all the various Christian sects that came to Thailand, ruling that Buddhism tolerated them all? If you walk down Bangkok's Silom Road past the bank skyscrapers, the McDonald's, the hotel towers, the Sri Mariamme Hindu temple and the headquarters of Thai Airways International, you will pass a lot that is boarded up, like a site awaiting development: push at a faded old doorway and you will catch a vista of whitened tombstones and fancily carved sepulchers stretching back as far as the eye can see. This is the Catholic cemetery donated by the king, an unexpected reminder of the Christian presence in an overwhelmingly Buddhicized city.

The Christian missionaries were in fact disappointed: very few Thais took theology sufficiently seriously to endure the wrench of leaving the Buddhist sociopolitical frame. More biddable were the Vietnamese and Chinese immigrants, some of whom, like the founder of the Sarasin family, had been softened up for Christianity in the more receptive ground of South China around Canton and Hong Kong. So the American and European missionaries in Thailand often found themselves tending a mainly Chinese flock. A few Thais reveal themselves as Christian, as did Thawin Rawangphai, a former Lord Mayor of Bangkok. But it is the Thai Chinese, "Sino-Thai" and Vietnamese communities which most often produce a Christian—like Chatri Sophonpanich of the Bangkok Bank, who is Catholic.

New Christian proselytizing can be misunderstood. There is a Buddhist Protection Group, which may sound like a contradiction in terms. It has detected a Roman Catholic plot to make Buddha a disciple of Christ (jumping the centuries, as it were) and to absorb Buddhism into the Holy See. The group rallied a thousand Thai monks to protest and vow their opposition. One of them, Phra Soponkanaporn, wrote a stirring tract entitled *The Plan to Destroy Buddhism*. What had upset them most was the Catholics' decision to indigenize their presence in Thailand by using Thai words for the various ranks in the Roman hierarchy.[9] A Mormon church leader was facing criminal charges in 1991 for saying that Buddhist monks do not normally understand the prayers they chant.

Luckily, such things stand at the periphery of Thai Buddhism. The heart of it is its address to human emotions, its wise tempering of them in the interest of developing a sound, balanced human being. Most religions tell you about goodness and its rationale: Buddhism goes further and offers practical, precise, *physical* guidance on how to discipline your body in order to attain it. Compassion is an exhortation in the Christian book, but Buddhism makes it something you can use with meaning.

Its teaching ranks second to none. Who would not be moved by Buddha's consoling words spoken to a grieving mother unable to accept her child's death: "All that is needed to bring your child back is one grain of mustard seed from a house where there has not been a death"? The woman races off eagerly, but soon realizes that every house has its death, and in that way begins to come to terms with her loss.

And how supremely relevant, in this age of economic development and political corruption, is the jewellike answer given to the greedy question, "If you catch a big fish, how can you make it provide for you throughout the year?" The possible solutions flash through the mind. Dry it? Salt it? Sell it for money to buy other things? No, the answer is much simpler. Share it with neighbors, so that they will share with you when *they* catch one.

Buddhism today has many different faces, some backward looking, some more aligned with the individualistic urbanism of the twentieth century. Women are still disqualified from attending Buddhist schools, entering the central shrine of the *wat* or becoming monks. The only female monk,

Voromai Kabilsingh, was ordained as a Mahayana monk in Taiwan, the Mahayana adherents being more liberal in this respect than the Thai Theravada *sangha*. This lady, now 84, heads a small nunnery of about 60 nuns and novices in Ratchaburi province. They go back to the original Buddhist texts to argue that the Buddha himself did not discriminate against women, but the male chauvinists who run the *sangha* are not convinced.

These old traditions might have faded away with modernization. But Buddhism proved resilient to meet the new challenges. Old-fashioned monks have little to say that is helpful about current practical problems, so new sects have emerged to meet those needs. Most of them turn their backs decisively on all the paraphernalia of the old temple setup—fortune-telling, lotteries, amulets and charms. They respect the Buddha image but do not worship it. They retreat from the pointless old collective rituals and march firmly into the liberated social arena where selves cry out for cultivation, either by being shown suitable avenues of individual moral action or by honing their social efficacy through meditation techniques. These sects are the nearest counterparts of the "protestant ethic" supposedly driving some northern European societies.

The most famous of them is Santi Asoke (meaning "Peace and No Sorrow"), founded by Phra Bodhirak, an aggressive former TV producer and singer, half Chinese, who was ordained at 36. Apart from not worshiping images, Santi Asoke adherents do not shave their eyebrows, are strict vegetarians—and wore brown robes instead of the usual saffron-yellow until they were excommunicated by the *sangha* in 1989 and forced to wear white. Bodhirak's quarrel with the *sangha* went across the board. He dismissed the Patriarch's ruling on politics on the ground that monks are involved with people and must necessarily therefore be involved in politics. The point of that had become clear in 1979 when the pious General Chamlong (later governor of Bangkok) declared his sympathy with the sect. The monks helped Chamlong's Palang Dharma party in election campaigns, though since the excommunication, the party has played down its connection.[10]

Santi Asoke has been plagued by difficulties. There was a scandal when bogus royal decorations were discovered in the sect's temples. But the worst blow came when Bodhirak, never renowned for his modesty, claimed in an interview that he had personally attained the same level of enlightenment as the Buddha himself—something no Thai had ever dared to assert before. Despite such excesses of zeal, this sharp, communicative, socially engaged priest is popular in the new Thailand. What he says is relevant to the issues of the day. He declares that the "silent majority" in the monkhood support him against the *sangha*. But he is choosy about his Buddhists, and is not at all sure that the Dalai Lama, for example, deserves support. He questions the Dalai's "devotion to society."

Dhammakaya (meaning "Body of Truth") is like Santi Asoke in officially discouraging magic and worship, but has come more decisively to terms with the material, and especially financial realities of modern Thailand. It was founded in 1970 by Phra Dhammachayo, then 26 and a economics graduate of mixed Thai, Chinese, Lao and Song ancestry. His deputy is Thai-Vietnamese. These two abbots do not believe in selling their sect cheap. They go out in a Rolls-Royce or Mercedes for morning alms, in robes made of Swiss cloth—all thanks, they explain, to lay generosity. Their sect is not inhibited about making money to keep itself going. It runs a profitable personal savings fund and holds industrial investments. In a neat matching of *karma* and property management, Dhammachayo and his monks persuade lay supporters to donate land to the sect with the promise that they will enjoy more land in their next life.

Dhammakaya is far from being revolutionary in social terms. It accepts the status quo, justifying the existing social structure and hoping merely to help individuals within that structure to feel better. It has developed a particular kind of meditation technique where you visualize Buddha internally within your body, and this is found helpful by many followers. Those include General Arthit Kamlang-ek, one-time Supreme Commander of the armed forces and deputy prime minister. With patrons like that, Phra Dhammachayo could go far in his quest for Rolls-Royce Buddhism.[11]

The sheep in the pack is Suan Mokh (meaning "Garden of Liberation"), which is older, saner and calmer. Its leader, Buddhadasa, preaches what he calls Dhammic socialism, a decentralized noncompetitive form of social cooperation in self-contained village republics free from greed. It is a beautiful concept, though the means of reducing or suppressing greed are not clear. Greed is the foundation of capitalism and is usually acceptable provided the capitalism produces wealth—and the greed can be kept from overreaching itself. All Thais worry about this problem. Buddhadasa offers an idealistic solution, and for that he is widely respected if not eagerly followed.

Regardless of sects, some sensible monks contribute individually to their locality's modernization. Abbot Nan Suntasilo of the Samakkee temple near Surin persuaded the villagers nearby to conquer their poverty by giving up land to build a new road to the city. The result was the constant roar of motorcycles, a mass invasion of consumer durables, a surge of gambling and drinking and higher debts. The abbot told the villagers they needed to acquire "spiritual immunity" to fight the influx of consumerism which was burying them in debt. Meditation was used. Abbot Nan proceeded to establish a fertilizer bank using donations to the temple, from which villagers could borrow without having to go to loan sharks. They still pay high interest, but as the abbot explains, "the temple's money is the people's money."

Then a rice bank was established to ease the hunger created by drought. "Friendship farming" was introduced, villagers donating their labor to plant rice on communal land also donated. The rice harvested from this went to the rice bank to help other villagers. Asked to comment on the traditional view that monks should not take part in life outside the religious sphere, Abbot Nan replies: "We monks are indebted to the people. They feed and take care of us. We cannot ignore their plight by saying that it is not our job to help." He was the first to warn that there is no set formula for this kind of work, every locality being different. The most important thing, he says, is to acquire "spiritual immunity" through meditation, and use the clear and calm mind which results from that to give strong practical leadership to the people. There are about 300 "development monks" who concentrate on the real needs of rural life, like Abbot Nan.[12]

At the other extreme are monks like Phra Kittivudho, who not only maintained a "wife" and smuggled arms across the borders but gave his full blessing for the killing of communists—for whom the Buddhist prohibition against taking life did not, he argued, apply. He too acquired many military followers, though he lost face in 1990 when the government closed his school down because its teaching standards were too low. On the fourth day of the 1991 coup Kittivudho drove up to a government office in his brand-new Mercedes-Benz—not to lobby for a religious cause but to ask the Ministry of Commerce to buy rice from his institute's cooperatives![13]

Buddhism is struggling to find a new persona in Thailand, and the options for citizens seeking various kinds of religious experience, reassurance, guidance or technique are widening. That modern monks prefer the stimulus of urban society to lifetimes of village uplift is not surprising. Buddhists today want to be where the action is. Hopefully their monks will eventually restate the Buddhist canon of morality in a modern industrial context. That is what people most ask from the men in saffron. Buddhism has the role of maintaining people's sanity in this period of fast economic growth.

7

A Fast Growth Economy:
Consolidating for Another Spurt

The political roller coaster has carried Thailand through many democratic ups and dictatorial downs. Management of the economy, by contrast, has been steadily successful, being largely left to civil service technocrats because they are the only ones who understand it. The Thai leaders were astute enough to choose free-enterprise capitalism and respect for market forces at a time when these policies were being rejected and even ridiculed in most neighboring countries. Thailand's adherence to reason and common sense made its position in Southeast Asia uncomfortable at times. Left-wing Indonesians, Vietnamese, Burmese and Chinese used to pour scorn on Thailand as a lackey of the United States in both business affairs and diplomacy.

Time may show that the antibodies that European rule produced in colonized Asia were antipathetic even to such fundamentally desirable aspects of European public life as capitalism. The Thai technocrats knew better. Their immunity to Western colonialism enabled them to see clearly the high levels of economic development and standards of living that the capitalist countries of Europe and North America had attained. Today the neighbors watch Thailand's rapid progress with envy, and most of them have belatedly tried to switch course toward the new capitalist direction. Meanwhile Thailand consolidates its economic lead over the other states of Southeast Asia with greatly superior economic growth rates.

Thailand, already a mixed economy under the absolute kings and Marshal Phibul, steered very firmly in the direction of private enterprise when Marshal Sarit was dictator in the late 1950s. By then, American influence was strong, and both the World Bank and the United States Agency for

International Development pressed the Thai government to abandon state enterprises and encourage private entrepreneurs instead.

Free enterprise actually has a long pedigree in Thailand. The thirteenth-century inscribed tablet of King Ramkhanghaeng decreeing that "whoever wants to deal in goods deals" is now suspected of being a creation, for thoroughly laudable reasons, of the nineteenth-century King Mongkut, who claimed to have discovered it. Whatever its vintage, it is a forthright statement of policy which has been followed since Mongkut if not before—even if the state corporations and their powerful trade unions still exist. The king's factories gave up their monopolies long ago, and foreign analysts admire the way enterprises are not cosseted as they are in, say, India, but rather exposed to the rigors of competition.

Ex-Premier Pote Sarasin remarked in the 1960s that if the state allowed the making of things or the performing of services to be "privately profitable," then people would do them.[1] That kind of realistic rationalization of free-enterprise capitalism was rare in the Third World then. It has been the premise of Thai economic policy throughout. Finance Minister Pramual Sabhavasu pledged in 1990: "The role of the government will shrink and the private sector will increase. We will only supervise at a distance, and unless it becomes necessary we will not supervise." He fell from power soon afterward, but his successors have reaffirmed this position.

Some Thais like to boast of their achievement. Others more modestly attribute it to Buddhism. "We were the chosen one for Southeast Asian growth," says one of Thailand's cleverest technocrats, with all the satisfaction of a man who knows he has been virtuous and is getting his reward. It was not always obvious, however, that Thailand would come out ahead of the Southeast Asian pack to qualify as a Newly Industrialized Economy, or NIE. The Philippines, after all, had been hailed as the model Southeast Asian economy before Imelda Marcos started buying shoes in the 1960s. Malaysia was neck and neck with Thailand in rate of growth until very recently—and still boasts higher income per head.

But now Thailand has achieved average real growth in Gross Domestic Product of 6.7 percent a year over the 40 years since 1951, and double-digit growth for five years running, 1986-90 inclusive.[2] Even with the Gulf War, growth in 1990 notched up a very satisfactory 10 percent, and the 1991 performance was 7.5 percent in spite of the military coup. Most projections for 1992 saw Thailand growing at about 7 percent, faster than most other developing Asian countries, in spite of the political upheaval.

Average income per head is approximately U.S. $1,200, and the Seventh 5-Year National Economic and Social Development Plan for 1992-96 has a

Developing Asia's Economic League

Growth Average real GDP annual growth rate 1980-90		Wealth GNP per head in 1989 dollars	
1. South Korea	8.0 %	1. Singapore	10,450
2. Taiwan	7.7 %	2. Hong Kong	10,320
3. Thailand	7.5 %	3. Taiwan	6,889*
4. Singapore	7.3 %	4. South Korea	4,400
5. Hong Kong	7.0 %	5. Malaysia	2,130
6. Malaysia	6.1 %	6. Thailand	1,170
7. India	5.9 %	7. Philippines	700

* GDP per head

[Newly Industrialized Economies (NIEs) in bold type.]

Sources: World Bank Atlas 1990, Baring Securities Economic Report on Thailand 1990, The Asian *Wall Street Journal,* 14 October 1991, and *Far Eastern Economic Review Yearbook, Asia* 1991.

target of $3,000 by the end of 1996. Industry already provides a third of the Gross Domestic Product and two-thirds of exports. The accolade of NIE-hood is confidently anticipated in the second half of the 1990s. Thailand would then join Korea, Taiwan and the two city-states—Hong Kong and Singapore—in belonging to developing Asia's economic elite. "The Thai economy," the Bank of Thailand concludes, "exhibits high potential, and its ability to expand is unlimited."

The 5-Year Plan aims at 8.2 percent average annual growth in GDP—3.4 percent in agriculture, 9.5 percent in industry, and 14.7 percent in exports. It also envisages significant expansion of infrastructure, reduced dependence on imported energy and inflation below 5.6 percent. The goal is to maintain steady growth with good distribution of income and improved environment.[3]

There are two views in Thailand about this prospect. Most businessmen and economists are delighted. "We have looked forward," says Sumitr Pitiphat, Thammasat University's dean of sociology, "to getting more wealth. Yes, we worry about the erosion of the old culture. But the obsolete must go." Excessive sentimental concern about the social cost of rapid economic growth is dismissed by this school of thought: People do not mind change if it puts money in their pockets and they can choose how to spend it. "Growth liberates people," says a Bangkok Bank director, "and in any case the old tradition of mutual help is still strong."

Such self-confidence about an economy changing shape and stride before their very eyes is not shared by a number of pessimists and conservationists, who include several intellectuals from the liberal arts, on the ground that Thailand's economic progress is failing to spread itself widely enough. A common complaint is the benefit gained by land developers, who can easily persuade farmers to sell when land prices escalate, with no concomitant economic benefit to society.

Fast growth makes people greedy, says Sulak Sivaraksa, the upholder of tradition, and then they start misbehaving, treating others badly, upsetting society and disrupting the family, that bedrock of social organization. King Bhumiphol, who is normally no admirer of Sulak, agrees with him on this point: growth should be slowed down to ease the burden of adjustment on the poor.

The great Dr. Puey Ungpakorn, who as a government official and advisor set the economic course for the 1960s, afterward regretted having neglected the unwanted social side effects of growth, especially the disparity of incomes. When material technical advances alter the nature of your social relationships and cultural values inexorably and swiftly, the whole society can become unstable and resentful. Puey's successor, Dr. Snoh Unakul, promoted to be deputy prime minister after the 1991 coup, also felt that the economy in the late 1980s had grown too fast, making people not only greedy but callous. The Gulf War of 1990-91, according to this view, came as a "blessing in disguise," to calm things down a little.

Tongroj Onchan, an agricultural economist at Kasetsart University, believes that the frenetic pace should be deliberately slowed down in order to give ordinary people the time to adjust, time to prepare themselves and their families, time to train themselves for new work. The government also needs more time to prepare its contribution to training and social adjustment. Another economist notes that more attention is currently being paid to the speed of growth than to its pattern or direction: economic policy can itself be a victim of rapid growth!

Such critics accept that there would be a cost to slowing down—less money, and fewer goods and services to go around. "We should slow down to serve justice," says the ex-governor of Bangkok, Major General Chamlong Srimuang, "even if we lose something else." There is a continuing suspicion that the extra goodies created by rapid growth mainly accrue to those who are already rich and are therefore best able to manipulate the market and the economic system. That is the opinion of the soldiers who seized power in

February 1991, though they would hope to have the best of both worlds through well-selected economic policies.

Doubts about the NIE label spring from other considerations besides the anxiety about fast growth. Thailand has already begun to suffer trade disadvantages, especially in the American market, arising from its better economic performance. The Thai export surplus with the United States is now at the $2 billion-a-year level, enough to provoke dissatisfaction in Washington. The United States took Thailand to the General Agreement on Tariffs and Trade (GATT) to pry open its market to American cigarettes and permit cigarette advertisements—as Japan, Korea and Taiwan have already done.

The United States also complains of dumping of Thai products on the American market, while Thai rice exporters complain about subsidized U.S. exports to world markets. The office of the U.S. Trade Representative has placed Thailand on a "priority watch list" for failing to legislate for the protection of intellectual property rights. Copyrights, trademarks and patents (especially for pharmaceuticals and computer software, but also for brand-name T-shirts and cassettes) are the main issues in this controversy. Brazil, Mexico and China are also on the list.

When you are poor, you qualify for special trade preferences and economic aid and are not pressed to open up your markets. Once you start becoming rich, you are expected to forgo such special treatment, abide by the same rules as everyone else and observe "reciprocity" of treatment vis-à-vis countries 30 times wealthier. NIE-hood has become a benchmark for such graduation from indigence to full membership of the club, and Thai exporters lobby for another kind of label which would do them less harm.

Another quarrel with the NIE acronym is that almost everyone takes it to mean going all-out for industrialization. That was certainly true for the two virtually wholly urban city-states, Hong Kong and Singapore, Even the two other NIEs—Korea and Taiwan—have emphasized industry to the point where it overshadows the relatively modest agricultural sectors. Thailand is different. Thai agriculture is famous all over the world and provides a livelihood for 30 million people. The kingdom's agricultural and forestry resources are far superior to those of the original NIEs. Agriculture plays a key role in Thailand's social structure and is closely bound up with Thailand's monarchy and national identity. Many alternative acronyms have therefore been floated, such as Newly Agro-Industrializing Country (NAIC), or Newly Agro-Industrializing Service Economy (NAISE). The former premier, General Chatichai, told a European audience that Thailand did not really mind what it was called—though it would settle for being known simply as a NICE country.[4]

The NIE label is thus ambiguous. Some Thais are proud of the international prestige it will bring, others are apprehensive about the domestic damage it may wreak. A senior MP pointed to the change in Japan (the prototype NIE), where traditional Buddhism had stressed simplicity and modesty, "but the NIE version of Buddhism is regimented and commercial," and that might also happen to Thai Buddhism. Dr. Snoh, with his fine sense of balance, has argued that Thailand's strong cultural heritage and social integrity should save it from the harsher consequences of the new status and allow the quality of life and social well-being to be preserved. Others are less sanguine.

Dr. Snoh talks fondly of the Buddhist philosophy underlying the stability, diversification, decentralization and cooperation between public and private sectors, which characterized the early and mid-1980s—the Prem years, before the economy began to sprint. A successor of Snoh's as governor of the Bank of Thailand declared: "We have taken the modest path, the Buddhist way, the middle path. . . . We have almost equally developed agriculture and industry."[5] For two bank governors to attribute prosperity to Buddhism shows the strength of the traditions which helped to keep a check on technical change, at least until the late 1980s. Today it is doubtful how much religion can help: daunting decisions about the speed of growth will have to be made, and the forces of the free market are raging almost uncontrollably through this land of the Buddha—some of whose monks now drive to morning alms in Rolls-Royce limousines.

With an experienced civil service and an unshackled Chinese business community, Thailand has been able to advance steadily to provide an attractive business environment obscured only by the fact that Thailand does not follow Anglo-Saxon institutional laws or models. Its officials do not necessarily speak English, and the bureaucratic obstruction, arbitrariness and corruption at the petty level can be off-putting to foreigners. With the gradual infrastructural improvement, Western businessmen, traders and investors from the West are surprised to discover what opportunities lurk beneath a sometimes unpromising exterior.

There was a left wing, of course, and indeed it was touch and go in the 1940s whether Thailand would not become an early case of Asian socialism. Of the two would-be dictators who fought it out to rule Thailand after having separated the king from his absolutism in 1932, Pridi Panomyong, the "Sino-Thai" Paris-trained economist and dedicated democrat, spoke for the left. He proposed to nationalize the land. It would not, he claimed, destroy farmers' incentives, but would on the contrary release altruistic nationalism to replace egoism. The love of the Thai race would prevail over the love of self. Everyone in this classic Left Bank blueprint would work for the government and draw a salary through cooperatives. It would represent a utopia and, yes, the golden age of Buddhism.

Pridi was a powerful and clever personality who inspired many of the idealistic young people of postwar Thailand. He might in other circumstances have become Thailand's Ho Chi Minh. His continuing legacy was seen in the left-wing program of the military Young Turks and Democratic Soldiers in the early 1980s, to partially nationalize banks and mines, implement land reform, control high finance and compile a hit list of a hundred businessmen to be "eliminated."

Ajarn Saneh, one of the few surviving adherents to the old Marxist "dependency theory," grumbles about Thailand's close imitation of the Western industrialization model, calling it inappropriate and "destructive." Market forces, once aroused, are too strong for Thailand to resist, he argues. They manipulate the national elite instead of the other way round. Saneh, who runs a local development institute in Bangkok, would like to seal off the kingdom in order to develop it more slowly and correctly. But that, he concedes, is impossible now that the demand for economic growth and modernization has been generally unleashed.

It was all the more significant, therefore, that under General Prem's statesmanlike adjustment to civilian rule in the 1980s, farsighted bureaucrats were allowed to exercise exemplary fiscal and monetary restraint, curb foreign borrowing, hold wages down and devalue the *baht* twice—by 8.7 percent in 1981 and by 14.9 percent in 1984. All these measures were opposed by vested interests, and Prem was quite untrained in finance or economics.

Even better, Prem's technocrats were able to bring together the self-righteous officials of the economic ministries and the bruised private entrepreneurs who had been hindered by arbitrary regulation and demoralized by Young Turk threats. The Joint Public-Private Consultative Committee on Economic Problems, set up in 1981, was a landmark in postwar policy. Its advocates had failed before, in the 1970s, because the private businessmen were not ready for such dialogue. They did not feel at ease with officials, and could not articulate their needs—could not even speak Thai, in the case of some Chinese tycoons!

When at last the committee did get off the ground, the private sector leaders were so critical and arrogant that some economic Ministers stopped attending. General Prem was himself suspicious of the capitalists, and reluctant to "get his hands dirty." Yet he wanted to attract foreign investors. Dr. Snoh Unakul, then Governor of the Bank of Thailand, and his supporters brought Prem round by asking him how foreign businessmen could be convinced to invest when domestic investors were holding back? It was eventually agreed that no risks would be taken: the committee's agenda would be carefully screened, and the meetings efficiently organized to focus on national, not personal interests, with everything on the table and nothing underneath it. No one would get his hands "dirty."[6]

Under the prime minister's personal chairmanship, these leaders of the two equally necessary sides of the nation's economic effort met in Government House every month and tackled the age-old complaints of business-men—taxes, customs duty, licenses, regulations. Among the committee's early successes were freeing tourism and gem exports from red tape and convening regional meetings where local issues could be tackled with the help of newly formed provincial chambers of commerce.

For the first time businessmen were able to influence the government collectively through their associations, and share in the making of public policy. From being merely tolerated on the fringes of the economy and economic planning they now acquired social acceptability, even equality of treatment with government officials while traveling abroad on missions. Dr. Snoh and his fellow officials were actually criticized by traditionalists for heaping too much honor on merchants.

The change of mood opened up the possibilities of privatization, though that word is not generally used. "We do not like the term 'privatisation,'" said Phisit Pakkasem, secretary general of the National Economic and Social Development Board. "We describe it as increasing the role of the private sector in development of state enterprises." The discovery that drivers for state enterprises were earning more than middle-ranking government offi-cials helped to disarm some of the opposition from bureaucrats. The Erawan Hotel, Bangpa-In Paper Mill and various rice and jute mills were privatized. The government largely resisted the temptation to sell off profitable concerns to favored domestic groups, and the whole exercise was carried out effi-ciently. Thai Airways International, among other state enterprises, is ex-pected to follow as Thailand continues to tap the international money market.

Foreign investment has indeed flooded in. In the decade of the 1980s it totaled about $8 billion, most heavily in electronics, chemicals, property and tourism. Japanese companies led, followed by Chinese (from Hong Kong, Taiwan and Singapore), Korean and American. These foreign investors are now responsible for half of Thailand's industrial output and employ one-fifth of the industrial work force.

Japan became the largest foreign direct investor in Thailand in 1986, overtaking the United States, Hong Kong and Singapore. Cumulative Japanese direct investment during the 1980s (1980-89) was around $2.5 billion. A financial journalist recently complained that it was easier to list Thai projects that lack Japanese participation than to name those that have it. There is some anxiety that this growing dominance of Japanese capital could in the long run affect the flexibility of Thai economic decision-making and have unfortunate political ramifications.[7]

The Thai government has, however, shown skill in diversifying its sources of investment and technology. As far back as the 1930s a Danish company had been chosen over Mitsui for an important construction project because the government was worried even then about excessive Japanese influence over the economy. Today, 60 years on, the same strategy is used. Big oil-refinery, petrochemical and telecommunications contracts are awarded not purely on corporate competitiveness, but also to balance the national factors as much as possible—something which has helped such British companies as Shell and British Telecom.

There is also now a reverse flow of investment. The Saha Union Co. of Thailand has bought a textile mill in Georgia, and Unicord, GSS Electronics, Bank Asia Finance One and Regional Container Line have purchased overseas companies in the United States, Hong Kong and Singapore. In one instance a British company was bought by Advanced Electronic Systems of Thailand.[8]

The foreign-investment boom in Thailand reached a climax at the end of the 1980s, with $1.1 billion directly invested in 1988 and $1.7 billion in 1989. Portfolio investment totaled $1.9 billion for those two years together, and the total investment amount represented 2.5 percent of Thailand's Gross Domestic Product in 1988, rising to 4.4 percent in 1989. Most of the direct investment is export-oriented, coming from industrialists in Northeast Asia and North America who seek to take advantage of significantly lower manufacturing costs, especially labor, as their own economies are affected by inflation and falling competitiveness.

The Thai government is doing a great deal to keep costs down as a stimulus to investment. The *baht* is a stable currency, pegged to the U.S. dollar and much in demand in neighboring countries. It is well managed, and the judgment of the Bank of Thailand technocrats usually prevails—as it did when the army leaders clashed with Prime Minister Prem Tinsulanond over the 14.9 percent devaluation of 1984.

Usually, though not always, the minister of finance in recent administrations has been an ex-bureaucrat or ex-banker. There have been differences of opinion between bank and ministry, particularly when the finance minister is a politician. In 1989 one bank governor clashed with the businessman who was then minister of finance, Pramual Sabhavasu, and was removed. Pramual was a pillar of the Chart Thai party then leading the government under Premier Chatichai. But a technocrat was then made finance minister in his place, and the independence of the bank was swiftly recognized.

At the end of 1991, the *baht* appeared to be slightly undervalued. The inflow of overseas funds was so large in the past two years that a *baht* revaluation might have been expected as a measure to cool down the economy by slowing exports and increasing imports. The government, however, chose to hold the *baht* down, with foreign exchange reserves approaching $1.6 billion.

The consequence of this was to boost inflation, which hovered around 6 percent in 1990 and 1991, and fell below 5 percent in 1992. Expected to rise further, it was unlikely to exceed the real rate of economic growth. There continues to be concern all the same about the adequacy of capital for investment in the coming period of further, albeit somewhat slower growth that lies ahead in the 1990s.

There is a shortfall between domestic savings and investment, and the volatile Stock Exchange is not yet capable of providing all the funds needed, though its capitalization doubled in only a few months in 1990. There is now a greater interest from abroad for Thai shares. The exchange offered a handful of new brokerage seats in 1990, and one of the companies selected included a foreign financial institution as partner. The Stock Exchange exploded in 1989, when prices more than doubled and trading volume soared. The estimated 500,000 investors patronizing the exchange (many of them Japanese, Taiwanese and other foreigners) had a field day, despite a government bombshell about taxing capital gains from stock transactions and some talk of raising interest rates. Total market capitalization reached $32 billion by September 1991 (equivalent to about a third of Thailand's Gross National Product).

The Stock Exchange is still described by jaundiced foreign residents as "a crap shoot." To see hundreds of traders, many in tennis shoes, jumping from desk to desk, hopping on and off the furniture and bouncing on and off each other like snooker balls, is hardly reassuring. "The floor," an American visitor to the Exchange said recently, "seems more like a place for slam dancing than trading securities." The Exchange is vulnerable to artificial demand, and lacks adequate supervisory mechanisms. The Bank of Thailand governor, Vijit Supanit (trained at Bristol University in the United Kingdom and at the Bank of England), was at the end of 1991 pushing through several reforms, including tighter listing procedures and better computers, to bring the exchange up to international standards.

Thailand's long-term external debt stood at about $16 billion at the end of 1990. But the ratio of long-term debt service payments to exports has been declining, averaging only 10 percent in the years 1989-91. Foreign exchange reserves at that time were equivalent to cover five months of imports, so the underlying position is healthy.[9]

The Anand government of technocrats in 1991 put in train a substantial liberalization of financial markets, foreign exchange controls and capital movements and the dismantling of many other controls. More foreign banks are expected to be allowed to open to stimulate the domestic market. The goal is to strengthen and supplement what local banks can offer in order to provide local enterprise with the capital it needs to expand. But no offshore trading role is envisaged to emulate Hong Kong or Singapore. If the financial facilities available in Bangkok are used by foreigners, that will be a welcome spin-off. Bangkok will, if domestic banks respond to the opportunity, become a subregional or Indochinese finance center for neighboring countries already using the *baht* (Vietnam, Burma, Laos and Cambodia), but not yet a Southeast Asian regional finance center.

The domestic banks, whose enthusiasm is necessary for assuming an Indochinese role, are overprotected. The World Bank's advice to allow banks to collapse if they are badly managed is not considered "Buddhist," and successive governments have preferred to salvage such candidates for bankruptcy, and protect their (often politically influential) shareholders and creditors. In 1983 when the Prem administration was pursuing its new and more rational economic policy, nineteen financial corporations were allowed to collapse. But another ailing 26 were salvaged through government takeover in the three following years.

Successive technocrats—Dr. Snoh Unakul in the 1970s and Boonchu Rojanasathien in the 1980s—tried to break up the big bank groups, or else press them to go public, but with little success. When he was finance minister, Boonchu ordered the Bangkok Bank, in which he had worked for over twenty years, to divest half its shares to small individual shareholders. In 1975 the bank went public, but the Sophonpanich family continued to hold, directly or indirectly, over 40 percent of the equity. Such reforms are more difficult to pursue in "democratic" governments openly dominated, as Chatichai's was, by businessmen. This perhaps is the kind of action which only a nonelected technocratic government like that installed after the 1991 coup can successfully carry out—showing the usefulness of the occasional military-bureaucratic coup.

The Bangkok Bank is the success story of Thai banking, standing now as the biggest commercial bank in Southeast Asia. It took off in the 1960s and 1970s when Boonchu built up first a tight network of rural branches, giving low-interest loans to small farmers, and then a similar one for the textile industry. Over those two decades the bank grew by an average of over 20 percent per year. When Boonchu was headhunted to be finance minister in 1975, a bureaucrat, Dr. Amnuay Viravan, became the chief executive. By the 1980s the bank had become fully professionalized.

When the founder, Chin Sophonpanich, died in 1988, there was some uncertainty. His eldest son in Bangkok, Chatri, was the obvious successor. But whereas Chin had an instinctive sense of whom to lend to (and usually did so on trust), his son lacked that nose for a good creditor and soon experienced collection problems. Staff loyalties were divided between Chatri and his brother Chote, who was easier to deal with, but not so sharp a businessman. In the end Chatri asserted his claim and formed a triumvirate with Dr. Amnuay and Damrong Krishnamara, the top Thai executive and Boonchu's former right-hand man, to run the bank's affairs. The bank is an active equity holder in new ventures and an innovator in every financial area. It could more than adequately hold its own against foreign competition, though many of the smaller banks could not. Sometime soon there will have to be a shakeout among the Thai domestic banks, however much the politicians may dislike it.

What lies ahead for the Thai economy in the early 1990s is an initial period of "growthflation." Output of goods is likely to continue growing vigorously. Once post-uprising investment resumes, the main concerns will be inflation and the current account deficit, which increased to 8.6 percent of GDP in 1991 but was expected to fall back to 7.5 percent in 1992.

Since 1989, long-term and short-term overseas borrowings have greatly exceeded the amount of direct investment from abroad. The boom in domestic demand drew in overseas finance to make up for the lack of local savings. In other words, the current account deficit was increasingly financed by the influx of hot money. Overheating had become apparent at the end of 1991, with accelerated consumer goods imports and higher inflationary pressures. The government intended to pursue deflationary policies to depress demand growth with higher interest rates and control of the growth of lending.

Thailand's foreign trade position is extremely healthy, with exports much better balanced as between commodities and between its overseas markets than other Asian countries. The only shadow is Thailand's failure to reduce its oil dependence. As a consequence, the rise in oil prices caused by the Gulf War in 1990 hurt Thailand more than its competitors in the region.

A major weakness for the future of the Thai economy is the poor development of infrastructure to cope with the rapid growth of the economy as a whole. Thai policymakers are slow to take the necessary steps to remove bottlenecks in the economy. There are vested interests, both business and political, which need to be satisfied in traditional Buddhist fashion, which usually means some kind of compromise. The frequency of changes in government is another hazard, and the overall result is often a delay in tendering procedures which leave international companies frustrated. There are exceptions which prove the rule, a notable one being the Electricity Generating Authority of Thailand (EGAT), which has succeeded in tripling its expansion programs without too much difficulty. Overall, however, the physical constraints of power and communications may hamper the future expansion of the economy and prevent Thailand from reaching its true potential.

As an American analyst has recently put it, there is not only a "recognition lag" in identifying the needs of double-digit growth, but also a "decision lag" even when the need has become clear and finally an "implementation lag" when vital projects are realized at an infuriatingly leisurely pace.[10]

The cost to industry of the overburdened port facilities, inadequate power generation grid, inefficient telephone network and transport system, is a nuisance to all, although it has not actually prevented double-digit growth. However, areas where economic growth demands action include essential expressways to relieve Bangkok's traffic jams, rapid mass transit systems, new electricity-generating stations (and possibly nuclear power), elevated railways through the center of Bangkok, the faster development of the new deep-sea port of Laem Chabang (which will eventually become a major port with five berths for containers, general cargo and bulk sugar) and three more deep-sea ports at Mabtaphut, Phuket and Songkhla. After lengthy negotiations under the Chatichai government, a major agreement between the CP (Charoen Pokphand) Group and the Anand government for an additional two million telephone lines in Bangkok was signed in mid-1991.

Rising prices, escalating wages, higher interest rates, infrastructural bottlenecks, labor shortages and a widening current account deficit suggest that the peak of the present growth cycle of the Thai economy has been passed and that the early 1990s will see a certain degree of consolidation, possibly followed by a modest slowdown. The thrust of economic growth, however, is still strong, in spite of the increasing problems. The defensive robustness, resilience and stability of the Thai economy should certainly save the country from any slump across the board—including the brief destabilization of May, 1992.

The best prognosis must be that the expected adjustment in the early 1990s will, with proper economic management, be moderate and controlled. Thailand will then be ready for another sustained burst of economic growth in the late 1990s and early 2000s that will carry it to new levels of development.

8

The Price of Economic Success: Inequality, Pollution and AIDS

The fastest growth in the world brings to Thailand concomitant problems of success. The natural and human resource base is under more strain than it has ever experienced. Environmentalists and egalitarians have never been more critical of their government's policies.

The obvious case is the progressive destruction of the natural environment that vitally affects the country's resources, production, climate and public health. Bangkok was an idyllic "village of wild olive groves" when the Chakri kings founded their capital there 200 years ago. There were only 12,750 registered motor vehicles in the city when King Bhumiphol was born. Today there are 1.75 million, belching into the air more than a metric ton of lead, not to mention quantities of other toxic matter, every day. "Everyone is dying slowly in Bangkok," says Bhichai Rattakul, a former deputy premier, ". . . because of the gas and smoke that they breathe in."

Three quarters of the nation's factories are in the Bangkok area, where lead has been found in umbilical cords of newborn babies. Levels of carbon monoxide, sulphur dioxide and nitrogen monoxide are dangerous. Taxi drivers, street vendors and policemen are at high risk from the dust and toxic gases that periodically droop in thick white clouds over central Bangkok.

The rivers are in a disastrous state. At the mouth of Bangkok's Chao Phraya River the mercury contamination in the sea water is between 7 and 40 times the accepted level, and accumulated heavy metal in fish and shellfish is 10 to 20 times above safety standards. The Thailand Development Research Institute calculates that by the end of the 1990s there will be no oxygen at all left in the Chao Phraya River, and aquatic life will cease. The river will die, and it will cost $1.75 billion to bring it back to life.[1]

Things are no better in the countryside, where farmers have for decades been applying too much chemical fertilizer and insecticide. Their malignant residue remains in canals, rivers and reservoirs, in fish and in the soil. Thailand's rich wildlife is now at risk from the march of commerce and industry.

Worst of all, the forests, of which Thailand used to be so proud, are falling to the axe, with their acreage diminishing by about 1.5 percent a year. For decades logging was uncontrolled. This led directly to the exceptional floods of 1988 washing whole villages away in the south, or burying them and their inhabitants in mudslides. After one such landslide caused by heavy rain on denuded hill slopes, the government belatedly braved the vested commercial interests and banned logging. Outstanding timber concessions were revoked. But wood was still wanted for construction and manufacturing, so many logging companies, including some army enterprises, negotiated alternative contracts across the border in Burmese or Cambodian forests. The Thais have begun to export their environmental problems.[2]

Other local lobbies succeeded in protecting their environment against development damage. Popular opinion buried the important Nam Choan dam scheme in 1988 despite determined efforts of successive governments to launch it. Most dramatic of all, the $44 million tantalum plant at Phuket, constructed against intense local opposition that believed its pollution would scare tourists away, was actually burned to the ground in 1985 after 50,000 people had demonstrated outside it.[3]

The climate of opinion is thus moving in favor of environmentalism. Influential opinion leaders are not just talking, they are taking action. Chin Sophonpanich's energetic Australian-trained daughter Chodchoy, for example, is president of the Thai Environmental and Community Development Association, which launched a program to clean up Bangkok's river and *klongs* (canals).

The underlying problem remains the incapacity of governments to act forcefully against the short-term financial interests of their own members and their business friends and patrons. That will take years to remedy. There is one small piece of comfort. "They raped the country," a foreign resident says of the Thai leadership. "There was no conservation, but it made them learn the hard way, from their own mistakes, not those of others." When the tide does turn, hopefully during the 1990s, it will be a decisive turn made from firsthand exposure to life's realities with no one else to blame. That is the advantage of having hung on to national independence.

The second malady which could, if unchecked, spoil Thailand's economic chances, is the polarization of incomes. "We are going to have a revolution by the people," Bangkok's ex-Governor Chamlong warns, "if the widening gap between rich and poor is not closed." In the countryside the bottom 10 percent of farmers enjoy only 1 percent of the cultivated land, whereas the top 10 percent control one-third of the land.

There are 15 million poor, dispossessed peasants, unskilled urban workers and slum dwellers—almost a quarter of the total population—whom Thai officials are surprised to discover have not substantially shared in the general economic boom of the 1980s. They fall below the poverty line as defined by the World Bank. [4]

A recent study by Suganya Hutaserani published by the Thailand Development Research Institute shows that if you divide the population into five bands each containing 20 percent of the total, the share of the total income gained by the top band is 55 percent, whereas that of the lowest band is only 5 percent. And the trend is for polarization to get worse. Over the thirteen years 1976-89, the top band gained 6 percent, and the other four bands lost 1 percent or 2 percent each.

That is not an earthshaking deterioration. Yet the figures are much quoted in angry newspaper columns by excited academics. "If the Thai economy has been growing impressively, and there is expectation that Thailand will become an industrialised country in the near future," writes Dr. Likhit Dhiravegin of Thammasat University in *Thailand Business,* "how would one justify the state of imbalance in income distribution?" General Chaovalit made much reference to these figures in the late 1980s. [5]

The top band in Thailand does get on average eleven times the income of the bottom band. But many of those at the bottom are farmers whose subsistence foodstuffs and some other purchases are cheaper than in the cities. They are partially outside the market economy, and their relative poverty is not quite as bad as it appears. Disparities exist in all countries, and the Thai figures are not disgracefully worse than those of the Asian NIEs.

The Thai Development Research Institute study concedes that "in contrast to the trend of income inequality, which has worsened over time . . . the poverty trend is decreasing." In the 1970s some 30 percent of Thais were "poor." Now the proportion has dropped to a quarter. Perhaps Thai intellectuals should worry less about figures, and recognize that in this kind of economic revolution some groups will be more ready to take advantage than others. It would be more constructive to worry about specific remedial measures for those "dropping out." A draft social security bill was, for example, passed through the legislature only in 1991, after a wait of 35 years.

Others argue that with 97 percent literacy, and widespread rural health centers and electricity diffusion, the next rural priority must be education. Two children in three are not attending secondary school, a much worse performance than the NIEs or Malaysia.

The most appealing initiative to beat inequality is the recent scheme for "social capitalism," where big companies "adopt" a village—not just out of charity but to hand on their basic financing, marketing and management expertise to enable villagers to earn more from their farming. The organizers hope villagers can be shown how to avoid the punitive rates of interest required by rural moneylenders. Meanwhile the companies can take advantage of cheap rural labor on the spot, without the social disruption of moving people into the cities.

In the ideal case a company might draft a market plan, bring a bank in, send the middlemen packing, improve the quality of the seed and fertilizer the village buys and find ways to reduce the prices paid for equipment and supplies. Villagers would hold a small equity in the "joint venture" and would not therefore feel exploited.

Bata, for example, is already interested in having its leather uppers sewn in villages under this scheme. Bangkok Glass adopted Baan Na village in Prachin Buri province, where villagers are now making labor-intensive, high-value-added colored glass and Tiffany-style lamps with design and marketing help from the Bangkok company. Volvo has taken up three villages.

There are good practical ideas to beat inequality in the cities, too. In the 1960s devastating fires largely destroyed the slum area in Bangkok called Rama IV. Although they were squatting illegally on private land, Rama IV's 1,200 families had set up their own markets, schools, banks and cinemas. Now all that was gutted, and the developers waited to move in. But an angry young pediatrician practicing nearby, Dr. Somporn Surarith, took up the slum-dwellers' cause. She interested the media and the local university in the case. Passions ran high. For a time Dr. Somporn hired a bodyguard, and on one occasion she even felt obliged to leave the country until things cooled down. Eventually someone suggested land-sharing and a deal was struck: the residents "gave up" 78 percent of the land to the developers, in return for getting multistory apartment buildings to live in on the rest.

One of the standard jokes in the capital is that Bangkok (whose population is bigger than either Singapore's or Hong Kong's) could become a NIE on its own, leaving the rest of the country to its agricultural status. Bangkok is embarrassingly richer than the rest of the country. It has only 3 percent of the nation's poor, whereas the Northeast has 37 percent. Bangkok's production per head is valued at ten times that of the Northeast, and its medical facilities are also about ten times better.

In other countries, provincial cities develop apart from the capital, but in Thailand, Bangkok monopolizes everything. The "power" factor attracts everyone to Bangkok regardless of convenience. The Bangkok Metropolitan Association has asked for a small new national capital elsewhere but nobody pays much attention. This accentuates the urban-rural polarity.

There has, however, been a successful establishment of a new industrial center on the Eastern Seaboard, and the technocrats plan to follow that with a similar Southern Seaboard project.[6] These should eventually take some of the strain off Bangkok and encourage a more widespread urbanization. In the end Bangkok might even solve the problems by itself sinking below the water. An Asian Institute of Technology expert predicted twenty years ago that this would happen by 1991. Built in a riverine delta with what used to be a Venetian-style network of *klongs* or canals (now mostly built over), Bangkok is descending at the rate of an inch or so a year—more in some districts.

The speculation is getting wild. Will Bangkok become a pond? A metropolitan hydrographic department official seriously suggested that the whole city might "just collapse under its own weight" one day. Or the city might, others joked, become the world's first submarine capital. Like a lazy animal, another commentator wrote, "when the water rises, it will have to get up off its belly and seek the higher ground."

Nart Tuntawiroon, advisor to the premier on environmental matters, said, "leave Bangkok alone and let it decay."[7] It would be too expensive to salvage, and the money would be better spent in the provinces. Meanwhile calm fatalism reigns even in the season of floods.

Polarity of incomes is prevalent in all societies undergoing rapid modernization. Millions of Chinese and Bangladeshis would dearly love to live on Thailand's poverty line. If the present distribution of the national income were perpetuated, that might indeed spark a revolution in the end. But the polarity, having reached its extreme, is likely then to contract.

Discounting the temporary and localized effect of particular natural disasters, almost all Thais are living a little better each year, and that fact is not altered by the success of some rich Thais in living very much better each year. Capitalism creates opportunities. It does not simultaneously enlarge everybody's innate capacity to exploit those opportunities—that comes more slowly. What is the alternative? The god of communism has failed, and Buddha was not interested in wealth creation.

Health questions are also central to the future of the Thai people. There was one basic but sensitive issue central to economic planning on which the Thai government was a late starter. For years it stubbornly refused to endorse any kind of family planning or population control, even though the Thais were reproducing so fast that they were set to double their numbers over twenty years—and stay poor. Prime Minister Phibul in the 1940s even imposed a punitive tax on bachelors, to keep the national numbers up. "Thailand," the government insisted as late as 1966, "is still a wide country, and the population is not yet sufficient."[8] The then prime minister, Field Marshal Thanom Kittikachorn, spelled it out that birth control would not be needed until the population hit 50 million (which it did in 1983).

But Thanom revealed a racial motive when he remarked: "If we cut down Thai births, and the aliens keep on producing babies, we will one day become a minority race."[9] The government's leading technocrat, Dr. Puey Ungpakorn, stood up for the silent Chinese by commenting that they would limit their families, too, if everyone else did. But the general dislike of the whole idea was conveyed in a newspaper cartoon of Dr. Puey prowling about in the night, lifting up the mosquito nets to stop couples from making love.

Yet the ordinary women of Thailand voted with their feet by flocking to the first family planning clinic started at Chulalongkorn University in 1965. Buses were chartered from the provinces to visit this clinic. Its customers soon proved that the pill and the loop could be accepted rapidly and fearlessly, in disregard of rural superstitions and without even the stimulus of nationwide publicity. Marlon Brando breezed through Bangkok in 1967 in the course of making the movie *The Ugly American*. Why not sell birth control, he kept telling everyone, like hair oil?[10]

One man heard him. Mechai Viravaidya had just returned from Australia with an economics degree. His Thai father and Scottish mother were both doctors. Tall, outspoken, mischievous, flamboyant and workaholic, Mechai became the Mr. Family Planning of Thailand. He founded Community-Based Family Planning Services in 1974 and used it to train 12,000 village volunteers. The population growth rate was halved to only 1.5 percent a year in the two decades of the 1970s and 1980s, and Mechai claimed that his little organization—later renamed Population and Community Development Association—had enabled ten million births to be prevented.

"I'm trying," Mechai explains, "to break down inhibitions about sex and contraception. Once people accept the idea that contraceptives are just one more item you can buy at the market, like soap or toothpaste or dried fish, they'll be more likely to use them. If I can accomplish that by blowing up condoms or filling them with water, then fine, I'll do it." He disarmed religious objections by discovering a Buddhist scripture which read, "many births make you poor," and recalled that Buddha himself had only one child. His reward is to have monks willingly bless condoms, individually or by the packet, and even sprinkle them, on request, with holy water.[11]

Mechai's salesmanship was inspired. He opened family planning supermarkets at bus terminals and persuaded traffic police to distribute condoms to motorists caught in jams. He used the resulting game of "Cops and Rubbers" to gain the interest of schoolchildren. When consignments of free American condoms arrived, there were complaints about their being too big. So Mechai enrolled five intelligent massage-parlor girls as temporary research assistants. "They measured more than five hundred of their customers," he explains, "so that we could come up with a Thai national size. You can't be shy about these things if you are going to succeed."

He has a record of achievement in the number of vasectomies performed, despite coyly refusing to say whether or not he himself has had one. He opened a restaurant called Cabbages and Condoms—"the only place where you can have a vasectomy between courses." He organized condom-inflating competitions, with a national championship cup, and his T-shirts made Thai sartorial history. One showed Winston Churchill giving his V-for-victory sign, with the legend, "Stop at Two." Another reads: "My Pigeon Flies High—It's Vasectomized". Mechai's name card is a brightly colored condom stapled to an order form. His own daughter used to take condoms to her kindergarten to give to her friends and teachers.

Mechai made the condom mentionable, popularized its use, and brought the population growth rate down. He went on to run the Asian Center for Population and Community Development, where people from 40 countries trained in his methods. In the later 1980s he became deputy minister for industry, senator and government spokesman under Premier Prem and was again a minister under Premier Anand in 1991. He has also expanded his organizations to cover reforestation, village development and rural education as well as family planning. He could easily be, as some admirers say, a future prime minister.

Tragically, having so unexpectedly defeated the specter of overpopulation, Thailand now faces a grim prospect of decimation through AIDS. Thai officials once feared that AIDS was being brought in by foreign tourists, but today they are alarmed to find it so extensive within Thailand itself that foreign tourists may stop coming. "The Thai male propensity to consume sex is immense," says Mechai Viravaidhya, the first to sound the alarm about the disaster.

An eminent doctor, Prawase Wasi, described AIDS as "worse than any war. It will destroy every fibre of our social and economic life. We need a movement so intense that it can uproot men's sexual habits. . . ." The minister of health and Princess Chulabhorn added their weight to the warnings, yet complacency persists. At the beginning of 1991 some 24,000 Thais had been tested HIV positive. The official estimate of the number of carriers was 75,000 but Mechai believes it is actually more than double that. He gloomily forecasts that by the end of the 1990s there could be up to 20 million Thais with the HIV virus and 2 million with full AIDS.[12]

Mechai's persuading the army not to dismiss soldiers with the HIV virus was a turning point. He led the AIDS prevention movement from 1987 almost single-handedly, using time on the army TV and radio stations, and allowing nightclubs, bars and gay rights groups an active role in distributing information about the problem. The virus has become so widespread within Thai society that only extraordinary measures will offer any hope of containing it. Students are becoming sexually active at a younger age than before, and the university custom of seniors taking freshmen to brothels for their "first sex" (*khuen kroo*) still continues.

Trying to shock his compatriots into action, Mechai described AIDS as "ceaselessly advancing without barriers among labourers, prostitutes, farmers, civil servants, students, entertainers, housewives and respectable professions." One third of those infected are of working age. To highlight the impact on the economy, he estimated that the lost earnings of AIDS victims who die before end-1999 could be $5 billion. Mechai has campaigned for a temporary closure of brothels and massage parlors, to be reopened with tighter medical control after a cleanup.

When substantial numbers of deaths begin to occur, Thailand will have to adjust its permissive attitude toward sex. By then the economic bubble may have been pricked by the collapse of tourist revenue and by the impact of the disease on employment and health care expenditure. Already the prospect of employers paying for the AIDS-related medical expense of employees is being talked of. The impact of all that on politics is likely to be damaging to dithering democracy, and tempting to military authoritarianism.

These three problems—environmental pollution, polarity of incomes and AIDS—are the major socioeconomic issues capable of forcing Thailand to postpone its legitimate ambitions for economic development. None of them are peculiar to Thailand, but the permissiveness that allowed free enterprise to flower so brilliantly has also failed to stem the rape of the natural environment, the widening of extremes of income and the alarming advance of AIDS. With population growth, on the other hand, a combination of leadership, education and monetary incentive allowed Thailand to overcome in about two decades a danger which many other developing countries have found intractable. That suggests a potential for tackling the other problems, if only at the last minute. AIDS is perhaps in a different category, with inexorable permanent damage going on beneath the surface and not yet accepted by political or public opinion as the emergency which it really is. All of these problems are the somber underside of Thailand's undoubted economic success: problems which must be addressed if that success is to be sustained.

9

Farm and Factory:
A Giant in the Making

The real heroes of rapid Thai economic growth are the producers—the farmers and industrialists and their 30 million workers throughout the kingdom. They took advantage of government policies and good preconditions to bring Thailand into the international club of important agricultural and industrial nations.

There is a new breed of Thai farmer typified by Farmer Prasit, now waiting for his son to return with his degree from the Agricultural University before building a new pigpen. Farmer Prasit is a tiny, imperturbable man with an intelligent face and an air of amused serenity about his situation. He is privileged, as one of the 50 shareholding farmers in the Nong Wah Agricultural Village in Chachoengsao province, backed originally by the local government, the Bangkok Bank and the Charoen Pokphand (CP) Group.

Having paid off his bank loan, Prasit now owns ten acres of land, his custom-built two-bedroom house, the pigpens and all their tools and equipment. He earns a minimum of $160 a month, which, with relatively few outgoings, is a very desirable income in the Thai countryside. His son will have innumerable ideas for scientifically rationalizing the pig farm. Two of the neighbors' children have already gone through university. One is helping on his parent's farm, the other has bought a unit of her own in the village project.

The women respond well to these new opportunities. Fifteen years ago Tawin Chuchit of Nuensaensut village found the returns from his tapioca on difficult dry soil disappointing. He was one of the first to sign a contract with the local feedmill to raise broiler chickens. He did well, and today his two daughters are carrying on the business. They raise 200,000 broilers a year and earn $20,000 a year, an unheard-of income for Thai farmers a few years ago. What do they do with it? "Eventually," says one of them, "I would like to save up enough money to travel to Europe!" The most successful farmers now boast pickup trucks, TV sets, refrigerators and other consumer electrical appliances.

Rearing livestock under cover is the lighter end of farm work. Most of Thailand's farmers have to labor by hand, or, if they are lucky, with a buffalo, out in the paddyfields or tapioca plantations under the burning sun and driving rain. It is a common experience to have too little rain or else too much, and big irrigation and water control works do not cover the whole ground. In an unusually severe drought a few years ago, one farmer dug 60 feet down to get water!

Most farmers do at least own their own land—90 percent is the usual proportion cited, though millions of rural Thais live illegally on forest or other public land and cannot claim the right of ownership. There is much tenancy farming, even in the rich Central Plains. But the majority of farmers are owner-farmers, and that gives Thailand more social and economic stability than her neighbors. Yet agricultural prices are often depressed and Thai farmers are worse off financially than urban workers.

The land in the Central Plain is fertile, and monsoon rains are normally ideal for agriculture. In the 1960s and 1970s farmers grew more for the expanding market by opening up new fields to cultivation. By the 1980s there was little suitable land left, and harvest increases had to be induced mainly by the use of chemical fertilizers on existing fields. The miracle rice IR-8, which did wonders in other Asian countries, was not so effective in Thailand, whose farmers found it too short, easily flooded and less immune to disease. A more suitable high-yielding hybrid rice, Suphan-60, was introduced in the 1980s, but proved disastrously vulnerable to the brown plant hopper, which devoured $100 million worth of it in the fields in its first year. The creatures which would normally prey on the hoppers had been felled by chemical pesticides![1]

One man who says "I told you so" is Wibul Khemchalerm, who farms four acres in Chachoengsao province, growing 400 types of fruit, vegetable and trees. He rebelled against modern techniques, and uses no chemical fertilizer, pesticide or insecticide. Instead he uses natural fertilizers, and deters (not kills) pests with herbal sprays, following the example of the proselytizing Japanese farmer Fukuoka Masanobu, who has been doing this for 50 years. After a few years of this regime, the natural balance of the soil was restored. The birds flocked back to prey on the insects. Dr. Prawase Wasi, a crusader against pollution, calls it "Buddhist farming" because Wibul is harmonizing with his environment and controlling rather than multiplying his needs and desires. "I grow things for myself now," Wibul says, "not for the marketplace."[2]

Modern farming does not come painlessly to tenant farmers traditionally at the mercy of their landlords and moneylenders. "In my grandfather's days," says Tawee Kanthong, a farmer in his early forties in the Central Plain of Thailand, "natural food was still abundant. Land was ample. To pay debts we could always sell land and clear the forest further. Labor was also free under the traditional . . . system by which farmers took turns to help one another. Now, the forests are no more. Food is scarce. Ploughing machines have replaced buffaloes. There is no free labor. Everything is money. And interest is counted by the day. For tenant farmers it is a life of slavery. There is no chance to be free."

The new machine ploughs need to be repaired, and they consume oil. These farmers miss the days of the buffaloes. "At least we are still using indigenous rice," says Tawee. "If we use high-yield rice as in other areas, we will have to invest so much more in chemical fertilizer and pesticides." For tenant farmers like this, the "Green Revolution" can bring as many problems as benefits—and there is no reserve to cope with them.

The Thai farmer is burdened by the growing competition around the world in agricultural products, the declining supply and productivity of agricultural resources in Thailand, especially land and forests, the generally low level of education and the consequent lack of bargaining power, which make it hard to sell his products and get credit at affordable interest rates when he needs it.

The new trend on Thai farms is for rice to be abandoned in favor of products which earn more on the market—fruit, vegetables and livestock. Farm laborers are increasingly attracted to construction and other urban work. From about 65 percent of the national total today, the rural work force is expected to fall to only 40 percent by the next century.

An American anthropologist, Dr. Michael Moerman of the University of California at Los Angeles, has been visiting a northern Thailand village, Ban Ping, for more than 30 years. His picture of the changes over that period is revealing. In 1959 it took him several days to reach the village, but now the drive is a matter of minutes from the town. The natural landscapes of grassland and forest are replaced by rice fields and corn. Where there were traditional primitive longhouses, there are now modern homes covered with metal or tiles with cement houseposts. The households are much smaller. The ownership of the farmland is less equitable. Everybody used to own something, but now half the people of the village have nothing. In 1959 there was only one laborer, now there are twenty. And now only one household in three actually farms, and three-quarters of those get important income from remittances of city workers and other nonfarming specialist work.

Thirty years ago these villagers grew 30 varieties of local rice, but now they use only the 2 or 3 government-issued varieties. "The rich genetic bank has been impoverished," Moerman observes. "Rice farming now stands on a narrow and more fragile ecological base, one more susceptible to disease, pests, drought and flooding." The new rices need chemical fertilizer that kill crabs and fish, and to get it you need to know something about bureaucracy and officials—so you need the new organizations, such as the farmers' associations. On the other hand the villagers have modern district hospital services. They know they can do something about illness. Knowledge of public health is widespread, and family planning has been adopted. Officials used to be regarded as a threat, but are now seen as a source of help. But there has been a loss of traditional culture.

The question of the price of rice is politically charged. It perplexed that sage monarch King Mongkut, toppled Field Marshal Thanom from his comfortable dictatorship, and dashed Premier Kukrit Pramoj's hopes of establishing a popular welfare state. Kukrit guaranteed higher prices for the farmers and seemed to be preparing the ground for a nationalization of the rice trade. He talked of rural communes, common ownership of farmland and nationalization of the paddyfields in exchange for government bonds. His experiments were cut short, perhaps luckily for the nation, in view of the fate of such policies elsewhere.[3]

But the issue was not buried there. In 1980 Thai rice exports, the biggest Thai export commodity, usually meeting 30 percent or 40 percent of the world market, collapsed. A new rice subsidy was introduced. The move was widely criticized, particularly since Thailand had joined other regional food-producing countries in protesting against European and American farm protectionism.[4]

Ammar Siamwalla, a leading agricultural economist, believes that a degree of farm support, of the kind which Japanese, Korean and Western farmers enjoy, will be needed if rice is to survive as a crop. The alternative would be to import inexpensive rice and other foodstuffs, to give Thai city dwellers cheaper food—as a result of which they could keep their industrial wages down and retain their international competitiveness. Thai agriculture, Ammar argues, is one of the least supported in the world, an argument which is usually a prelude to protectionism, which would rally rural support for the government at the expense of urban consumers.

Thais easily overenthuse about their farm sales overseas. With rice exports still hitting $2 billion a year, and rubber, maize, tapioca, prawns and sugar adding another $3 billion or more to account for one-fifth of the kingdom's total exports, Thais may be excused a certain self-satisfaction. "One day, we will feed a quarter of the world," boasted Paul Sithi-Amnuai, a London School of Economics graduate and rising star of the Thai business world, in 1988.[5] General Chaovalit used to express the same idea in barrack-room terms when he talked of Thailand's becoming an "agricultural super-power." But Sithi-Amnuai's financial empire collapsed, and the general has lowered his sights.

The kingdom has become the world's largest exporter in some new lines, notably canned pineapple (one in every two cans opened in America is Thai) but also canned tuna. Export prospects for poultry and several other farm products are also excellent. But rice has a cloudy future. Many of the Asian countries which used to buy Thai rice now grow enough themselves, thanks to the "Green Revolution." At the lower-quality end of the world rice market, Vietnam has begun to challenge with sharply lower costs. Only China and Hong Kong are steady customers for the dearer and more nutritious rice which Thai farmers excel in growing.

The former Soviet Union still buys Thai rice, but for how long will the Russians be able to afford that? India now grows more rice than it wants and may not need to buy from Thailand again. It may even compete with Thailand in other markets. All farm exports are vulnerable to protectionism. During the 1980s the European Community made Thailand cut its tapioca exports, though at least it funded a switch to alternative crops—mung beans, for instance, and rubber—to soften the blow for the Thai farmer.[6]

It is the reared or captured creature—chickens, pigs, prawns and tuna—that may now save the day for Thai farmers as their crops lose their appeal. The story of Thawin and his two daughters demonstrates the attraction of broiler rearing. Another successful chicken contract-farming project is at Sriracha, where farmers found cassava crops were losing yield and leaving the soil infertile. A nearby feedmill in an agribusiness chain organized a broiler project in 1976. A bank lent the money for poultry houses and an operating fund, while the feedmill guaranteed the loans and showed the farmers how to produce and market the chickens.

There are now 145 families in the project, each earning about $350 a month after having paid off the bank loan to become owners of the broiler houses and equipment. Legally they may sell their chickens to anyone, but "most of them stay with us," the feedmill representative explains. The work is demanding and constant attention is needed. Rats and mongeese may break in for a midnight feast. But insurance and modern technical aids take the edge off the worry and the work, and at any one time there are usually 1.5 million chickens in this project, all destined for the same commercial slaughterhouse. One of the participants in this project, gap-toothed farmer Jaran, has seen his own land appreciate in value a hundredfold in the last decade.

Tuna fishing is another food industry which has begun to flourish recently on modern mass-production lines. Unicord has become Asia's biggest exporter of tuna, commanding one-fifth of the world market, after buying the third-largest U.S. tuna canner, Bumble Bee Seafoods. Its "total fish" approach allocates the white meat to Western consumers, the red meat for pet food, part of the head for medicine, the skin for fishmeal—and waste water from the cleaning goes into soap manufacture. Under the Bumble Bee deal Unicord will ship frozen tuna to the United States to be canned there and retail more cheaply than imported cans from Thailand (because U.S. import duties are higher on cans). Unicord's President Dumri Konuntakiet has also negotiated a joint venture with an East German state herring canning enterprise, as a beachhead in Europe.

The victim of Thai agricultural success is forestry. Thirty years ago two-thirds of the kingdom was covered with rich natural forest, but now, to serve the needs of a population that has just about doubled in only one generation, the forests have been halved. In some areas the practice of "slash-and-burn" agriculture progressively destroys the forests to provide firewood and crop soil, while in other areas commercial logging to meet the timber market has felled trees by the thousand.

The slash-and-burn phenomenon can be tackled at source. In 1980 the Royal Forestry Department launched a project, with United Nations help, to restore the forest near Nakhon Ratchasima on the Khorat Plateau. Here a community of 8,000 families had slashed and burned through successive stands of trees without knowing any other way of life. Most of them wanted to stay and farm, and just over half of the land area was suitable for agriculture. So the government reforested the remaining areas to prevent erosion and watershed damage and gave the farmers certificates of usufruct, guaranteeing the right to use and inherit the land but not to sell it—because it was national forest land. Cotton, soybeans, peanuts and other new crops were introduced, along with beekeeping, fruit trees and cottage industry. Miles of road and nineteen small dams were built, so there is not only water in the dry season but fishing all the year round.

Meanwhile the royal foresters planted pines, acacias and paper mulberry trees on the steep slopes and fast-growing eucalyptus around the villages.

(Recently eucalyptus has fallen out of favor because it takes up too much water and nutrient from the soil, starving nearby crops and ruling out intercropping between the trees: angry Khorat villagers have uprooted eucalyptus saplings by the thousand.) To see Saen Kampolkrang, one of the reformed "slash-and-burn" farmers, surrounded by baskets of mango, jackfruit, tamarind, cotton and corn produced from his land, delight oozing out of every wrinkle on his face, is to understand the possible good future for the forests.[7]

Government officials used to try to guard the forests as national property, but they never had a chance of policing such a huge area effectively and lacked the manpower even to replant the lost areas. What took them 30 years to plant is now lost in only 1 year. The Nakhon Ratchasima "forestry village" represents a new and more realistic policy of encouraging citizens to use the forests constructively without unnecessary damage. Foresters and farmers used to argue bitterly; now the attempt is being made to reconcile them and get them to work together. They call it "social forestry." The goal is to recapture hundreds of thousands of square miles to make the forests cover 40 percent of the total land area instead of only 28 percent as at present. That could happen if the example of Nakhon Ratchasima spreads quickly and widely enough across the kingdom, and if the government puts its full weight behind these policies.

While such scenes of improvement unfold in the farms and forests of the countryside, seven business-suited men assemble in the thirtieth-story penthouse of Bangkok's tallest building on Silom Road. Here the decor is discreet 1930s pastel. The Chinese food served at the lunch table comes in modest helpings but is mouth-watering. It is chosen by an epicure. Across the table a shy-seeming, twinkling-eyed man looks to see if you enjoy the dishes and half raises his glass of mineral water to encourage you (he is a teetotaler and does not smoke, so a little gourmandizing is to be condoned). This is Dhanin Chearavanont, the dapper Thai Chinese who chairs the agribusiness Charoen Pokphand group, currently turning over $2.5 billion a year and poised to become the nation's biggest enterprise in a few years' time. "There won't be a supermarket anywhere," Dhanin declares, "without a CP product on its shelf or in its freezer." Shyness does not extend to being modest about corporate goals.[8]

His story begins in the South Chinese port of Shantou, which used to be known as Swatow. In the 1910s the Chia family, fallen on hard times, won a living by growing seeds and selling them in a Shantou shop. The teenager Chia Ek Chaw unexpectedly became head of the family farm and shop at a time when new customers were badly needed. Why not, he thought, sell to the overseas Chinese kinsmen in Southeast Asia? So in 1921 he and his bother Seow Whooy sailed to Thailand, which they believed would be their best foreign outlet because it was not ruled by Western colonialists. The Chia Tai Seed and Agricultural Company duly opened a shop in Bangkok's Chinatown, and when Mao Zedong's Red Army marched into Shantou in 1949 the two brothers made Bangkok their new headquarters.

Chia Ek Chaw fathered seven sons, who diversified and developed the company's business, taking the Thai family name of Chearavanont. Jaran, the eldest, gave up his chance of a good education in order to work in the company and allow the other boys to go through school. Montri and Sumet, the next two, both served the company diligently. But it was the fourth boy, Dhanin, today in his early fifties, who was the man of ideas and who propelled the little seed business to heights its founders never dreamed of.

Dhanin was born in Thailand in 1939. His father sent him to the family's ancestral village and to school in China. He began a university course in Hong Kong but did not complete it because the family firm needed him. In 1958, not yet twenty, Dhanin returned to Bangkok to work in the seed shop. Difficult decisions were being mulled over by the family. Charoen Pokphand (the name means "commodity development") had already been registered as a company. Jaran, the eldest brother, had started an experimental feedmill which rapidly outgrew the local demand. Where should the family go next? Dhanin had the answer. They must raise the level of Thai chicken-rearing from the cottage to the industrial scale, and thus enlarge the demand for feed.

Dhanin crossed the Pacific in 1970 to negotiate a 50-50 joint venture with Arbor Acres of the United States, and introduced in Thailand its integrated farm-to-market system for broilers. In Bangkok CP launched the Bangkok Livestock Processing Company to replicate the American system, and eventually Dhanin came to preside over a regional network of profitable chicken-breeding, feedmill, hogmill and ancillary businesses not only in Thailand but also in Taiwan, China, Indonesia, Singapore and Malaysia and even Portugal and Turkey. CP is now the fifth-largest feedmiller in the world, and the world's largest prawn-feed producer. "Seed-feed-breed-food," the blue-suited yuppies seem to chant as they scan their pay envelopes and dividend notices on the various floors of the $40 million CP Tower on Silom Road.

At this point Dhanin's judgment failed him. Carried away by the need to get all those extra chickens eaten, he opened a franchised fast-food chicken chain. The public was not quite ready for it, and it folded. Today, fifteen years on, Bangkokians cannot get enough fast food, and CP is involved with some of the foreign household names in chicken outlets. Dhanin learned the lesson of keeping the wish sequestered from the market study. His latest prediction, that prosperity and changing taste will swing Asian consumers away from dark meat to white meat, as has already happened in the West and Japan, is well based. His future plans therefore emphasize fish and marine shrimp processing.

Having made contract farming succeed for chicken and pigs, CP now advocates a controversial program of massive contract farming for about one sixth of the kingdom's paddyfields. Thailand, it argues, is ripe for commercial farming. It has got by for all these years with mostly small farms averaging ten acres, from which farmers would reckon merely to meet their own family needs for food. But the optimum size for a farm producing commercial crops, able to use tractors and other machinery, is a thousand times bigger.

CP points out that an American corn farmer gets seven times more from each acre than a Thai farmer because of better seed, fertilizer, water, methods and machines. "There is no need for this discrepancy to continue," Suphat Wibulseth, Agricultural Communications Manager for CP, stoutly insists. Suphat describes the group's strategy as "based on providing an incentive not only for the farmer to cultivate his lands, but for him to be able to educate his children and have them want to stay on the land. By achieving this goal, the company would create a sound modern agricultural base for the country, which would make Thai products competitive on both the domestic and world markets and turn farmers into the kind of consumers that industry needs to grow and prosper."[9]

So the first model is the contract farm system for broiler chickens, later extended to pigs. Farmer Tawin and his daughters at Nuensaensuk, and gap-toothed Farmer Jaran at Sriracha, are examples of that. The second model is the integrated farming settlement for crops and livestock, as launched experimentally in Panomsarakam in eastern Thailand and Kamphaengphet in the north. Farmer Prasit, waiting for his son to graduate, illustrates that prototype. Finally, CP has a third experiment of contract farming for corn and rice, where good farmers contract to train others in modern methods, buying their produce for resale to CP. This gets technology transferred into the field and cuts out the middleman. Dhanin believes this policy would attract poor farmers into the more developed farmlands, which would be preferable to their drifting into the cities.

Not everyone likes contract farming. King Bhumiphol is said to be concerned lest farmers lose their rugged independence and become sheeplike operatives on a big-business assembly line. CP would put it differently, that more interdependence will bring more income and a richer life-style to farmers as well as more profits to agri-businesses like itself. It points out that so far, only one contract farmer in five has opted out of his agreement with CP. New wealth can undermine the incentive to work, but the problems of Farmer Prasit and Farmer Jaran do not seem to center upon loss of independence. The king's romantic image of his loyal yeomen does not square with the city feed salesman's more pragmatic assessment of the farmer as a potential customer and supplier for mutual advantage.

Dhanin does not confine his exceptional energies to Thai agriculture. To the confusion of shareholders and financial editors, he has ventured into industry, property and communications as well. It was understandable, in view of the family origins, that CP would invest in feedmills in China. The wheel that was set rolling when Dhanin's father took a suitcase of seeds on the steamship to Bangkok came full circle 60 years later when a CP feedmill opened in Shenzhen in Guangdong province.

The agricultural know-how that the father conveyed to Thailand has been amply repaid by the sons. CP is now the largest Southeast Asian investor in China. CP furnishes its own experts, like Smutara Mekchaidee, manager of the Bangkok Livestock Processing Company's quality-control department, who in 1991 prepared himself for a four-year assignment in Beijing supervising quality in all the group's north China feedmills.

The big surprise came when Dhanin started assembling motorcycles and automobile parts in Shanghai with technical licensing from Honda. This revealed an unsuspected propensity to be a "Mr. Fix-it," capable of getting enterprises organized which are entirely outside his personal knowledge— and on a tri-national basis. Next came a brewery in China in partnership with Heineken—and this was only the beginning. With Solvay of Belgium, CP will from 1992 start producing vinyl chloride monomer—the raw material for PVC—in a $350 million petrochemical plant. It has VCM and PVC projects under way in Ningbo (in central China) and in Indonesia.

All those pale beside the $6 billion telecommunications contract that CP won, with British Telecom as partner, to add two million lines to the Bangkok system. The contract was renegotiated on a smaller scale after the military coup of 1991, but was still a big one. "We always do big things," was Dhanin's comment. Considering CP's previous lack of expertise in telecommunications, to secure control of such a large project, a major intrusion of the private sector into a state monopoly, and effectively to hold it on the political roller coaster, is a spectacular feather in the cap of the boy who started by selling seeds.

Dhanin Chearavanont's leap into petrochemicals and telecommunications dramatizes the potential of the two newer and more advanced sectors of the Thai economy—services and industry. These now contribute more than 80 percent of the Gross Domestic Product. Taiwan and Korea owed much of their postwar industrial success to the infrastructure built up by Japanese colonial authorities. Hong Kong and Singapore manufacturing industry similarly benefit from their British legacy. Thailand had no such industrial infrastructure bequeathed to it on a plate by colonial masters. That is why its industry was a slow starter and a late developer.

When the Thai leaders decided the time was ripe to push strongly for industrial development, Thailand was lucky enough to be subject to strong American influence, far short of usurping indigenous authority but passionately recommending the capitalist path. This has now resulted in a manufacturing industry supplying 36 percent of Gross Domestic Product and a string of service industries accounting for 47 percent of GDP.

Industry is able to count on a continuing surplus of labor, which gives it a cost advantage over the NIEs. It is a relatively new phenomenon. Apart from the king's very successful—though at that time monopolistic—cement plant, Thailand's industry before the war was modest. After 1945, like the other Southeast Asian economies, the kingdom started with a policy of import substitution. It tried to create industries which would remove the need to spend scarce foreign exchange on buying consumer goods from abroad. It was, as a later finance minister said, an "overnationalistic and protective" policy. Meanwhile the recommendations of the World Bank for the country's economic development were broadly followed. The Friendship Highway built across the nation by the Americans in the 1950s to help it resist armed communism opened up new vistas for better economic communications as well.

In the 1970s Thailand's economic administrators became more self-confident. They saw that Thailand could gain by joining the international system and could sell enough exports to earn the money to buy the necessary imports. Protectionism became discredited. "I would like to announce the arrival of Thailand Inc.," proclaimed Boonchu Rojanasathien, the first finance minister to set the new course. As a long-time Bangkok Bank chief executive, Boonchu knew intimately the virtues of private enterprise.

From then on official policies were geared to promote exports, liberalize foreign investment and encourage the multinational corporations. The big push came with the Fourth Five-Year Plan of 1977. This launched the Eastern Seaboard as the long-term site for large-scale heavy, medium and small industries. The target was to transform Thailand into an export-led manufacturing economy based partly on heavy industry and petrochemicals, especially two soda ash and chemical fertilizer plants on the Eastern Seaboard costing $800 million and using domestic natural gas. Once this new development had got into its stride, the World Bank put it to the Thai government in 1986 that the Sixth Plan could write the guidelines for fast growth on the Korean model with a huge increase in the amount of investment. Since then the dynamism has hardly faltered.

Conditions are not ideal for Thai industry. The infrastructure is not strong. Technology and technical training are another weakness. The modern scientific attitude is not found in the Thai educational tradition. New ideas were never highly valued and were even distrusted in the old days. The main practice in schools is still to master a fixed body of learning and repeat it like a parrot. This has not encouraged Thai science, though some breakthroughs have been made. Dr. Vitoon Osathanonah invented a new method of sterilization called minilaparotomy; Dr. Art-Ong Jumsai invented microwave ferrite isolators called Mikrotek; Thai doctors helped the World Health Organization to control thalassemia and a locally designed microcomputer was built in 1979. Dr. Salyaveth Lekagul has won awards for simplifying instruments and procedures for rural ear operations, and has demonstrated them in India and Kenya. But the total technological achievement remains small for a country of such size and development.[10]

For the same reasons, engineering skills are neglected. Most other Asian countries boast more engineers per head of population than Thailand. Korea and Taiwan have eight times as many. Only 3,000 engineering graduates are available in Thailand, yet the present need is for 10,000 newly qualified engineers *every year*. There will be a very large shortfall into the next century. Thailand is thus dependent on foreign technology, and is intellectually beholden to the West, while Thai PhD students go to the provinces for their research wearing amulets instead of safety belts.[11]

The first of four new engineering universities was to open at Suranari in the northeast in 1992, and Thammasat University plans new engineering and medical faculties. Its president, Dr. Krirkkiat Phipatseritham, is proud of having lured back five Thai lecturers, who were drawing higher salaries in their overseas posts, to teach in them. The success of the Thai economy is tempting many professionals back from positions in America or Europe, like Roy Jutabha, who had been in the United States since the age of four and became a Price Waterhouse accountant, or Chali Sophonpanich of the Bangkok Bank family. Jack Hu was recalled from his own retail business in the United States by his father to help him build up his steel enterprise in

Thailand, and now runs Sahaviriya, a $10 million-a-year office automation distributor. Many similar cases could be cited.[12]

The country did well to resist the initial temptation to construct heavy industry too large for its local market. But once a market appeared, steel and petrochemical industries followed. Thailand was exporting steel pipe to customers in Africa, in a joint venture with Sumitomo, as early as 1966. The discovery of natural gas in the Gulf of Thailand prompted the establishment of a National Petrochemical Corporation, the first stage of which was a plant near Rayong on the Eastern Seaboard to make ethylene and propylene. In the second phase starting in 1992, Thailand will move from basic to more sophisticated petrochemicals.

The Bangkok Bank is contributing one enterprise to this petrochemical development. The CP Group is also in the picture with its joint venture with Solvay of Belgium to make PVC from 1992. The big struggle is between Thai Petrochemical Industry, headed by the Leophairatana brothers, and Siam Cement, the aristocrat of Thai corporations with substantial royal ownership. Thai Petrochemical earlier spearheaded the plastics industry and will lead the second phase of the National Petrochemical Corporation expansion at Mabtaphut with a $95 million polypropylene plant.

Thai Petrochemical Industry has made that vital but often resisted move in Chinese-founded firms of easing off the tight fingers of family control to allow greater delegation to professional managers. Dr. Kosal Sindhavananda, managing director of the Thai Petrochemical Polyethylene Company, recalls that when he first joined the group, "the President had to sign contracts for hiring drivers." Now Thai Petrochemical is going into cement manufacture with German technology and funds, while Siam Cement is conducting the reverse operation, moving from its traditional cement, glass, tires and ceramics into plastics. It has two joint ventures with Dow Chemical for this; Siam Cement impresses potential partners because of its record of investing over $60 million in a Research and Development Center.

Although free enterprise is the slogan, there is much jockeying for position, and inevitably opportunities for corruption and influence peddling, because new entrants to an industry have to secure government permission. The Board of Investment and the appropriate ministries and officials decide which new companies can start, and how much they can produce, using tax holidays and similar incentives to get the results officials and politicians want. Originally Siam Cement had a monopoly in cement, but ultimately had to accept two rivals joining the field, Siam City Cement and Jalaprathan Cement. Siam Cement later sought, with an American partner, to crack the monopoly on the manufacture of sheet glass products, but the industry ministry refused permission on the ground that current production exceeded demand.

No-one failed to notice that the existing glass manufacturers were important financial supporters of Premier Chatichai's Chart Thai party, the leading party in the government coalition, and the party supplying the then minister of industry. Siam Cement had done well under the Prem administration in the 1980s, and did not expect such big favors under his successor. Such are the political perspectives of industry. This is not yet free enterprise, but the regulation is not destructive.

Thailand now claims to have a car industry, though it would be more accurately described as an assembly industry dominated by Mitsubishi Motors. Some of the Dodge Colt cars from the Thai plant have been exported to Canada, and these were followed in 1987 by Nissans to Brunei. Motorcycles and three-wheelers have been exported to the United States, Bangladesh, Sri Lanka and Nigeria. Local content of the automobiles is put at 58 percent. Eventually this will lead to automobile manufacturing, but that may take some time still. Again, Thailand did not take the risk of going all out for full-scale manufacturing before acquiring the assembling skills.[13]

Electronics is another burgeoning industry. Rice cookers and fans have been exported to the Middle East, America and Japan for several years, and some of the manufacturers are doing very well. GSS Electronics, now six years old, has acquired a Singapore company to gain customers and marketing expertise. GSS was started by an American, Gary Stickles, in partnership with Thai engineers, and now employs 2,000 people working around the clock. They make printed circuit board assemblies and magnetic disc-drive heads, and export to the United States, Japan and the European Community.[14] Another big name is Thaksin Shinawatra, unusual in hailing from the north of Thailand, who began by distributing IBM computers and now presides over a growing electronics empire with a work force that has grown tenfold over two years.[15] The multinationals, especially Japanese, are also on the scene: Fujitsu has invested $600 million to create its first integrated computer manufacturing system outside Japan. Thailand welcomes such investment from Japan while ensuring that its industry does not become dominated by it.

Many branches of the electronics industry require more state help if they are going to survive, and many companies depend on technology imports from abroad. They also face the threat of increasing restriction in overseas markets, especially the EC. British TV manufacturers were complaining as early as 1980 about the import of small black-and-white television sets from Thailand. There is an unmistakable vigor in this industry reminiscent of Hong Kong and Taiwan twenty years ago.

Hong Kong and Taiwan companies now have many manufacturing subsidiaries in Thailand—and it also happens the other way round. Stelux, the Hong Kong watchmaker, is controlled by the Wong Chiming family, whose head is the Thai Mongkul Kanjanapas. Mongkul started as a stallholder in Bangkok's Chinatown and was so successful at selling watches that he won the Seiko franchise from Japan for all of Southeast Asia. Over 40 years he and his eleven sons created a business empire turning over $450 million annually. The eldest son, Anant, started the Stelux manufacturing operation in Hong Kong in 1963. This is the pattern of the new Chinese multinationals ranging over all the markets of East Asia, in this case from a Thai base.

Textiles is the other mainstay for Thai manufacturers, drawing on expertise, technology, and capital from Taiwan, Hong Kong, Korea and Japan. The late Jim Thompson set an example for Thai companies in the way he used to sell his famous Thai silk fabrics. He would drape them over his arm in the lobby of the Oriental Hotel, knowing that some Westerner would stop and ask about them—and most likely place an order. He once went to a reception where the film star Paulette Goddard was so taken by the Thai silk suit he was wearing that she insisted on buying it on the spot. He retired to the men's room to take it off, and went home, a satisfied salesman, in his raincoat.[16] It took a *farang* to show the Thais how to create a new billion-dollar export industry out of a small traditional craft.

The 1990s should be Thailand's big opportunity to develop industry and manufacturing skills—because its labor costs remain lower and its reservoir of unskilled labor higher than in the NIEs. That is why so many companies from those NIEs relocated their production in Thailand in the 1980s.

The Thais are above all a practical people. If they want to work hard, or if they need to work hard, they will. Otherwise they will not. It is this individualism which irritates many foreign managers. The 300,000 Thais who went to work under long-term contract in construction projects in the Middle East, Singapore and Japan over the past decade or two went with the intention of working hard. Many come back with their pockets full of money, and their remittances home have already exceeded $1 billion.[17]

Generally, Somsakdi Xuto may be right when he remarks that the hard work that economic success demands is an un-Thai characteristic. Sustained, purposeful, collaborative hard work may not be common. But if you look at the construction sites in Bangkok and see the street vendors slaving away day after day for long hours in dismal conditions, you would not think that Thais are lazy.

Conditions in many Thai factories do fall below an acceptable level. A research study for the Asian Productivity Organization in Tokyo in 1988 concluded that conditions in small Thai textile factories "were universally less than fair. The working environments were dim, dusty, noisy and hot. The ergonomics of work station, neatness, work position and welfare facilities were ignored, neglected and abused. . . . (T)he hiring practices of small mills, whereby they select unsophisticated and docile workers to then work in nearly intolerable conditions, the inadequate community support, lack of proper nutrition and little access to necessary medical care all put added pressures on relatively unprepared individuals." That was the conclusion of an internationally backed researcher.[18]

There is nevertheless a current minimum wage, of about $4 per day, the second lowest of the ASEAN countries. Strictly speaking, it applies only to workers in registered enterprises, but in practice it is used as a yardstick for other workers in private industry.

Safety conditions are a major weakness in many enterprises, as in most developing countries. Child workers are another problem. There are said to be half a million below the age of fifteen, earning around $20 a month for a ten- or even fifteen-hour day. Some are below the minimum age of twelve. There are not enough inspectors. Enforcement of the law is lax. Penalties are light, and somehow there is always a loophole.[19] But complaints about conditions are not common, with unemployment at around 7 percent. There is someone ready to take your job if you leave it. Wages are in any case tending to rise and are better than what had been known before.

Only about one-tenth of industrial workers are organized in trade unions, which find it difficult to recruit members because of Thai individualism. Strikes have not been frequent since the sudden spate of them in the early 1970s, when half a million days a year were being lost. One of the earliest moves of the National Peace Keeping Council after the 1991 coup was to suspend the right to strike in the public sector and to impose further restrictions on the trade unions.

The Thais, a Japanese investor observes, "put their private life before their work and have a smaller sense of participation than the Japanese." One of the reasons why Jim Thompson's company was so successful was that he allowed his silk weavers to work on their own at home instead of in an ordered and standardized factory. He got better work out of them as a result.

The ugly incidents involving labor are usually the result of management excess. Managers sometimes demand money in return for giving a job to an applicant, and friends of the owners or administrators often have free rides on the payroll. Some of these practices are being reduced under the glare of public opinion, especially through the media and the political parties.

The *World Competitiveness Report* for 1990 finds Thai workers flexible, strongly motivated and productive, while Thai managers have education and initiative. A comparison with eight other developing countries with new industry, including the four NIEs of East Asia, showed Thailand ranking second or third for competitiveness of management and labor. Quality control circles have been operating in the Japanese joint ventures in Thailand since 1975 and in the Siam Cement Group since 1979.[20]

To their own surprise—and profit—the Thais have seen the annual wave of foreign tourists rise to over 5 million, so that the tourist industry now accounts for about 10 percent of Thailand's GDP. The numbers would probably have been almost 6 million in 1990 but for the Gulf War. Tourists are arriving at an average rate of 600 every hour, and each one spends about $1,000. That adds up to $5 billion a year—equal to half the country's exports.

Only one hotel in the world has been named "the best in the world" by travelers every year since 1981. It is not, as one might have expected, one of the grand hostelries in London, Paris or New York. It is the Oriental Hotel in Bangkok, so beloved of Somerset Maugham. That particular honor is partly due to good management led for some 25 years by a German, Kurt Wachtveitl, long married to a charming Thai lady—and thereby combining the graciousness of the East with the efficiency of the West. The Oriental also has long unbroken traditions of personal attention, including two staff members to every guest. On the business side, the $90 million Queen Sirikit National Convention Center, built with all the latest equipment for the World Bank/IMF annual meeting in October 1991, will attract large conferences for many years to come.

Thais enjoy serving other people, and do it well. The welcoming charm of the Thai people, the hot sunshine, the magnificent beaches and historical sites, the colorful festivals, the access to Buddhist meditation and the easy availability of sex add up to a powerful attraction for foreigners—Asians as well as Westerners.

The Thai economy is in a period of rapid growth, thanks to the natural endowments of the country and the forthright market-oriented enterprise policies of its political leaders. The price of success in terms of environmental degradation and human inequality *is* painful. But the initiative and vigor of the Thais working in the economy—from the agro-industrial barons such as Dhanin to the electronics whiz-kids and the farmers, factory workers and service personnel who make their dreams come true—should ensure that this national success will continue to flourish further in the twenty-first century.

10

Continental Diplomacy: The Hub of Southeast Asia

Thailand lies at the very heart of that restless and diverse Balkans-like corner of the Asian continent called Southeast Asia. It has extensive shores on both the Indian Ocean and the South China Sea, with one of the longest coastlines down both sides of the Malayan peninsula. But it is also an important land power, with long interior borders through difficult mountain and forest terrain in the north. Southeast Asia was historically a cockpit for the rival ambitions of five states—one being Thailand, and the others Indonesia, Burma, Cambodia and Vietnam. In the postwar period Thailand, the only one to escape colonialism, has stood out.

Look at any map of aviation routes and the importance of Bangkok becomes clear. It is on all the major flight paths through Asia, whether north-south or east-west. Thailand is the home of the United Nations Economic and Social Commission for Asia and the Pacific, as well as the Asian headquarters for many other world organizations including FAO and UNESCO. These are the fruits of Thailand's skills as a diplomatic survivor.

The Thais have interfused with their neighbors ever since the first Thai-type tribesmen began to migrate from China about a thousand years ago. The first wave to the west settled in the hills and forests of northeast Burma and became the Shan people. The second wave went east along the banks of the river Mekong to become the Lao people. The third wave penetrated to the upper reaches of the Chao Phraya River, which led down to a fertile plain and the sea. These were the ancestors of the present-day Thais.

As the Thais forced their way south down the Chao Phraya Valley they came into conflict with the Mon civilization in what is now southern Burma, and the Khmer empire centered in what is now Cambodia. By splitting asunder these two culturally similar civilizations (they were both Indian-influenced), the Thais laid the foundation for long, drawn-out conflict on both their western and eastern frontiers. A millennium of conflict forged the contemporary identity of the Thais, Burmese, Laotians and Cambodians, though it also resulted in much blending of cultures and intermarriage of peoples.

When European colonialists arrived in the nineteenth century a regional system of sorts was in operation. Thailand was a fairly united medium-sized kingdom, facing on the west a bigger and stronger Burma. The Thais suffered frequent invasions, twice losing their capital, Ayutthaya. At one point after successive defeats in the sixteenth century, Thailand became little more than a vassal of Burma. Only Burma's failure to maintain its own political unity enabled Thailand to hold its own, though scarcely capable of resisting Cambodian advances on its other flank. A Khmer force reached the outskirts of Ayutthaya in 1570.

Full Thai independence was not restored until the much admired King Naresuan pushed deep into Burmese territory and slew the Crown Prince of Burma in a duel on elephant back in 1593. But the Burmese later recovered the initiative and sacked Ayutthaya in 1767, vandalizing the richest collection of Thai treasure and cultural heritage, including Thailand's first Christian church, and carrying away great quantities of gold as well as 30,000 prisoners. The ruins of Ayutthaya are now a major tourist attraction, bringing in millions of dollars to the Thai treasury. What especially rankled was the Burmese mutilation of Buddha images in the city. Even after two hundred years Thais still resent the sacking.

Every time the royal barges are brought out for a regal ceremony on the river at Bangkok, it is remembered (and the press rubs it in) that the original barges were burned by the Burmese in that attack. When the Thai government celebrated the twenty-fifth century of Buddha in 1957, it invited many foreign dignitaries. One of them was U Nu, the prime minister of Burma, and the Thai government made sure that he saw the ruins at Ayutthaya and met the descendants of the people Burma had "wronged" two hundred years earlier.[1]

The response of the Thais to the Burmese sack of Ayutthaya in 1767 was to start all over again further down the river in Bangkok. There they went through the ordeal of resisting European conquest. King Mongkut (reigned 1851-68) sent missions to Europe to explore its technology and power, and the reports brought back were acted upon. Thailand never underestimated Europe. The spate of "open door" treaties signed in the 1850s, at the beginning of King Mongkut's reign, delayed the threat to Thailand's independence by satisfying the immediate commercial ambitions of the European powers.

, King Mongkut knew from seeing the humiliation of China in the Opium War of 1839, and the defeat of Burma by the British in 1824, that if it came to force of arms the Europeans could only win. The Thais therefore relied on skillful diplomacy, playing the colonial powers off against each other. Luckily by the 1890s the Europeans were reaching the limit of their territorial ambitions and capabilities, and although the British would not have allowed the French to take Thailand or vice versa, both were content to agree in 1896 to leave it "neutral." The wisdom of King Mongkut and his son King Chulalongkorn (reigned 1868-1910) paid off.

The staggered arrival of European colonialism distorted the politics of the region. The Burmese stopped attacking Thailand when they were themselves overrun by the British in 1824. The Thais were then able to force Cambodia and Laos into submission. In doing so, however, they encountered a new rival in Vietnam, which had designs on territory in the heartland of Indochina—a pattern to be repeated in the third quarter of the twentieth century. In the late 1820s a Vietnamese emperor seriously undermined Thailand's suzerainty of Laos, in retaliation for which the Thai king (Mongkut's elder brother and predecessor) sent his army into Cambodia in 1833 to clear it of Vietnamese troops, almost prefiguring the events of 140 years later. He went on to invade Vietnam itself, and that war dragged on for fourteen years before petering out in stalemate.

Cambodia and Laos acted for a time as buffer states between the Thais and Vietnamese. But the French colonial advance in Vietnam altered the balance again, and Thailand had to see its suzerainty rapidly reduced: France established a protectorate over Cambodia in 1863, and Laos in the 1890s.

At the peak of European colonialism in the nineteenth century, therefore, Thailand was on the defensive on all fronts. British-controlled Malaya nibbled away at Thai territory in the south, while British commercial interests based in Burma developed a presence in the northern Thai province of Chiang Mai, and the French pressed constantly via Cambodia and Laos.

But Thailand set the seal on its independence in the twentieth century by joining in the First World War on the side of the Allies. Thailand's subsequent participation in the Versailles peace conference and membership of the League of Nations raised her international prestige immeasurably. In 1922 Thailand signed a landmark treaty with the United States abolishing the extraterritorial rights it had to confer on the Western powers giving their nationals, for example, immunity from the Thai courts.

The Second World War, when Europe scuttled away and the Japanese marched triumphantly to take its place, was no less of a test for Thailand. As a Thai politician warned at the time, "Japan's intention is to chase away the white men from Asia and put itself in their shoes."[2] Thailand had exercised its usual caution when Japanese power began to direct itself toward Southeast Asia in the 1930s. It had abstained, for instance, when the League of Nations condemned Japan's attacks on China. One reward of that was Japanese help in regaining parts of Cambodia and Laos which had been lost to the French in earlier decades. Thailand won back the west-bank territories along the Mekong (though it had to return them again after the Allied victory in 1945).

Thailand could not stand alone against the imperial army of Japan, so Marshal Phibul struck up an alliance with Tokyo in 1940 to prevent a hostile takeover. He did not play the part of puppet, however. He refused to enter the Co-Prosperity Sphere of which the Japanese were so proud or attend the Greater East Asia Conference. The Thai government remained technically independent but with a strong Japanese garrison—never below 50,000 men—to remind it where its loyalties should lie. Meanwhile a "Free Thai Movement" developed in the United States and Britain, with links well into Thailand, so that when Japan was defeated, a new pro-Allied government was ready to take over in Bangkok. Pridi and the young Seni Pramoj replaced Phibul to negotiate with Mountbatten, who probably felt that Thailand had helped Japan more than was necessary, but who at least recognized Thailand's claim to independence. In a superb demonstration of shrewd diplomacy with weak cards, Seni was successful in averting a formal occupation by the British army (represented by Indian units).

As Southeast Asia emerged from the colonial era after the Second World War, indigenous national rivalries began once more to be a major factor in the politics of the region, though soon muted by the neocolonialist impulses of the Cold War.

Unlike Vietnam, Thailand had fended off both European rule and full-scale Japanese occupation. When the patriotic nationalists of Vietnam found the French coming back after the Japanese defeat, they united behind a leadership that happened to be largely Marxist, as it had been taught to be in Paris. The United States saw the contest as one between Asian communism and democratic capitalism, so it threw its decisive weight behind the French.

In 1950 Phibul, back in power after a brief disgrace, had signed a treaty of military and economic aid with the United States. Thailand thus found itself as an ally of the United States in the front line of the most savage war ever staged in Southeast Asia. Thais were gratified that the Americans were content to leave Thailand alone politically, giving it only economic aid. But the price was to join Pakistan and the Philippines as one of the three Asian founder members of the anticommunist Southeast Asia Treaty Organization (SEATO) in 1954, and to be host to U.S. bases.

In the case of Burma, colonialism substantially altered the balance of power in Thailand's favor. Burma was so traumatized and weakened by its experiences under the British that it no longer had the strength to threaten Thailand. Relations between Burma and Thailand in the postwar period were generally good. Quarrels flared up from time to time over opium smuggling, Karen rebels along the Thai-Burmese border, fishing disputes and Thailand's acceptance of political refugees—notably the Burmese prime minister U Nu when he was deposed. But these irritations were contained by virtually continuous dialogue and cordial, if not friendly exchanges—in spite of the continuing military dictatorship of General Ne Win and his successors.

To the east, it was more difficult. Thailand's relationship with Laos was marred, first by the Cold War and frequent border incidents along the Mekong River—and later by the Vietnam War. The Vietnamese sponsored insurgency in the remote border areas of Thailand adjoining Laos. Here were all the ingredients of trouble—alienated tribespeople, economically depressed Thai farmers, internal fighting going on just across the border, and occasional disaffected Marxist students fleeing from right-wing regimes in Bangkok.

Border incidents after the Vietnam War became more serious from 1975 when the Pathet Lao, militarily and politically close to the Vietnamese communists, came to power. As recently as February 1988, three hundred Thai soldiers died in a serious border clash. Now Thais are increasingly committed to opening economically to Laos in an effort to wean it away from Vietnamese influence. They could succeed if they can suppress their own propensity to exploit the weak by emphasizing the heavy-handed "big brother"–"little brother" syndrome instead of the commonality of history and language.

Thailand's success in avoiding colonization skewed the power relationship with Cambodia further in Thailand's favor. Cambodia's residual fears about Thailand's historical claims to provinces west of the Mekong, including Battambang and Siem Reap, deepened the political divide between the two countries. In the 1950s Thailand was ruled by a right-wing dictatorship closely allied with the United States, whereas Cambodia was governed by a left-wing king pursuing an idiosyncratic neutralism. As Cambodia became embroiled in the Vietnam War it began to lean on outside support in the shape of China. A series of border disputes beginning with the small but emotive issue of the Khao Phra Viharn temple kept Thai-Cambodian relations severed for much of the 1960s.

Things took a turn for the better after a right-wing coup ousted Prince Sihanouk in 1970. Cold War security considerations prompted Thai military aid to Cambodia, though with more caution after the Americans announced the withdrawal of their troops from Thailand. When Pol Pot and the Khmer Rouge gained their victory in 1975, Thailand, showing a sense of history as well as political acumen, was the first noncommunist country to establish relations with the new Cambodia. The communist success in the Vietnam War shifted Thai policy from a fiercely anticommunist stance to one dominated by fear of Vietnamese expansionism per se. Thailand could, after all, be the next "domino" to fall to the Red Flag in Southeast Asia! Cambodia was once more seen as a buffer state between Thailand and Vietnam, rather as it had been in the nineteenth century. Despite the apprehensions of many Thais about the brutal Khmer Rouge regime, historical and geopolitical factors had to prevail.

The alteration in Thailand's stance in the mid-1970s had deep historical roots. For the first time since the early nineteenth century, Thailand lacked either the status of a neutral buffer zone or the protection of a guardian superpower in its dealings with its neighbors and historical enemies. Laos and Cambodia were both communist by the late 1970s, but whereas Thai relations with Vietnamese-backed Laos were poor, its links with the Chinese-supported but rather independent Khmer Rouge in Cambodia were stronger, especially between the respective military establishments.

Until the 1970s, whatever underlying fears Thailand might have had about Vietnam were overridden by the Cold War conflict. Thailand had no diplomatic ties with the communist North, but cordial relations with South Vietnam, with which it shared close economic links with the United States and opposition to communism.

From 1966 onward Thai troops had been deployed in South Vietnam under SEATO. At the height of the Vietnam War in the mid-1960s half of the millions of bombs dropped by American planes on Vietnam originated from Thai airfields, and some Thais still feel nervous lest Vietnam eventually present them with the account for it. Thanat Khoman, then the Thai foreign minister, expressed such vigorous support for the anticommunists in the Vietnam War that he was variously dubbed the "most outspoken Asian statesman" or "the most hawkish U.S. ally in Asia."

Vietnamese communism was viewed as a threat by all Thai governments: even now Thai officials are not allowed to marry Vietnamese. Refugees from the fighting in Vietnam came across the border into Thailand by the thousand, especially in the 1970s. Some of them were organized by the communists, others were fiercely anticommunist; either way they made difficulties for the Thai government and military.

After the Americans lost the war and Vietnam was reunified, Thailand's traditional hostility focused on resolute opposition to the Vietnamese invasion and occupation of Cambodia in 1979. Between 50,000 and 80,000 Khmer Rouge forces resisting the Vietnamese fled to Thailand, and for a time a Vietnamese invasion of Thailand was a real threat. The Thais became deeply involved in stiffening up anti-Vietnamese resistance in Cambodia by both the Khmer Rouge and Prince Sihanouk and in keeping the Cambodian seat in the UN out of the hands of the Vietnam-backed government in Cambodia. The civil war in Cambodia continued throughout the 1980s.

By the late 1980s, the external geopolitical obstacles to a Cambodian solution began to disappear. The Cambodian war became the focus of the three key conditions that the Chinese laid down for a resumption of Sino-Soviet relations. Soviet pressure was a major factor leading to the final phase of the Vietnamese army's withdrawal from Cambodia in September 1989. Soviet-American détente also played a key role in this respect, diminishing the degree of mistrust between the Thais and Vietnamese. Another related development which eased the tension was the introduction of a degree of market-oriented economic reforms in both Vietnam and in Cambodia. In only a very few years, Cambodia and Vietnam, from Thailand's perspective, were transformed from being a major military threat, to providing a new and unprecedented opportunity for Thai economic development and investment, confirmed by the historic international agreement on Cambodia struck in Paris in October 1991.

How do the Thais of today view all these historically awkward neighbors? Most Thais are preoccupied by domestic events, and do not look outward much. To the extent that they are aware of the outside world, it is a haphazard mélange of Japanese comics, American movies, European pop music and, for a rather smaller circle, the antics of the Hong Kong and Singapore stock exchanges. But there is a very capable elite, split between government service, the universities and the media, that is interested in Thailand's relations with the world. These people view Thai diplomacy in Asia as being in four tiers. First there are the immediate neighbors in Indochina that have caused so much trouble in the past but could be useful economic partners in the future. Secondly there is ASEAN, the Association of Southeast Asian Nations, which is the principal forum for Southeast Asian external relations. Then there are the two regional titans anxious to have a say in Southeast

Asia, namely China and Japan. Beyond these three Asian tiers lie Thailand's important diplomatic relations with the West—notably Europe and the United States.

Some Thai intellectuals remember that in the mid-eighteenth century, before European colonialism arrived, virtually the whole of Cambodia and Laos and the eastern half of Burma—and even a small area of China's Yunnan province—were under Thai control. Cambodia, Laos and Burma lie across Thailand's northern frontiers, and Vietnam stretches behind Laos and Cambodia, in places only a hundred miles from Thailand. There used to be a buffer zone of hill tribesmen occupying both sides of this border area, loyal to neither. That is gradually changing. Thanks to the king's interest in a better breed of pig, the army's strengthening grip on the border areas and the impact of modern communications and consumer goods, the tribespeople have become less detached.

The minority Lao people who live in the northeast of Thailand, known as Isarn, are sometimes called, quaintly, "the Thai that have not yet come south," or, as has been said, "little brother," and are looked down upon by the Thais. Paler and taller, they are often more energetic than the Thais in the south. They mostly descend from Lao people forcibly removed to the Isarn when Thai troops sacked Vientiane in the 1820s. Indeed, there are more Lao speakers in Thailand than in Laos itself. The two peoples understand each other fully though they use a different dialect and in Laos there is a different script. Field Marshal Sarit, the famous dictator, came from this area, and was half Lao: one of his cousins became prime minister of Laos. That is the kind of kinship that Thailand has with Laos. The border is the river Mekong for most of the way, and in the dry season you can walk across its sandy bottom. Mukdahan in Thailand gets its fresh bread from across the river in Lao Savannakhet, and many Thai towns derive their electricity from a master hydroelectric power station in Laos.

Yet there is a fierce spirit of independence in Laos which prevents it from being absorbed into Thailand. Border disputes persist. The Vietnamese foreign minister once referred to the "seventeen provinces of Laos under Thai administration."[3] But Laos is small, poor and landlocked. Its seaborne trade is controlled by Thailand, the routes via Vietnam being more tortuous. It has been so riven by fighting that it welcomes what help it can get from Bangkok. Many Thai academics and officials have been advising the Lao government in the last few years. One expert was recently on his way to advise Laos on its economic plan when he was summoned to join the Thai cabinet as finance minister. Senior specialists from the Ministry of Industry have been staying for as long as seven months at a time to help Lao reconstruction.

Laos is not a threat to Thailand, unless it is controlled by somebody else—by Vietnam or China. That threat is, for the time being at least, removed. Now the proposed Thai-Lao bridge over the Mekong between Vientiane and Nongkhai is making the headlines, and Laos will be the chief beneficiary of the new $7.8 million foreign-aid program of the Thai government. Two more power stations are to be built in Laos for supplying the Thai grid through the Electricity Generating Authority of Thailand—EGAT—and further dams are planned.

Much of what has been said about Laos could also be said of Cambodia. Former Premier Seni Pramoj's aunt, who married one of Cambodia's last kings, observed: "Cambodia is like a little brother that should behave better—it's not a traditional enemy like Burma or Vietnam."[4] Linguistically, culturally and spiritually, a Thai writer observes, "The Laotians and Cambodians are much closer to the Thai than to the Vietnamese. Thailand can have great economic, social and cultural influence despite the fact that politically Laos and Cambodia belong to another ideological camp."[5] That camp has now disbanded, and as long as Thailand does not rush in too quickly to assert a kind of hegemony, these two countries could once again provide a kind of buffer between Thailand and Vietnam.

Unwilling to see influence and business opportunities in Vietnam go to other countries, General Kriangsak had put forward in the 1970s the idea of an opening to Vietnam. The opportunity had to wait until the end of the 1980s when Premier Chatichai made his famous pronouncement that all of Indochina should become a marketplace rather than a battlefield. Businessmen like Tawat Yip In Isoi, chairman of Thaiviet Invexim, are now leading the materialization of Chatichai's vision in trading and investment with Vietnam.[6]

There were voices of caution. Some of the Thai military were nervous about détente with a country still officially communist and possessing a very large army, however ill-equipped. Some Thai economists worried lest Vietnam under a capitalist style of management might steal Thailand's rice markets and overtake Thailand in light industry. But it was agreed by all that if Vietnam were linked with the world economy, its leaders would at least see some virtue in maintaining stable relationships with neighbors.[7]

With Burma, the overlapping of Shan tribespeople on both sides of the border, together with drug-running in the famous Golden Triangle spanning the border areas of Thailand and Burma, makes the relationship difficult. But Ne Win, the veteran Burmese dictator, used to cultivate the Thai royal family, the Thai military leaders maintain a dialogue whatever the changes in government on either side,[8] and Thai businessmen provide an outlet for sales of Burma's minerals and commodities. There is an illegal trade in the border region that benefits local bosses as well as some army officers. But Burma is for the time being so weakened by internal divisions, fighting and military dictatorship, which has led to ostracism by so many other countries, that it has little impact on Thailand. When some political solution is found in Burma, and its economy begins to develop again, Burma could well be drawn closer into the Thai orbit.

Thailand used to appear as an exposed state on the front line of communist expansion, and dependent on American support. Now, with communism no longer a threat and the Thai economy booming, Thailand sees itself instead as a regional power of some muscle, able to influence its neighbors directly, without patronage from the West. The apologetic capitalist weakling, which sought defensively to justify its pro-Western stance to the Asian neutrals, now prepares to nudge its communist neighbors toward a free-enterprise market-oriented ideology without firing a gun. (It may actually be subversive merely to invite Vietnamese, Cambodian or Laotian officials to Bangkok. The Thai capital is so developed, so affluent, so bubbling with life that visitors return home to lobby openly for Hanoi and Ho Chi Minh City to be developed like Bangkok. Expectations are raised simply by the dialogue.)

In a factual sense Thailand is already a center for the Indochina subregion comprising these five countries. The *baht* is widely used in all of them, and they mostly regard Thailand as their first and major option for trade and investment. General Chaovalit Yongchaiyudh talks about this subregion as *Suwannaphum,* or "golden land." He perceives Thailand as the economic engine spreading wealth and development through the subregion in a way that would benefit all. Thailand would not dominate such a grouping, he insists, but act as a center on which the other countries can rely. He thus distinguishes his concept from the "Greater Thailand" expansionism of Field Marshal Phibul in the 1940s.[9]

Some foreign critics call Chaovalit's blueprint "a new imperialism,"[10] an excuse for exploiting the natural resources of neighbors in place of the domestic ones that Thailand has already used up. This will be the tension of the coming years. The crucial factor will be whether Thais act with restraint in carrying out their new role, and whether the neighbors estimate it as minimally helpful to them or simply a national ego trip on Thailand's part. The brilliant young advisors of General Chatichai's government some-times revealed their sense of superiority to their hosts and counterparts in neighboring countries. Their certitude bordering on arrogance, and more particularly the greed of some Thai timber and mineral concessionaires, may have lost friends for Thailand, and if repeated could spoil the prospects for *Suwannaphum*.

Thai dominance may be a problem. But the prospects for Thai leadership should not be exaggerated. To take another indicator, there are no facilities in official Thai institutions to teach the Burmese or Vietnamese languages, and only a few students learn the archaic Cambodian offered at Chulalongkorn University. Any serious planning for a. long-term hegemonistic role would surely have provided for such necessary language skills. But Thais have to go to Harvard or London to learn these neighboring languages systematically. One may infer a certain lack of seriousness for the *Suwannaphum* objective.

One project has finally succeeded after many years of frustration, and that is a Thai-Vietnamese dictionary, which was a joint effort between scholars and institutions of the two countries. It almost failed because of communication difficulties and bureaucratic obfuscation on the Vietnamese side.

Intimately preoccupied with difficult land neighbors on her northern frontiers, Thailand rather neglects her partners in ASEAN, namely Indonesia, the Philippines, Malaysia, Brunei and Singapore. The Thais can rightly claim to have been the architect of this modestly successful regional grouping. In a controversial act of decolonization, the British in the early 1960s attached their two northern Borneo colonies of Sarawak and Sabah to independent Malaya in a new Federation of Malaysia, which Indonesia—the other occupant of Borneo—did not accept. A war of confrontation against the new federation was declared. It was the Thais who eventually brought the combatants together, and that reconciliation led to the foundation of ASEAN.

ASEAN did not diminish the sovereignty of any of its members, merely committing them to consult and collaborate, especially in economic development. Even this proved more difficult than anyone had thought. The six countries are at a broadly similar level of development and compete with one another. Military cooperation was deliberately rejected in order to avoid provoking other countries outside Southeast Asia, but there is a high level of bilateral defense collaboration. The Thai armed forces have a standing program of cooperation with their Malaysian and Indonesian counterparts. From time to time ASEAN becomes the forum for floating ideas about neutralizing the region, declaring it a nuclear-free zone, or regional collaboration with the East Asian states and Australia.

The most important result of ASEAN over 25 years is to have made the region's elites familiar with each other. The Thai foreign minister and his civil servants meet so frequently with their counterparts that they know one another intimately. Even ministers and bureaucrats in such fields as education, agriculture, and communications find themselves plugged in to a permanent network with the five others. This does not always mean common policies, but it does make for adequate consultation, and offers the means of quick communication to avert conflict.

During the bloody wars in Vietnam and Cambodia, the ASEAN governments took a common stand against communism without endorsing American intervention. Thailand, with its responsibilities to SEATO, actively assisted the American operations in Vietnam. Its attitude was therefore different from that of its ASEAN partners. But ASEAN was able to contain these differences, and even, in the Cambodian conflict, to take a lead in attempting to negotiate a settlement.

At the end of the 1980s Thailand suddenly switched round under the Chatichai government to befriending Vietnam and offering help in its economic reconstruction. Chatichai also informally suggested joint naval maneuvers with Japan, something which he had not discussed beforehand with the other ASEAN governments, and which was quite opposed to their thinking.[11]

ASEAN appears to be breaking down into two tiers—a northern tier comprising only Thailand, preoccupied with the events and prospects of its neighbors to the north, and a southern tier in which the remaining members of ASEAN have a common interest in maritime affairs but are rather more detached from the tensions of Vietnam and China. Thailand retains membership of ASEAN for a variety of useful global and continent-wide concerns, while having the freedom of maneuver to take a slightly different line on Indochinese questions. As Premier Anand put it in May 1991, Thailand will act as a bridge between ASEAN and the Asian mainland (especially Vietnam) but will continue to regard ASEAN as a foreign-policy anchor. Or as Korn Dabaransi, a minister in the earlier government of Premier Chatichai (his uncle) said, Indochina is Thailand's inner circle of involvement, ASEAN the outer circle.

Only Malaysia, of all Thailand's ASEAN partners, shares a frontier with Thailand. Like the other borders, it is made difficult by ambiguity. There are ethnic Thais long-resident on the Malaysian side, and vice versa. There is tension between Islam and Buddhism. The Malaysian states on the border were surrendered to the British colonial masters of Malaya as recently as 1912. The southern Thai provinces of Pattani, Yala and Narathiwat are as much Malay in character as Thai. While the towns are filled with Thais and Chinese, the countryside is largely Muslim. During the 1960s the insurgency by Thai communists, Malaysian bandits and the remnants of the Malaysian Communist party conducting terrorism in Malaysia made this a very difficult part of Thailand to govern. But it is not a flashpoint today.

Thailand would be most unlucky to experience substantial trouble in the coming decades from its Southeast Asian neighbors, though all its skills may be called in to play to insulate itself from such events as future upheavals in Burma and the potential clash between Communist party elders and young technocrats in Vietnam. Whatever happens, however, it appears that Thailand will be the major player in the Southeast Asian game for the rest of this century, and probably beyond.[12]

11

Dealing with the Bigger Powers: The Crocodile or the Whale?

Beyond the Southeast Asian horizon lie two ambitious giants in East Asia—Japan and China—and the three centers of European or Western power in the United States, the former USSR and the European Community. These relationships are crucial to Thailand's well-being and are carefully nursed by the Thais.

Beyond the Vietnam menace of the 1960s and 1970s had loomed the mysterious presence of China, the colossus whose foreign minister, Chen Yi, had specified in 1965 that Thailand would be the next target for revolution.[1] Luckily for the Thais, China became preoccupied for the next several years with its Cultural Revolution, and that was followed by a period of moderation in foreign policy. The Thais took advantage of this, treading in the American footsteps, when Premier Kukrit Pramoj and Foreign Minister Chatichai Choonhavan traveled to China in 1975 to restore diplomatic relations. Mao Zedong sought to reassure the Thais by observing that Thailand should not worry about the Thai Communist party. Not a single member of it, he said, had come to see him.

"Why didn't you say so at the beginning, Chairman?" the Thai premier gaily replied. "I'll send five of them over immediately."[2] This crucial rapprochement was furthered by the "Chineseness" of the Thai national elite. Many Thai diplomats and politicians had enough Chinese blood in their veins to be able to pretend, for the purposes of diplomacy, to be long-lost sons of the greater Chinese family. As such they could expect more favorable treatment than "strangers." (Phibul himself had used this ploy with the British to justify his China policy in 1941.)

The Chinese believed they were making an investment that would pay off, in time, in good relations with people they could understand. Deng

Xiaoping, China's strongman, told another Thai premier, General Kriangsak, a few years later: "I am proud to say that the domino theory does not apply to Thailand any more."[3] It demonstrated yet again the infinite capacity of Thai leaders for cool thinking, flexibility and charm, alongside an unswerving attachment to the Thai national interest.

Thailand does not share a land frontier with China. That is because British and French colonial cartographers decreed that it would be safer for everybody if Laos and Burma met over the top of Thailand in a thin strip of territory separating Thailand from China. But it was from South China that the Thais had emigrated many centuries ago, and they retain some cultural features which are similar to the Chinese. There is controversy as to where exactly the Thais came from in South China. The major research on this is necessarily conducted by Chinese academics like Chen Lufan, whose book *Whence Came the Thai Race?—An Inquiry* was published in 1990 in Kunming.[4]

Thailand's large Chinese population enables it to be more effective in dealing with China. The Charoen Pokphand Group alone has $1 billion of investments in China. But the "Sino-Thais" could also facilitate China's influence over Thailand. They constitute an organic connection between the two countries which could be used from either end, though the successful assimilation makes China's influence more shadowy. It is extremely unlikely that the Chinese embassy in Bangkok could raise a mob or torch a revolution. Mao Zedong is still admired by some "Sino-Thais," but almost all of them are committed to Thailand, which is their home and country.

Thailand tries all the same not to provoke China, avoiding antagonistic postures. Although it prides itself as a Buddhist kingdom, it would not allow the Dalai Lama to visit Thailand, knowing that he would plead the case for Tibetan independence, which would anger China. When Thailand joined SEATO in 1954, it was rumored that the government had made a secret arrangement with China promising not to use arms against Chinese territory. After Thai recognition of the People's Republic of China in 1975, the position became much more open, with General Chaovalit later traveling to Beijing several times to purchase arms and equipment. Much of that proved to be of such poor quality that the orders were not repeated. The purchases nevertheless cemented relations between the two armed forces, so that Thailand is again singled out in ASEAN as the partner conducting the friendliest military dialogue with China.

The 58 million Thais would feel safer having a reasonably friendly relationship with the 1,100 million Chinese. But from China's point of view, Thailand is a subregional player of only moderate importance, whose usefulness depends on its attitude toward other small countries where China has a particular interest, notably Laos and Cambodia. There Chinese and Vietnamese ambitions were for some time directly pitted against one another, at least until the tentative Sino-Vietnamese rapprochement of 1991. When Vietnam invaded Cambodia in 1979, the Thai armed forces automatically supported the Cambodian resistance movements fighting against the Vietnamese, including the Khmer Rouge—which has bases on Thai soil. Since China was also supporting the Khmer Rouge for the same reason, to keep Vietnamese influence out of the neighboring countries, Thailand and China found common cause.

When most of the Vietnamese army left Cambodia in 1989, Thailand reduced its support for the Khmer Rouge, no longer needing such a brutal ally condemned by world opinion. China, however, continued to patronize the Khmer Rouge until late 1991, and so Thai-Chinese relations cooled. The lesson was that Thailand must deal in the first instance with threats from its immediate neighbors and can only then expect to reach past these neighbors to have sound relations with the Chinese giant just beyond. The price of Chinese friendship will always be to follow pro-Chinese policies toward other countries of the region, and that will be Thailand's future dilemma.

It is possible that the Chinese, for their part, have persuaded themselves that the Thai Chinese and the "Sino-Thais" are potential instruments for China's influence in Thailand. Premier Zhou Enlai told then Foreign Minister Chatichai Choonhavan during his visit to Beijing in 1975 that China was an "elder relative" wanting to cooperate with Southeast Asia. The Chinese in Beijing sometimes talk about those with Chinese blood in Thailand in the way that Britons talk about Australians, as "chips off the old block" finding their own path in the world but basically responsive to the mother country's needs and ideas. If so, China is in for a disappointment. The assimilation has gone too far for that.[5]

If the Thais aspire to a special relationship with China, Asia's major political power, they make the same claim regarding Asia's only world economic power, Japan. Japan and Thailand have the same kind of constitutional monarchy, a similarly revered royal family, the identical experience of avoiding European colonialism, the selfsame Buddhist religion—and some equivalence of national character. The exchanges between the two countries go back to the fourteenth century. In the twentieth century the Japanese are grateful for the fact that Thailand was the only Asian country officially—though passively—supporting them in their drive against European control of Asia in the 1940s.

After the war Japan offered war reparations to help the Thai economy. The Japanese prime minister, Yoshida Shigeru, admitted quite openly that although the Asian recipient countries insisted on calling it reparations, "for us this is nothing but investment."[6] Japanese infrastructural loans continue even today to assist the extension of Japanese industry into Thailand and so promote Japan's influence. Japan accounts for 70 percent of the foreign aid currently being received by Thailand. And Thailand is the second biggest recipient of Japanese aid after China.

Occasionally there has been anger against Japan, partly in reaction to the arrogant behavior of some Japanese businessmen. A student group in Kasetsart University called for a boycott of Japanese products in 1971,[7] and more recently some Thai academics have campaigned against the violence depicted in Japanese cartoon magazines circulating to Thai children. A 1987 opinion poll showed only 20 percent of the Thai sample felt that the Japanese were honest, and only 10 percent thought them reliable. In one of the most admired modern Thai novels, Srirat Satapanavat's *Phaendin Nee Kong Krai* (Whose Land is This?), the brutal torture of a Thai lawyer by Japanese soldiers during World War II is described in horrifying detail.[8]

Yet the Japanese Ambassador was able to say, truthfully, in 1989 that "in the past two centuries of European and American domination of the world, Japan and Thailand were the only two countries which consistently maintained independence and preserved their traditional values."[9] There are Thais today who feel that the white Western domination of world affairs should be challenged on cultural grounds. Japan would inevitably assume a leading role in such a project. Many Thai intellectuals would like to see the power of the Anglo-Saxons rolled back to allow an "Asian personality" to emerge— but through peaceful adjustment, not by fighting, as in the 1940s. These views must, of course, be coupled with the continuing Thai wariness of Japan's regional power.

A recent foreign minister, Siddhi Savetsila, urged that Japan should play a bigger security role in Southeast Asia. Questioned about the threat of Japanese remilitarization, he replied: "Don't worry, Japan does not want war. But Japan has to play a security role."[10] This was a prelude to Premier Chatichai's remarks about joint naval maneuvers to the visiting director of Japan's Self-Defense Agency in 1990. A Malaysian critic commented that Chatichai's proposal would better have come from countries that had been occupied by Japan in the war, rather than one which had collaborated.[11] Clearly the division of Southeast Asia in the path of the Japanese advance during the war is still strong. There is latent resentment of Thailand's good fortune in the 1940s, in emerging from World War II in a better position than the other Southeast Asian countries, her economy less damaged and her public life surviving uninterrupted. But Thailand can be counted on to respond to future crises with the same realism, flexibility and practicality as in the past.

Thailand's affinity with Japan should not be overdone. Its test would come if Thailand had to choose in any dispute between Japan and China. The Thai instinct would be to put off the evil day as long as possible by trying to please both sides. In the end, if neither side were actually threatening Thailand, the Thais would probably prefer China to Japan. But the prime consideration would be to maximize Thailand's independence and security, perhaps by engaging in that reliable ancient strategy of the zigzag.

The Western powers used to seem to the Thais more powerful and threatening than China or Japan, but also more distant, and now their menace has almost disappeared. Thailand figuratively bordered on Europe for the century in which it was "boxed in" by British colonialism (in Burma and Malaya) on one side and French colonialism (in Cambodia and Laos) on the other. The West created a popular legend with its romantic fantasy *The King and I*. But the king in question, King Mongkut, could have turned the tables by penning an equally stirring and suspenseful drama called *The West and I*. He once described Thailand's dilemma as "whether to swim up the river to make friends with the crocodile, or swim out to sea and hang on to the whale." Initially ill-informed about the intentions of the powerful Western nations then advancing across every continent of the world, Mongkut had to devise strategies of appeasement and ingratiation to persuade Europe to halt at Thailand's gate. He offered President Lincoln a herd of elephants to fight in the Civil War,[12] and wrote billets-doux to Queen Victoria, always susceptible to such familiarities, as from a "brother" to his "sister."

King Mongkut succeeded. Thailand escaped the fate that engulfed all its neighbors and preserved its independence. But he was not merely the short-term savior of his country. His mind penetrated to the reasons behind Western superiority in trade and weapons. He launched Thailand into a sustained and comprehensive acquisition of the technical skills that would allow Thailand to become an equal of the West. That effort, not systematically imitated until much later by Thailand's neighbors, has continued without interruption ever since, and it still goes on.

Those neighbors of Thailand had a different experience: they had Western values, systems, customs and conventions—even language—thrust down their throats by European nations. Thailand was the only country which reached out voluntarily for those aspects of Western civilization it believed it needed. At first this made the process slower. The Thais had to find out for themselves where to go to discover things, whereas the Vietnamese, Burmese and Malayans had built-in access to basic Westernization provided by the colonial masters.

But in the longer run the Thais scored. Their sense of identity and cultural self-confidence never seriously weakened. Because the West never asserted an alien political power over Thailand, the Thais were not psychologically alienated from the Western possessors and teachers of the new skills Thailand needed. It was the difference between choosing one's own medicine for an illness and having it crammed into one's mouth by a draconian doctor.

For more than a century young Thais have been drinking at the fountains of Western knowledge and mixing with Western society. King Mongkut sent many of his sons to Europe, Chulalongkorn sent all of his to the West. Almost every Western country now has its share of the descendants of Thai royals, many of whom married into the local aristocracy. There is now an intellectual, professional and administrative elite in Thailand which can trace its Western connections back for several generations. These young people returned with scientific or professional knowledge. They also brought admiration for the political and legal systems of Western countries, which allowed their people to be individualistic within a strong framework of order and justice.

When communism first appeared, the Thai love affair with the West was already many decades advanced. Few Thais were attracted by Russian bolshevism or Chinese Maoism. The Vietnamese grasped Marxism as a means of toppling French rule; the Thais faced no such desperate choices. When basic policies for economic development needed to be set, whether by Mongkut himself at the very beginning or in the interwar period or during the crescendo years of the 1970s and 1980s, Thailand instinctively went for free enterprise.

The Thais are not immune from Asian nationalism. Dislike of America or Europe, distaste for the West or the white races, can easily be found in Thai student canteens, officers' messes, senior common rooms or professional clubs. Pongsak, editor of the Thai-language newspaper *Matichon*, complains of the Western foreign correspondents in Bangkok: "They think that because they are white men, they are the centre of civilisation. They put themselves on a pedestal and present their own hypothesis."[13] When Westerners pontificate about Thailand on the basis of rather superficial contact, Thais react just as strongly as any Indian or Chinese or Indonesian would in a similar case, though the famous smile might conceal it.

In the 1970s Thammasat University students published a book called *Bhai Kao* (or "White Menace"), warning about the evil intentions of foreigners, whether "yellow or white." American aid to Thailand was "a white man's menace," and the American military offices in Thailand were "aiming to murder Thai culture."[14] That was in the course of the kingdom's "American period," before and during the Vietnam War when SEATO—read "United States"—required Thailand to host the American bases from which targets throughout Indochina were bombed. It was also the period when the minuscule Thai Communist party was most attractive to students and intellectuals—for domestic rather than international reasons.

But these anti-Western feelings do not build on dark memories of British district officers or French colonial gendarmes kicking local members of the subject race around. The only trace of that kind of sentiment is vestigial resentment of the British for initiating in the nineteenth century the series of extraterritorial treaties which limited Thai sovereignty and for insisting on the return in 1945 of the disputed provinces on the Malayan border which Thailand had recovered under the Japanese.

There is also smoldering anger about the "theft" of ancient artwork from ruined sites, which almost exploded in the case of the eleventh-century Phnom Rung carved stone lintel which is exhibited at the Chicago Art Institute.[15] Artistic, nationalist and religious passions merge here to form a powerful lobby for bringing the Buddha figures home. Americans and Europeans take a legalistic view of such things, asking whether such objects were fairly or legally acquired in the first instance, whereas Thais see the matter in the different light of reciprocal respect for national cultures and treasures. A Thai princess sightseeing in Paris expressed relief that General Bonaparte never got as far as Thailand: "If he had, the Emerald Buddha would be in the Louvre."[16]

Thai foreign policy, it must be conceded, has gone through periods of great vulnerability. Thailand has always preferred to avoid foreign-policy commitments. A former foreign minister recalls that when he was representing Thailand abroad in the 1940s and 50s, he used to get cables from Bangkok saying, "Attend conference, do not (repeat do not) open your mouth." Another common instruction was, "Talk to our friends to see how they vote and then conform to their position."[17] That was how Thai foreign policy was conducted in the early postwar years when America, victor in the Pacific War and dispenser of aid, was king.

Thailand had not always been in full control of its international relationships. Marshal Phibul, when prime minister, told a Japanese envoy on the eve of the Pacific War that the Thai Ministry of Foreign Affairs *was* the "British Foreign Office"—because it was dominated by pro-British, British-trained officials.[18] Escaping colonialism did not magically endow Thailand with a cadre of skilled officials able to identify and protect Thailand's interests in a fast-changing world.

In earlier centuries individual charismatic *farangs* had been able to acquire unusual power. Constantine Phaulkon, the cheeky Greek adventurer in Thailand in the late seventeenth century, had one Thai king eating out of his hand, so that other foreigners dealt with him as a prime minister. Earlier in that century the Japanese Yamada Nagamasa had been a major player at the court, so that foreign governments competed for his favors. These days Westerners who become too involved in Thai politics are liable to expulsion.

In the earlier postwar period American officials had more influence than other foreigners, but the huge number of GIs in the 1960s later caused a backlash. The withdrawal of American bases following the end of the Vietnam War in 1975 did not wipe the slate clean of anti-Americanism. "Allies" against Indochinese communism in the 1970s, Thailand and the United States have become economic competitors reduced to squabbling over videocassette royalties and cigarette imports. For decades the Thais dutifully restricted their shipments of garments to the United States and other Western markets under the Multi-Fibre Arrangement negotiated in the GATT. When the Americans insisted on Thailand's opening its market freely to their cigarettes, even though this would hurt the Thai industry, it looked like a double standard.

For "pirated" videocassettes to sell at their own market rate in Bangkok seems to many Thais another expression of the free market. Thais ask themselves whether they are being asked to support the fine principles of international trading or merely help fill the coffers of American movie-makers and tobacco giants. The same resentment arises over American demands for reciprocal air traffic rights.

Some accuse the white industrial-military powers of clubbing together to dictate world affairs, which they see as nothing more or less than a racial policy.

The vast majority of officials, politicians and generals who govern Thailand are convinced all the same that Thailand's interests are best served by cultivating good relations with the West. Irritations over aviation or intellectual property rights will not undo the strong links between Thailand and America. King Bhumipol was born in Massachusetts, and many leading Thai personalities lived, worked and studied in America. The present generation of leaders in their late fifties and sixties was largely European-educated, but those who will succeed them mostly have an alma mater in the United States. Many senior officers of the Thai armed forces have been trained in the United States, and most of their equipment comes from U.S. manufacturers.

There is now an important overseas Thai population in the United States, especially on the west coast, including the king's eldest child. Thai leaders joke that these American Thais will soon be numerous enough to vote for their own representative in the U.S. Congress—who could then represent "Eastern" or Thai interests. An outstanding Thai novelist, S. P. Somtow, is one of these Thai-Americans, though as a minor member of the royal family he was educated at Eton and Cambridge.[19] This growing community will help to cement Thai-U.S. relations and tide them over temporary difficulties. Some of them are returning to live and work in Thailand using their American-acquired expertise to help realize Thailand's development as a Newly Industrializing Economy (NIE).

The positive side of the U.S. relationship was expressed by President Lyndon Johnson when he declared that the United States and Thailand were "Pacific brothers."[20] There is some hollowness in that kind of rhetoric. A few officials in Washington and some of the clever young men currently around the White House and the Departments of State and Commerce, as well as many academics, do have brotherly feelings toward their Thai opposite numbers. But the majority of American politicians and bureaucrats see Thailand as a small faraway country which needs to be brought to heel on such matters as intellectual property. There is a degree of unconscious cultural disdain here.

The Thais will go on trying, all the same, and they have no intention of abandoning the West. Premier Chatichai Choonhavan put it cleverly in 1989, when he defended a compromise that his officials had worked out on one of these American economic demands, in the words: "We have to give them a little concession. After helping other countries in the world they are getting poorer. Thailand should provide them a little help, since it has become a small millionaire."[21] This is the new factor—that Thailand has more room for maneuver by virtue of its economic success. That may strengthen the demand by some Thais to get tougher with the West, but it also makes the Thai economy more interdependent and especially more dependent upon the American and European markets. No dramatic change should therefore be expected.

It is, however, time that Thailand was taken more seriously in Western foreign ministries. There is still a tendency to regard Thailand as one of many small Southeast Asian countries, occupying a minor strategic area in world communications and not powerful enough to count in global decision making. For the 1990s and beyond, the scenarios will be more complicated. At one level Thailand will be ordering her relations with the neighboring small states of Southeast Asia, probably to form a subsystem in the northern tier for mutual development and security, while collaborating with the other ASEAN countries in the southern tier to realize the region's Asia-wide and global goals.

At another level Thailand is likely to cultivate both of the strong Asian powers, China and Japan, simultaneously—rather as she did in the nineteenth century with another pair of rivals, Britain and France, and then in the 1930s and 1940s with Japan and America. At the global level, Thailand will seek good relations with all major powers, seeing them as markets, arms suppliers and potential guarantors of the Southeast Asian system. This will include Russia, now in retreat from regional power, and the European Community.

The momentum of fulfilling Premier Chatichai's idea of Indochina as a marketplace rather than a war zone—with Thailand dominant—is likely to continue. But in the long term Thailand will probably compete, at first with a Vietnam growing economically (and therefore politically) stronger and even later perhaps with an increasingly wealthy Indonesia. In due course the West may have to make some strategic choices as these interrelationships develop. For the foreseeable future, Thailand is more strongly placed than the others, because of its vibrant economy and firm position of independence.

The West would do well to understand why Thailand is becoming the Southeast Asian leader and gear its policies accordingly. For the West—and particularly the United States—to make short-term demands in order to meet global economic targets, dictated by American or European commercial lobbies, without an attempt to compromise or negotiate to reach a middle path, is to do a disservice to the West's real lasting interests in Thailand and Southeast Asia. The United States regards itself as a "major player" in the growing economic stakes of the Pacific basin. As a Pacific power it has more to lose than Europe does. In Thailand, patience and long-term vision will offer the United States significant diplomatic and economic rewards well into the twenty-first century.

The West's interest for now is to support as far as possible the political system of the country most likely to exercise constructive leadership in Southeast Asia. With Western military power effectively withdrawn from Southeast Asia, it falls to Thailand to seek to keep the unruly peninsula in some kind of order. It will not use armed force, but it will use all kinds of pressure and ploys. The Thai military will seek to disarm and patronize the leaders of neighboring armed forces. Businessmen will offer trade and investment. Diplomats will present attractive solutions of local problems and seek mutually beneficial political ties.

In all these endeavors Thailand will gain national advantage. It will also assist the security of the entire troubled region, one in which the West would serve itself by recognizing Thailand's maturity and supporting its exertions. Better to cultivate the leader of the Southeast Asian pack, especially when it has declared its preference for the West.

Conclusion:
Alone and Free at Last

An American reporter, comparing Thailand in 1950 with its neighbors, then emerging groggily from a century of European colonialism, complimented the kingdom for being "still largely its own, not a bastard product of two civilisations . . . a jewel of (almost) unblemished easternism shining on the junk heap of the wrecked empires."[1] Thailand is now about as modernized as other Asian countries, but it enjoys the great advantage of having lost less of its own tradition and values in the process. By circumventing colonialism, the Thais retained a continuing clarity and certitude about the source of domestic authority, a sense of cultural and psychological independence and a quiet determination to do better by their own efforts. As a prime minister once put it, "never having been colonised, we can only blame ourselves for our problems."[2]

Modernization in Asia came from *above* rather than below, but in this case it was at least a Thai "above" and not a foreign one. The purpose of King Mongkut and his successors in modernizing Thailand, from the creation of government departments to the imposition of surnames and hats, was not to transform Thai society for its own sake. As in Meiji Japan or the dying days of imperial China, the goal of modernizing was rather to preserve the underlying traditional system by making it more resilient in resisting foreign pressure. Thailand responded to the pressures of the West as China did ("Chinese learning for essence, Western learning for practical use") or as the leaders of the self-strengthening movement in Japan did ("Eastern Morality, Western Science"). But overambitious Japan invited military defeat and occupation at American hands, while China turned the knife on itself with debilitating civil war.

Paradoxically, a degree of voluntary modernization in Thailand on the British model tempered the British temptation to annex the kingdom. In the colonies which the Europeans did conquer, social and economic transformation was undertaken on the order of Europeans to facilitate European rule, by brainwashing the "natives" into dependence on European culture and education.

Thailand's uninterrupted independence, bought at some price and with certain territorial concessions, has not been sufficiently recognized as the boon that it in fact was. It was not a case of backward-looking archaic rulers being allowed to keep their subjects in innocent ignorance in order further to enjoy the perks of an anachronistic absolutism. It was much more a case of sensible and farsighted kings being able to put in train momentous changes in their society, of their own choosing and at their own speed—with the goal of strengthening their society's capability to resist the military and territorial encroachments of powers that, though from a distant continent, were far stronger than weak little Thailand.

Only now, in the 1990s, do we see the real importance of this history as Thailand emerges, measurably advancing over her neighbors recently released from the colonial yoke. Compared with Burma and Vietnam or Indonesia, the three large countries of equal potential to east, west and south, which were absorbed in the British, French and Dutch empires respectively, Thailand is demonstrably ahead in terms of education, economic growth, standard of living, urbanization, modern industry, cereal harvests, social freedoms, the rule of law, political participation and all the other hallmarks of modern society.

Pride and self-confidence are the key. Every Thai knows that King Bhumiphol is the direct descendant of the earlier kings of the great Chakri dynasty and fully inherits their magical properties. Because of this, he is an acceptable reconciler of political conflict. There is no such figure in Vietnam or Burma, or in most other Asian countries for that matter.

The Thai system has been allowed to develop naturally and organically from the absolutist tradition that King Mongkut inherited down through the many reforms that he and his descendants initiated. That evolution of social and political institutions was allowed to take place without serious break. There was no colonialism to undermine the traditional authority. There was no violent social revolution of the kind that the Russians lived through in 1917 or the Chinese in 1911, 1927-49 or 1966-67.

The "revolution" of 1932 in Thailand was entirely peaceful, with no loss of life. The monarchy continued, though without the absolute powers that it had already agreed to give up. No changes were imposed from the outside, in the way that the Japanese ravaged and dismembered China in the 1930s, or in the way the Americans told Japan how to reorder its polity in 1945-52. Thanks to an imaginative and supple diplomacy, Thailand was left unscathed by the Second World War.

Outsiders detect instability in Thailand because prime ministers, cabinets and dictators change so frequently. But this is an instability of persons and of temporary groups, not of the underlying system itself. Below the surface of those visible changes, the system has evolved steadily to deliver the goods that Thai people want. It has ensured the uninterrupted independence of the Thai state. It has preserved Thai unity, though at the cost of some marginal border provinces disputed with neighbors.

It is a system that has allowed a large measure of political participation for the people. When a German scholar recently compared politics in Chiang Mai, Thailand's second city, with those in comparable Malaysian and Philippine cities, he concluded that the Thai city was the best placed of the three to broaden the participatory process. Its municipal political scene disclosed less social inequality, more mobility and more participatory pressure on the formerly dominant forces. There were chances for upwardly mobile persons or groups in Chiang Mai to integrate into the political process without extraordinary disruption.[3] The outside world may smile when it reads of yet another Thai military coup d'état, but the equally frequent and sometimes more significant general elections under universal franchise (including the votes of women) often go unnoticed in Western newspapers. Thailand has vastly more real experience in democracy than her neighbors.

The system has also delivered social peace and much freedom to the people, in a measure without parallel in the region. There is more room in Thailand for free thought, free assembly, political lobbying and the activities of voluntary religious, cultural or social groups, than in other parts of Southeast Asia. The rule of law is by no means perfect, and there are still aspects of Thai culture which hinder it, but it is in better shape in Thailand than in the countries surrounding it.

The system also favors economic uplift of a more successful kind than almost anywhere else in developing Asia except possibly Korea and Taiwan. There are immense problems, notably pollution of the environment, AIDS and also the disparity of incomes between rich and poor, urban and rural communities. But solutions to these problems are constantly debated and are made easier to implement by the vigor of 10 percent annual economic growth over the past four years. It is likely, given the momentum which Thailand has been able to build up, that the 1990s will see a further spurt of public and private investment, both domestic and foreign, which will consolidate Thailand's lead in the region.

Private enterprise and the market economy have been allowed to produce their best results, greatly helped by the "Sino-Thais." Thailand is not yet heading along the path of economic egalitarianism pioneered by Taiwan and

Korea, but economic power is sufficiently dispersed to facilitate economic growth on the basis of keen competition. The specter of the AIDS time bomb does cloud the chances of Thailand's becoming the economic powerhouse of its region. The natural attitude to sex maximizes risks, but then it also maximizes solutions by the relative ease of spreading the use of condoms.

The Thai system encompasses a built-in safety mechanism which stops any one force in the political arena from becoming absolutely supreme. There will always be a coalition by the others to prevent such an abuse or excess of power. This is the Thai system of checks and balances, involving the king, the army and the political parties. This might not have been possible if the Thai army had acquired the kind of overweening power and prestige that the nationalist or "freedom" forces won when fighting colonial rule in other Asian countries.

Given the experience of the colonized countries, the king would not have inherited his present powers if Thailand had been a colony; indeed he might not have inherited anything at all. Where are the kings of Burma, Cambodia or Laos now?* Thailand might have been left with an impotent figurehead president lamely trying to keep the lock on the barracks gate.

The reward of this political history is Thailand's exceptional ability to absorb freely from the world outside. A merging of influences into the country was permitted; the government did not intervene or attempt to supervise. It was left to natural forces, consistent with national self-respect. First Chinese and then Western culture were allowed to influence the society without subjecting it to foreign dictation. Those were the ideal conditions for modernization.

The success of Thailand in absorbing and assimilating millions of Chinese immigrants to the extent that their descendants consider themselves fully Thai is largely to be explained by the Thais feeling themselves secure and unthreatened in their own inviolate kingdom. There were no exaggerated feelings of inferiority or superiority: the Chinese were admired for their proficiency in business and economic matters. Buddhism makes no distinction of race or culture. The Thais voluntarily allowed the Chinese in, whereas the Malays, Vietnamese and Burmese distrusted their Chinese immigrants,

---

* King Vattana of Laos succumbed in a remote prison hut in 1979, after his deposition by communists, ending a 600-year-old dynasty. King Sihanouk of Cambodia abdicated in 1955, though he retained power as a prince at the head of a political faction until 1970 and could again become a head of state in a future Cambodia. King Thibaw of Burma was seized by the British in 1885 and exiled to India.

seeing them as introduced by European rulers in order to prop up colonialism. Thailand was able to acquire with virtually no social indigestion a body of Chinese workers and entrepreneurs who, with their descendants, have contributed enormously to Thai modernization. Only now in the 1990s are other Southeast Asian governments beginning to understand this Thai attitude—and envy the Thai record.

The Chinese were only the latest of many nationalities to be absorbed into Thai society. Thailand is surprisingly heterogeneous, with Muslim Malays, Vietnamese, Cambodians, Laos and hill tribespeople—all in some degree Thai-ized—living side by side in the same state. When the prime minister goes to the southernmost provinces he needs an interpreter in Malay. Indeed, the first prime minister of Malaysia had a Thai mother. The political unity of Thailand is more robust than that of some of its neighbors. The king himself has led the drive to integrate the minority hill tribespeople of the north into the mainstream of Thai society.

In the moving equilibrium of Thai politics, the army may intervene against a wrong-headed government. The king, because of his personal qualities and history of service, reinforcing the godlike sanctity of his line, can deflect the ambitions of generals—though that does not necessarily mean that the monarchy will be as effective in the hands of King Bhumiphol's successors. The politicians, civil servants and generals together would restrain any damagingly intemperate king in the future, though at the possible cost of permanently weakening the monarchy and forfeiting its mediating role in future crises. So far these checks and balances have been carried out with very little conflict because of the nature of the Thai people, the teaching of their religion and the character of their polity. Only the events surrounding the student revolutions of 1973 and 1992 could in any sense be called violent. The contrast with neighboring countries is indelible.

Thailand finds itself recompensed for its intrinsic virtues and favored by geography and geopolitics, becoming an important player not only in the region but also wider afield. During the colonial period Thailand's ambitions were limited to staying clear of Western domination. Later Thailand was necessarily caught up in the long succession of wars and ideological confrontations of postwar Asia. It ultimately became a target for communist subversion and an ally of the United States in the effective military defeat of expansionist Southeast Asian communism, exposing itself as a Southeast Asian domino. That agenda is now completed.

A new scene now emerges where the former colonial powers lack influence. Even the two superpowers which followed them in seeking to dictate Southeast Asian politics exert a declining leverage. Russia no longer has the capability or will to act in Southeast Asia. The United States, the sole remaining superpower, is enlarging its global economic canvas and humanitarian responsibilities in the light of the new needs in Eastern Europe and seems increasingly to be regarding its presence in Southeast Asia as a declining proportion of its overall (growing) international responsibilities.

China and Japan present quite different problems to Thailand. China is almost a neighbor, and is closely involved in the developments in the Indochinese countries from Burma to Vietnam. In the long run the Chinese may seek a dominant role in, or at least some kind of veto power over, the policies of these small neighboring countries, which would embarrass Thailand and make difficulties for the Thai government. But that prospect is diminished by China's continuing economic weakness and the possibility of strong centralized power giving way to a looser system in the future. Japan has no direct political interest in the Indochina countries, but has such an overpowering economic role that any possibility of a more overtly political diplomacy on Japan's part would have to be taken very seriously by Thailand. It may, however, take some time before Japan can gear itself for anything more than a relatively passive and reactive diplomacy in Southeast Asia.

Thailand is left in the position of being the richest and most successful country, politically and economically, in Southeast Asia. It naturally aspires to leadership in the Indochina states neighboring it as well as in ASEAN. Fate beckons it to such a position in that bloc of small countries around its northern borders, extending from Burma to Laos, Cambodia and Vietnam. The marketplace cry of General Chatichai Choonhavan's government in the late 1980s exactly reflects the genuine interests of those countries and accurately embodies that key feature of Thai life and history, the avoidance of conflict.

Being human, the Thais may be tempted to boast in their new role. They would be wise to suppress such emotions if they hope to realize their ambitions. But this is a minor side product of the extraordinary achievement of Thailand in turning itself into a major regional power. With a population larger than France's, an area the size of France and Britain combined and a Gross National Product bigger than that of all its land neighbors put together, Thailand feels itself to be in a strong position.

For a long time, over many epochs, other states called the tune in Southeast Asia. Before European colonialism they were Vietnam, Burma and what is today Indonesia. The Burmese sacked the Thai capital only just over 200 years ago. By the nineteenth century, states from another continent, with quite different cultures and religions, came to dominate the region—Britain, France and Holland, followed eventually by the United States and Japan. Then in the twentieth century communism, whether Soviet or Chinese, seemed set on enclosing Southeast Asia into its empire. Meanwhile many Thais feared that the American response to communism was itself, because of its size and transparency, constituting a kind of imperialism. Only now in the 1990s have these ogres vanished. Only now does Southeast Asia stand, a little nervously, entirely on its own—free from both the greedy attentions of expansionist outside powers and the insistent demands of supportive but overbearing allies.

Lying at the maritime crossroads of the globe, on the major shipping and oil tanker routes of the industrialized world, Southeast Asia knows that it is not forgotten in world affairs. It is only to be expected that at some time in the future other countries might take a closer interest in Southeast Asia and its sea-lanes than is either warranted or comfortable. Disputes in other parts of the globe could easily spread to this region and require unilateral or regional action by the Southeast Asian states. Potential conflicts between China and Japan, the two future superpowers of Asia, could well result in Southeast Asian fallout, and the region's Chinese population might become a pawn in any such confrontation.

Meanwhile the economies of Southeast Asia, gathering momentum as a free-enterprise, market-oriented zone, with their huge natural resources, can only make an increasing impact on the global economy. The *Economist* has predicted they will form the fourth major area of capitalism in the world after Europe, North America and Japan.

In these circumstances Thailand stands ready as the most prepared and best-equipped Southeast Asian state to deal with any difficult situations that may arise. Malaysia has not yet come to terms with destructive racial envy between Chinese and Malay; Singapore is too small to wield a big stick, and Indonesia is still busy grappling with a low level of economic development and a high level of authoritarianism. Thailand was instrumental in bringing Indonesia, Singapore and Malaysia together after their confrontations in the 1960s and in forming ASEAN and ASPAC, the two significant regional groupings to be forged from within. Thailand is likely to take similar initiatives again when the need arises.

Thailand was long dominated, successively, by her neighbors, by the European colonial powers and more recently by the United States in the context of defeating communism. One after another, foreign states have tangled with Thailand's destiny. Thailand has survived the experience intact and made good use of all its enforced close contacts to ensure its growing modernization.

A few Asian states have already mounted the bandwagon of sustained and diversified industrialization. Now it is Thailand's turn to climb aboard. Other countries, within or outside the region, have determined Southeast Asia's fortunes. Now it is Thailand's turn.

Epilogue:
Yuppies Brave the Bullet

Thailand's image was damaged by fatal confrontations between the military and civilians in May 1992. General Sunthorn Kongsompong and General Suchinda Kraprayoon, who led the military coup in February 1991, kept their word about holding elections under a revised constitution. But that revised constitution turned out to allow the military to control the Senate and thus act as a brake on any elected government. It also allowed the elected assemblymen to appoint a prime minister who was not elected. Given the strength of the new military-sponsored political parties, the constitution gave the armed forces a much bigger say in the government. The generals publicly promised that they would not run for the premiership. Most Thais assumed that the armed forces would be satisfied.

But the premiership became the center of dispute and rivalry the moment the results of the March 1992 election came in. At first, the three major parties forming the ruling coalition in the Assembly proposed one of their number, Narong Wongwan, as leader of the Samakkee Tham party, which had been formed by the military with civilian "front men." Narong, a Chinese tobacco magnate nicknamed "Godfather of the North," was viewed with some distaste by the Thai middle class. When it emerged that he had earlier been denied a U.S. visa for alleged involvement in drug trafficking, his colleagues searched for a new candidate. It was due to these circumstances that they proposed General Suchinda himself, in spite of his earlier refusals. This time Suchinda agreed, and he became prime minister on 7 April 1992. To the disgust of the liberals, he appointed a cabinet containing many ministers from the Chatichai government, which he himself had overthrown the previous year. Some of them had been singled out by the army for special investigation on suspicion of gross corruption.

These two features of the incoming government—its unelected military premier and its old and distrusted faces from the Chatichai regime—stung a dissident general, Chamlong Srimuang, into action. Basking in his party's sweeping victory in 32 of the 35 Bangkok constituencies, ex-Mayor Chamlong warned the ruling coalition that it would risk a popular uprising by choosing an unelected prime minister. On the night of 20 April a huge crowd demonstrated to demand Suchinda's resignation. Several rallies of growing intensity followed. General Chamlong himself laid a thin straw mat out in front of the parliament building and declared that he would fast to death on it if Suchinda did not resign.

This was the cue for tens of thousands of protesters to gather in the streets of Bangkok, just as they had done in the early 1970s when the issue had been democracy versus dictatorship. But this time they drove in their Nissan and Volkswagen automobiles and took their mobile telephones and video cameras to record and report on the demonstrations. This time it was not only students who risked life and limb for their political beliefs but a middle class that was newly enlarged and self-confident, tired of being governed either by generals or by corrupt politicians elected by peasants.

On 8 May a large crowd marched toward the Royal Palace and the parliament shouting for an elected premier and a reduction in Senate powers. Suddenly the disputants met to defuse the quarrel, and Suchinda appeared to agree to changes. Chamlong ended his fast. But the government coalition parties reneged on the pact, the rallies resumed, and Premier Suchinda decreed a state of emergency on 17 May.

A fateful four days of disorder and violence flashed onto the world's television screens as the international media looked on. On the first day, the demonstrators were opposed by policemen using water cannons and truncheons. They tried to scatter demonstrators who threw stones and bottles at them and at public buildings.

On the second day, when about two hundred thousand people massed on the streets, Suchinda withdrew the police and put in conscript infantrymen and other units from the army. On 19 May, the confrontation reached its almost predictable climax when paratroopers appeared, at first firing their machine guns in the air but then turning them into the crowd and killing indiscriminately. General Chamlong was arrested, along with many of his followers, a police station was burned to the ground, and many unarmed civilian protesters were beaten and killed by troops in the area around the Royal Hotel. Some officers blamed the killings on the confusion of orders coming down the line of command.[1]

The king had held back until now, perhaps unsure of his capacity to give orders to the army. But just before midnight on 20 May he held an audience at which he chided Suchinda for his actions. "You have not followed the people," King Bhumiphol said. "You talk about democracy but you don't do anything about it. You are losing the country." These words were spoken to

Suchinda in the presence not only of his principal rival, General Chamlong, and the elder statesman, and ex-premier, General Prem Tinsulanond, but also of television cameras, which presented to Thai households and to viewers in other countries the dramatic sight of Suchinda's grovelling on his knees before a seated and rebuking king. The king, whose earlier hesitation had caused dismay, now regained the respect of his people, while Chamlong was ranked as Suchinda's equal in a skillful reapportionment of "face."

An armistice was established after four days of savage violence during which at least 48, but possibly more than 100, Thai civilians died and many more were injured. It was now obvious that the discontent was not merely felt by radical students and subversive communists, as Suchinda claimed, but was far broader and deeper than anything that had happened in 1973. This time university teachers and even officials and businessmen were involved. The coalition parties quickly agreed to withdraw their backing for Suchinda, and he resigned on 24 May after issuing a controversial decree of amnesty for those involved in the violence on both sides.

The killings changed the climate for military action in political affairs. "We cannot accept soldiers using weapons paid for by taxpayers shooting down Thai citizens," said one student leader, Jaturporn Pronpan. It was a cardinal mistake by the military to allow its soldiers to shoot unarmed, young, middle-class Thai civilians. And it was greedy of the military leaders to think that they could take the premiership as well as retain control of both the National Assembly and the Senate.

The military's ineptitude and overreaction to events were made worse by open factionalism within the army. Suchinda found himself standing not merely against civilian politicians but also against his former commander, General Chaovalit Yongchaiyudh, who had emerged as the biggest opposition personality in the Assembly; against General Chamlong, with whom he had already quarreled much earlier; and against Air Chief Marshall Kaset Ronjanil, the ambitious leader of the Air Force and an architect of the Samakkee Tham party, who was also openly ambitious to become premier.

The temperature was brought down in June 1992, after the coalition parties, led by the military-backed Samakkee Tham, failed twice to unite around an alternative person for premier. This time the king intervened more promptly, appointing Anand Panyarachun, the interim premier during 1991, to hold the reins of government once more (pending another general election later in the year). This neatly extracted the bruised party leaders in the Assembly from the nation's dilemma. Anand was greatly admired both by the business community and by the middle class for his honesty and efficiency during his previous period of office. After all, General Suchinda had selected him in the first place to head the caretaker government after the military coup, so the army could hardly complain—although they had soon found out that Anand was independent enough to stand up to military pressure.

The wheel had thus come full circle. Military rule had been tried and had been grudgingly accepted as long as it was temporary and allowed the economic "miracle" to continue. Then Thailand gained a very brief elected government that turned out to be controlled by the military through constitutional devices. For the ensuing months Thailand was destined to be run under the king's command, Bhumiphol having directly appointed Anand as premier under the previous constitution. The royal authority had swelled with the respective disgraces of both the military and the political parties.

For the election of March 1992, Anand's government set up a voluntary monitoring organization to observe the polling and reduce irregularities. It worked primarily in Bangkok, but even so, those who took part in it mostly estimated that about half of the votes (especially in rural areas) had been bought in advance. The same monitoring was organized for the subsequent election of September 1992. The parties' coffers would be virtually empty so soon after the extravaganza of March, so vote buying might have been less significant this time. One new move is that of a group of leading businessmen, who have started a fund to help candidates who are opposed to vote buying.[2]

No machinery is yet in place that will keep eager military hands off the helm of government if generals remain greedy for power and are offered no regular role in government.[3] The military did, in the end, accede to civilian demands in mid-1992, and the king did succeed, belatedly, in defusing the tension.

The political upheaval of 1992 dented the Thai kingdom's economic prospects. Most predictions of annual growth for 1992 were brought down a percentage point—from around 8 percent to around 7 percent (still one of the highest growth rates in the world). Tourist earnings suffered an immediate and significant setback, and there was an inevitable hiccup in the inflow of foreign investment and foreign aid—which should eventually resume unless Anand is unable to contain further conflict.[4] In due course Thailand should find itself again in a more favored position than its neighbors and competitors in Asia. Its underlying advantages relative to others have not changed.

The 1992 confrontation left the Thai people more capable and confident of addressing their problems. A marked heightening of political consciousness could be observed in those tense days and in the weeks of military-civilian standoff that followed. There is a larger middle class that is more sophisticated, more educated, and more cosmopolitan than before—and more capable of dealing realistically yet toughly with the overriding problem of a recalcitrant and obsoletely motivated army.

The traditional Thai pattern is for conflict to be suppressed for a long time and only then to come out in the open—and then vigorously. The Suchinda affair brought new middle-class forces out into the open, after which no one could be in any doubt of their vigor and resolve. The old mechanism of checks and balances, the moving equilibrium in Thai politics, played out its latest scenario. Civilian forces outplayed a powerful military and look increasingly capable of containing it. The monarchy still occupies its umpire's seat, and 7 percent economic growth is forecast even in a year of turbulence. Thailand's turn is coming.

NOTES

Prologue

1. See Dominic Faulder, "The Royal White Elephants," in *Sawasdee Magazine*, vol. on H. M. King Bhumiphol Adulyadej (Bangkok: Thai Airways International, 1988), p. 41.
2. This is a taboo subject in Thailand. Rayne Kruger's *The Devil's Discus* (London: Cassell, 1964) investigates the question, and Antony Grey's *The Bangkok Secret* (London: Macmillan, 1990) refers to it in a fictional context.
3. Interview with Denis Gray, *Sawasdee Magazine*, January 1987.

Introduction

1. William Overholt, *B. T. Brokerage Review* (Hong Kong), May 1988.
2. *The Guardian*, London, 22 October 1977. *The Times* leader on the same day declared that a coup in Thailand attracted no more attention than "a small earthquake in Chile."

Chapter 1

1. *Japan Times* (Tokyo), 10 March 1991.
2. *The Nation* (Bangkok), 25 February 1991.
3. *Far Eastern Economic Review* (Hong Kong), 4 May 1989.
4. Boonchu Rojanasathien, quoted in *Far Eastern Economic Review* (Hong Kong), 21 April 1983.
5. Puey Ungpakorn in *The Guardian* (London), 25 January 1974. See generally Tai Ming Cheung, 'Immovable Object,' *Far Eastern Economic Review* (Hong Kong), 25 June 1992.
6. See R. Bates Gill, "China Looks to Thailand, Exporting Arms, Exporting Influence," in *Asian Survey* (Berkeley, CA), June 1991, p. 526.
7. See Chai-Anan Samudavanija, Kasuma Snitswongse and Suchit Bunbongkarn, *From Armed Suppression to Political Offensive*, (Bangkok: Chulalongkorn University, 1990), pp. 78-79; and Suchit Bunbongkarn, "The Thai Military's Efforts to Institutionalise its Political Role," in *Pacific Review* (Oxford), vol. 1, no. 4, 1988.
8. See the same authors in *Far Eastern Economic Review* (Hong Kong), 26 November 1987.
9. J. L. Taylor, "New Buddhist Movements in Thailand," in *Journal of South East Asian Studies* (Singapore), March 1990, p. 146. See also *Bangkok Post*, 29 March 1992.

10. Chai-Anan Samudavanija, Kasuma Snitswongse and Suchit Bunbongkarn, *From Armed Suppression to Political Offensive*, p. 147.
11. *The Guardian*, 6 April 1987.
12. *Bangkok Post*, 27 October 1990.
13. Suchit Bunbongkarn.

Chapter 2

1. Richard Hughes in *Far Eastern Economic Review* (Hong Kong), 25 November 1977.
2. A Mahidol University lecturer quoted in Yuangrat Wedel, *The Thai Radicals and the Communist Party*, (Singapore: Maruzen Asia, 1983), p. 12.
3. *Japan Times* (Tokyo), 22 September 1989.
4. Quoted by Jackson, "The Hupphaasawan Movement," in *Sojourn* 3, no. 1 (1988).
5. Kukrit Pramoj, in *Far Eastern Economic Review* (Hong Kong), 9 December 1977.
6. Dr. Suntaree Komin, *Psychology of the Thai People* (Bangkok: National Institute of Development Administration, 1990), p. 154.
7. *Far Eastern Economic Review* (Hong Kong), 12 May 1990.
8. *Bangkok Post*, 22 December 1966.
9. *Far Eastern Economic Review* (Hong Kong), 28 December 1967.
10. *International Herald Tribune*, 4 March 1981.
11. *New Society* (London), 29 February 1968.
12. *New Nation* (Singapore), 26 September 1979.
13. Wedel, *The Thai Radicals and the Communist Party*, pp. 15-24.
14. *Far Eastern Economic Review* (Hong Kong), 23 January 1976.
15. *Far Eastern Economic Review* (Hong Kong), 14 and 28 August 1981.
16. *Bangkok Post Weekly*, 23 September 1990. Songtham's comment was "The General does not have a democratic heart."
17. *Bangkok Post*, 29 March 1992; *The Nation* (Bangkok), 1 April 1992.
18. *Far Eastern Economic Review* (Hong Kong), 19 July 1984.
19. Judith Stowe, *Siam Becomes Thailand* (London: Hurst & Co., 1991) p. 10.

Chapter 3

1. *South* (London), July 1982; *Far Eastern Economic Review* (Hong Kong), 30 June 1988; *Asian Finance* (Hong Kong), 16 January 1991.
2. See, for example, Derek Davies, "A Right Royal Example" in *Far Eastern Economic Review* (Hong Kong), 23 January 1986, p. 22.
3. *The King of Thailand in World Focus* (Bangkok: Foreign Correspondents Club of Thailand, 1988), p. 108-9.
4. Davies, "A Right Royal Example," p. 23.

5. *Illustrated Handbook of Projects Undertaken Through Royal Initiative* (Bangkok: Rattanakosin Bicentennial Committee, 1982).
6. Voice of the People of Thailand Radio, cited in *New Nation* (Singapore), 2 April 1977.
7. See *International Herald Tribune*, 2 September 1986; Ben Barber in *Toledo Blade*, 6 September 1988, and *Sunday Telegraph* (London), 10 February 1980.
8. Sulak Sivarakse, *Siam in Crisis* (Bangkok: Thai Interreligious Commission for Development, 1990) pp. 175-6, 322.
9. David Lomax in *Sunday Telegraph* (London), 10 February 1980.
10. *Asiaweek* (Hong Kong), 23 April 1982.
11. *The Observer* (London), 4 October 1987; *Japan Times*, 6 October 1987; *Sunday Times* (London), 6 December 1987; *Far Eastern Economic Review* (Hong Kong), 21 January 1988.

Chapter 4

1. This stung the *Washington Post* leader-writer to a famous comment in which he referred to the Thais as "the best allies that money can buy." *Bangkok Post*, 3 June 1969; *Far Eastern Economic Review* (Hong Kong), 12 June 1969.
2. *Far Eastern Economic Review* (Hong Kong), 28 August 1981.
3. Likhit Dhiravegin, "Demi-Democracy and the Market Economy: The Case of Thailand," *Southeast Journal of Social Science* 16, no. 1 (1988), p. 16.
4. Suntaree Komin, *Psychology of the Thai People* (Bangkok: National Institute of Development Administration, 1990), p. 226.
5. *Daily Telegraph* (London), 27 January 1987.
6. Kukrit Pramoj, address to Pacific Area Travel Association, 31 January 1969, in Steve Van Beek, ed., *Kukrit Pramoj, His Wit and Wisdom* (Bangkok: Duang Kamol, 1983), p. 163.
7. Ibid., p. 203.
8. *Bangkok Post*, 5 September 1970 and 9 January 1972.
9. Quoted in Peter Jackson, *Male Homosexuality in Thailand* (Elmhurst, NY: Global Academic Publishers, 1989), p. 223.
10. *Bangkok Post*, 4 November 1990.
11. *Bangkok Post*, 12 September 1971.
12. Sulak Sivarakse in *Siam in Crisis* (Bangkok: Thai Interreligious Commission for Development, 1990), p. 114, describes the loss of the name Siam as the "first step in the psychic dehumanization of its citizens." But see also *Bangkok Post*, 16 November 1973.
13. Thak Chaloemtiarana, *Thailand, The Politics of Despotism* (Bangkok: Thammasat University, 1979), p. 62.
14. *Far Eastern Economic Review* (Hong Kong), 27 July 1989.
15. Herbert Phillips, *The Thai Peasant Personality*, (Berkeley, CA: University of California Press, 1965).
16. Thanin Kraivixien, then a judge, in a Rotary Club speech said: "Give me back the old days [meaning before 1932] when a man could have as many wives as

he liked and his chief wife would even go through the trouble of finding mistresses for him" (*Bangkok Post*, 27 July 1967). It is arguable that economic growth harms the status of poorer women: see Darunee Tantiwiramanond and Shashi Ranjan Pandey, "Dutiful but Overburdened: Women in Thai Society," *Asian Review* (Bangkok), vol. 3, 1989, p. 41. On General Sunthorn see *New York Times* and *International Herald Tribune*, 2 August 1991.

17. Van Beek, ed., *Kukrit Pramoj: His Wit and Wisdom*, p. 253.

18. See, for example, Thak, *Thailand, The Politics of Despotism*, pp. 336-7.

19. Kirrkiart Pipatseritham, quoted in *The Guardian*, 12 May 1987.

20. Kukrit Pramoj, in *Far Eastern Economic Review* (Hong Kong), 18 January 1968.

21. Sulak Sivaraksa, *Siamese Resurgence* (Bangkok: Asian Cultural Forum on Development, 1985), p. 423.

22. Prasoet Beunson, quoted in Jackson, *Male Homosexuality in Thailand*, p. 33.

23. Van Beek, ed., *Kukrit Pramoj: His Wit and Wisdom*, p. 253.

Chapter 5

1. Steve Van Beek, ed., *Kukrit Pramoj: His Wit and Wisdom* (Bangkok: Duang Kamol, 1983), p. 162.

2. Jiang Yingliang, *The History of Thai* (Sichuan: People's Press Chengdu, 1983) p. 644.

3. Botan, *Letters From Thailand* (Bangkok: DK Book House, 1977), p. 13.

4. Quoted in Peter Jackson, "The Hupphaasawan Movement," *Soujourn* 3, no. 1 (1988), p. 151.

5. The Patpong story is colorfully told by Alan Dawson in *Patpong* (Bangkok: Thai Watana Panich Press, 1988) pp. 1-21.

6. See Cristina Blanc Szanton, "Thai and Sino-Thai in Small Town Thailand," in Peter Gesling, ed., *The Chinese in South East Asia*, vol. 2; and Jacques Amyot, *The Chinese and the National Integration in South East Asia* (Bangkok: Chulalongkorn University, 1972), chapters 4 and 5.

7. *Bangkok Post*, 6 July 1974.

8. Survey in Boonsanong Panyodyana, *Chinese-Thai Differential Assimilation in Bangkok, An Exploratory Study* (Bangkok: Chulalongkorn University, 1971).

9. Carl E. Blandford, *Chinese Churches in Thailand* (Bangkok: Suriyaban, n.d.), p. 46.

10. Quoted in Jackson, "The Hupphaasawan Movement," p. 151. See also foreword and preface to Phya Anuman Rajadhon, *Essay on Thai Folklore* (Bangkok: Duang Kamol, 1968).

11. Quoted in Boonsanong Panyodyana, "The Changing Status and Future Role of the Chinese in Thailand," in *Trends in Thailand* (Bangkok: Institute of South East Asian Studies, 1973), p. 60-1.

12. Botan, *Letters from Thailand*, pp. 344, 389.

13. Ibid., p. 142. See also "Chinese in Bangkok: Living a Double Life," in *Bangkok Post,* 8 October 1988; and "Paying Homage to the Gods," by Wasant Techawongtham, in *Bangkok Post,* 11 February 1990.
14. Blandford, *Chinese Churches in Thailand,* p. 39.
15. *The Economist,* 26 January 1991.
16. Kenneth Landon, *Siam in Transition* (Westport, Conn.: Greenwood Press, 1968), p. 87.
17. Quoted in Boonsanong Panyodyana, *Chinese-Thai Differential Assimilation in Bangkok, An Exploratory Study,* p. 1.

Chapter 6

1. Herbert Phillips, *The Patterning of Interpersonal Behaviour in the Village of Bang Chan* (Berkeley: University of California Press, 1965).
2. Somsakdi Xuto, ed., *Government and Politics of Thailand* (Oxford: Oxford University Press, 1987) p. 195; *New Nation* (Singapore), 27 April 1978; *The Times* (London), 17 December 1990.
3. *Bangkok Post,* 11 March 1970.
4. Jackson, "The Hupphaasawan Movement" in *Sojourn* 3, no. 1 (1988).
5. *Far Eastern Economic Review* (Hong Kong), 14 July 1983.
6. William Warren, *Jim Thompson, The Legendary American of Thailand* (Bangkok: Thompson Thai Silk Co., 1990), p. 122.
7. *The Asian Wall Street Journal* (see *South China Morning Post* (Hong Kong), 1 September 1989).
8. See Sulak Sivarakse, *Siamese Resurgence* (Bangkok: Asian Cultural Forum on Development, 1985), pp. 19-20.
9. *Far Eastern Economic Review* (Hong Kong), 14 July 1983.
10. J. L. Taylor, "New Buddhist Movements in Thailand," *Journal of South East Asian Studies* (Singapore), March 1990, p. 146ff.
11. Ibid., pp. 140-43; *Far Eastern Economic Review* (Hong Kong), 4 July 1991. See also Sawanna Satha-Anand, "Religious Movements in Contemporary Thailand," *Asian Survey* (Berkeley, CA), April 1990, pp. 395, 400.
12. Sanitsuda Ekachai, "The Buddhist Approach to Fighting Rural Poverty," *Bangkok Post,* 11 March 1990.
13. *The Nation* (Bangkok), 16 November 1990; *Far Eastern Economic Review* (Hong Kong), 18 June 1987.

Chapter 7

1. Address to the Asia Society, New York (*Bangkok Post,* 1 October 1966).
2. See Mushkat Miron, *Will the Jewel in the Southeast Asian Crown Continue to Shine?* (Bangkok: Baring Securities, Thailand Research, October 1990).
3. *Far Eastern Economic Review* (Hong Kong), 19 September 1991.
4. *The Nation* (Bangkok), 16 October 1989, and *South China Morning Post* (Hong Kong), 24 October 1989.

5. Kamchom Sathirukul (*Japan Times*, 30 October 1988).

6. See Anels Laothamatas, "Business and Politics in Thailand, New Patterns of Influence," *Asian Survey* (April 1988), p. 451.

7. See Kavi Chongkittavorn in *The Nation* (Bangkok), 6 April 1990; also Ambassador Hisahiko Okazaki in *The Nation* (Bangkok), 9 August 1989; and see generally Kamchai Laismit, "Economic Nationalism and Trade Deficit in a Bureaucratic Economy: An Alternative View of the Japanese Trade Dispute," *Asian Review* 1 (1987), p. 121; and Kunio Yoshihara, *Japan in Thailand* (Kuala Lumpur: Kyoto University, 1990).

8. *The Nation* (Bangkok), 2 October 1990. See also *Far Eastern Economic Review* (Hong Kong) 2 July 1992.

9. See, for example, Smith New Court *Asiawatch* (Thailand), 12 June 1991.

10. Mushkat, *Will the Jewel in the Southeast Asian Crown Continue to Shine?* p. 35.

Chapter 8

1. See Dr. Suntaree Komin, *Social Dimensions of Industrialisation in Thailand* (Bangkok: National Institute of Development Administration, 1989).

2. See *Far Eastern Economic Review* (Hong Kong), 12 January 1989 and 31 October 1991. A good instance of constructive action on the forests is at Ban Sup Tai: see *Network News* (Biomass Users Network, January 1990).

3. Phillip Hirsch and Larry Lohmann, "Contemporary Politics of Environment in Thailand," *Asian Survey* (Berkeley, CA), April 1989.

4. Suntaree Komin, *Psychology of the Thai People* (Bangkok: National Institute of Development Administration, 1990), pp. 22-26.

5. *The Nation* (Bangkok), 4 October 1990. See generally Robert J. Muscat, *Thailand and the US: Development, Security and Foreign Aid* (New York: Columbia University Press, 1990).

6. "Ambitious Plan for Prosperity," *Bangkok Post*, 30 June 1991.

7. *The Guardian* (London), 24 June 1982, and *Far Eastern Economic Review* (Hong Kong), 25 June 1982.

8. *Bangkok Post*, 13 April 1966.

9. *Bangkok Post*, 19 July 1966.

10. *Bangkok Post*, 25 April 1967.

11. *Asian Wall Street Journal*, 8 September 1976.

12. *Bangkok Post*, 5 March 1991.

Chapter 9

1. *Financial Times* (London), 5 December 1990; see also *Bangkok Post*, 3 July 1967.

2. *Japan Times*, 4 October 1990.

3. *Far Eastern Economic Review* (Hong Kong), 30 January 1976. On Kukrit's role, see Steve Van Beek, ed., *Kukrit Pramoj: His Wit and Wisdom* (Bangkok: Duang Kamol, 1983), pp. 124, 135-36.
4. *Far Eastern Economic Review* (Hong Kong), 17 January 1991.
5. *Asian Finance* (Hong Kong), 15 October 1988.
6. *Far Eastern Economic Review* (Hong Kong), 22 August 1985.
7. See William N. Raiford, "Social Forestry," in *World Development* (New York: UNDP, November 1988), p. 12.
8. On Dhanin's career see *Asian Finance*, 15 November 1988; Peter Janssen, "The Not-so-Simple Art of Creating Wealth in Thailand," *Billion* (Hong Kong), 1987; and *World Executive's Digest*, March 1987, p. 26; on his agribusiness see Sanya Theimsiri, "CP Group propels Thailand into role as Regional Poultry Leader," *Agribusiness Worldwide*, March 1986, p. 23.
9. *Agribusiness Worldwide*, May 1986, p. 23.
10. See *Science and Technology in Transition*, (Bangkok: Thai Life, National Identity Board, 1985).
11. Supachai Lorlowahakarn in *Bangkok Post*, 22 October 1990; and *South China Morning Post*, 24 October 1989.
12. See *Asian Finance*, 15 March 1990.
13. See *Bangkok Post*, 7 November 1987 and 30 June 1991.
14. *Financial Times*, 8 November 1990.
15. *The Economist*, 26 January 1991.
16. William Warren, *Jim Thompson, the Legendary American of Thailand* (Bangkok: Thompson Thai Silk Co., 1990), pp. 68, 72-3.
17. We are indebted to Professor Patya Saihoo of the Chulalongkorn University Anthropology Department in this discussion.
18. Dr. Malinee Wongphanich, *Health and Safety Conditions in Manufacturing: Japan and Thailand* (Toyko: Asian Productivity Organisation, 1988), p. 54.
19. See Kunio Yoshihara, ed., *Thai Acceptance of Japanese Modernisation* (Kuala Lumpur: Falcon, 1989), p. 106.
20. Professor Thirasak Kumbanaruk of Thammasat University, "Japanese QCC in Thailand," unpublished; see also Surasak Sananukool, *Productivity Improvement Through QC Circles in Service Industry*, (Tokyo: APO, 1987).

Chapter 10

1. A well-traveled Thai businessman told a Western friend that Burma's present problems could be a delayed vengeance for the 1767 desecration of images at Ayutthaya. (William Warren, *Jim Thompson, the Legendary American of Thailand* (Bangkok: Thompson Thai Silk Co., 1990), p. 92.
2. Vichit Vatakan, quoted by Kamon Pensrinokun in Chaiwat Khamchoo, ed., *Thai-Japanese Relations in Historical Perspective* (Bangkok: Innomedia, 1988), p. 132.
3. *Far Eastern Economic Review* (Hong Kong), 12 June 1981.

4. David van Praagh, *Alone on the Sharp Edge, The Story of M. R. Seni Pramoj* (Bangkok: Duang Kamol, 1989) p. 113.
5. Sulak Sivaraksa, *Siamese Resurgence* (Bangkok: Asian Cultural Forum on Development, 1985) p. 274.
6. Joyce Rainat, "Building Bridges into Vietnam," *Asian Finance* (Hong Kong), 15 February 1991.
7. See the discussion by Atthavibool Srisuworanan and Pongsak Srisod in *The Nation* (Bangkok), 29 March 1990.
8. On General Chaovalit's visit to Burma in 1988, see, for example, *Bangkok Post*, 15 December 1988.
9. *Bangkok Post*, 23 February 1989.
10. See, for example, a Philippine report cited in *The Nation* (Bangkok), 16 October 1990.
11. For Chatichai's foreign-policy initiatives see Leszek Buszynski, "New Aspirations and Old Constraints in Thailand's Foreign Policy," *Asian Survey* (Berkeley, CA), November 1989, p. 1057; see also *The Nation* (Bangkok), 29 March 1990, 9 May 1990 and 19 October 1990.
12. See generally Suchit Bunbongkorn and Sukhumbhand Paribatra, "Thai Politics and Foreign Policy in the 1980s: Plus Ça Change, Plus C'est La Même Chose?", in *ASEAN in the Regional and Global Context* (Berkeley, CA: University of California Press, 1986), p. 52.

Chapter 11

1. "We hope to have a guerrilla war going in Thailand before the year is out"—Chen Yi quoted in *Far Eastern Economic Review* (Hong Kong), 10 February 1966.
2. Steve Van Beek, ed., *Kukrit Pramoj: His Wit and Wisdom* (Bangkok: Duang Kamol, 1983), p. 143.
3. *The Times* (London), 16 June 1980.
4. See also Du Yuting and Chen Lufan (of the Institute of South East Asian Studies, Kunming), "Did Kublai Khan's Conquest of the Dali Kingdom Give Rise to the Mass Migration of the Thai People to the South?" *The Journal of the Siam Society* 77, part 1 (1989), p. 33.
5. See generally Sukhumbhand Paribatra, *From Enmity to Alignment, Thailand's Evolving Relations with China* (Bangkok: Chulalongkorn University, 1987).
6. Quoted by Chaiwat Khamchoo in Chaiwat Khamchoo, ed., *Thai-Japanese Relations in Historical Perspective* (Bangkok, Innomedia, 1988), p. 263.
7. *Bangkok Post*, 15 January 1971.
8. *Bangkok Post*, 3 March 1991.
9. *The Nation* (Bangkok), 18 March 1989 (Ambassador Okazaki).
10. Quoted in Chaiwat, ed., *Thai-Japanese Relations in Historical Perspective*, p. 259.
11. Chatichai's remark was to Yozo Ishikawa, director of the Self-Defense Agency. The Malaysian comment was by Dr. Noordin Sopiee, director General

of Malaysia's Institute of Strategic and International Studies. See *The Nation* (Bangkok), 15 May 1990.

12. Abraham Lincoln courteously refused; see his letter to King Mongkut of 3 February 1862 in Abbot Low Moffat, *Mongkut, the King of Siam* (Ithaca, NY: Cornell University Press, 1961), pp. 94-5.
13. *Far Eastern Economic Review* (Hong Kong), 19 July 1984.
14. *Bangkok Post,* 9 March 1971.
15. See *Far Eastern Economic Review* (Hong Kong), 5 May 1988.
16. Princess Poon Pismai Diskul, *My First Impressions of Europe* (Bangkok, 1972) pp. 46-47.
17. *Bangkok Post,* 1 December 1970.
18. Benjamin Batson and Shimizu Hajime, "The Tragedy of Wanit," *Journal of South East Asian Studies* (Singapore), 1990, p. 37.
19. He wrote *Vampire Junction* (1984) and *The Shattered House* (1986).
20. *New York Times,* 31 October 1966.
21. *Far Eastern Economic Review* (Hong Kong), 8 June 1989.

Conclusion

1. John Stanton, *Time Magazine,* 3 April 1950.
2. *The Economist,* 25 June 1988.
3. Jurgen Ruland, "Continuity and Change in South East Asia," *Asian Survey* (Berkeley, CA), May 1990.

Epilogue

1. See Paul Handley in *Far Eastern Economic Review* (Hong Kong), 28 May and 4 June 1992.
2. *Financial Times,* 19 June 1992.
3. See Michael Richardson in *International Herald Tribune,* 22 May 1992; and also William Branigin (of *Washington Post*), 'Thai Generals Cling to their Posts and Corporate Seats; *International Herald Tribune,* 20 June 1992.
4. Jonathan Friedland, 'Cost of a Crisis,' *Far Eastern Economic Review* (Hong Kong), 28 May 1992.

SELECT BIBLIOGRAPHY

Anek Laothamatas. "Business and Politics in Thailand, New Patterns of Influence," *Asian Survey,* (Berkeley, CA), April 1988.

Botan. *Letters From Thailand.* Bangkok: DK Bookhouse,1977.

Chai-Anan Samudavanija. "Thailand: A Stable Semi-Democracy", in Larry Diamond ed., *Democracy in Developing Countries: Asia,Vol. 3.* Boulder, Co.: Lynne Rienner, 1989.

Chai-Anan Samudavanija, Kusuma Snitwongse, and Suchit Bunbongkarn. *From Armed Suppression to Political Offensive.* Bangkok: Institute of Security and International Studies, Chulalongkorn University, 1990.

GATT Trade Policy Review: Thailand. Geneva: GAM, June 1991.

Gray, Denis, ed. *The King of Thailand in World Focus.* Bangkok: Foreign Correspondents Club of Bangkok, 1988.

His Majesty King Bhumiphol Adulyadej, articles from *Sawasdee* magazine. Bangkok: Thai Airways International, 1988.

Jackson, Peter A. *Buddhism, Legitimation and Conflict: The Political Functions of Urban Thai Buddhism.* Singapore: University of Singapore Press, 1989.

Keys, Charles F. *Thailand—Buddhist Kingdom as Modern Nation-State.* Bangkok: Duang Kamol, 1989.

Klausner, William J. *Reflections on Thai Culture.* Bangkok: Prachandra, 1984.

Mulder, Niels. *Inside Thai Society, an Interpretation of Everyday Life.* Bangkok: Editions Duang Kamol, 1990.

Mushkat Miron. *Will the Jewel in the Southeast Asian Crown Continue to Shine?* Bangkok: Baring Securities, 1990.

Nostha Chartikavanij and David Scott. *A History of Thai Politics.* Bangkok: W. I. Carr, 1990.

———. *A History of Business in Thailand.* Bangkok: W. I. Carr, 1990.

Overholt, William H. "Thailand, A Moving Equilibrium", *Pacific Review* 1 (1988).

Pisan Suriamonkon. *Institutionalisation of Democratic Political Processes in Thailand: A Three-Pronged Democratic Polity.* Bangkok: Daneree Indrasuksri, 1989.

Rong Syamananda. *A History of Thailand.* Bangkok: Thai Watana Panich, 1977.

Somsakdi Xuto, ed. *Government and Politics of Thailand.* Oxford: Oxford University Press, 1987.

Stowe, Judith A. *Siam Becomes Thailand: A Story of Intrigue.* London: Hurst, 1991.

Suchit Bunbongkarn. "The Thai Military's Effort to Institutionalise its Political Role," *Pacific Review* 1, no. 4 (1988).

Sukhumbhand Paribatra. *From Emnity to Alignment, Thailand's Evolving Relations with China.* Bangkok: Chulalongkorn University, 1987.

Sulak Sivaraksa. *Siamese Resurgence.* Bangkok: Asian Cultural Forum on Development, 1985.

————. *Siam in Crisis.* Bangkok: Thai Inter-Religious Commission for Development, 1990.

Suntaree Komin. *Psychology of the Thai People.* Bangkok: National Institute of Development Administration, 1990.

Taylor, J. L. "New Buddhist Movements in Thailand: An Individualistic Revolution, Reform and Political Dissonance," *Journal of South East Asian Studies* (Singapore), March 1990.

Thak Chaloemtiarana. *Thailand, the Politics of Despotism.* Bangkok: Thammasat University, 1979.

Tonkin, Derek. "The Art of Politics in Thailand," *Asian Affairs* (London), 1990.

Van Beek, Steve, ed. *Kukrit Pramoj, His Wit and Wisdom.* Bangkok: Duang Kamol, 1983.

Van Praagh, David. *Alone on the Sharp Edge, The Story of M. R. Seni Pramoj.* Bangok: Duang Kamol, 1989.

Warren, William. *Jim Thompson, the Legendary American of Thailand.* Bangkok: Thompson Thai Silk Co., 1990.

Yoshihara, Kunio, ed. *Thai Acceptance of Japanese Modernisation.* Kuala Lumpur: Falcon, 1989.

————. *Japan in Thailand.* Kuala Lumpur: Falcon, 1990.

Yuangrat Wedel. *The Thai Radicals and the Communist Party.* Singapore: Maruzen Asia, 1983.

INDEX

Thai names have been listed by first name, as is customary in Thailand, not by surname.

Acharn Suan 99
Advanced Electronic Systems 115
Africa 143
Agriculture 111, 131-40
AIDS 63, 78-9, 127-9, 177
Air Force 22, 62, 185
Ajarn Saneh xiii, 113
Akihito, Emperor xxiii, 56
Amerasians 73
Ammar Siamwalla 134
Amnesty International 32
Amnuay Viravan xiii, 118
Ampha 83-4
Anand Panyarachun ix, xiii, xviii,
    10, 25, 46, 91, 117, 119, 127,
    160, 185-6
Ananda Mahidol, King ix, xvii,
    xxiii, 37
Anant Kanjanapas 145
Anek Srisanit xiii
Animism 97
Antique shops 100
Anuman Rajadhon, Phra 88
Arbor Acres 138
Armstrong, Louis xviii
Arms procurement 13, 164
Army 3, 7-25, 58
    and business 12-13, 23, 115
    and politics 14-22, 178
    factions 22-24, 185
Arsa Sarasin xiii, 92
Art-Ong Jumsai 142

Arthit Kamlang-ek ix, 7, 15, 21, 23,
    40, 44, 105
Asia Trust Bank 68
Asia and Pacific Council 181
Asian Center for Population and
    Community Development 127
Asian Institute of Technology 125
Asian Productivity Organization 146
Association of Southeast Asian Na-
    tions (ASEAN) xii, 146, 155,
    159-60, 164
Astrology 87, 98
Australia 89, 91, 122
Austria 9
Automobiles 144
Ayutthaya 41, 84, 150

Baan Na 124
Bacho 56
Baht xi, 113, 115-7, 158
    devaluation 113
Ban Ping 133
Bang Chan 76
Bangladesh 25, 125, 144
Bangkok 121-25
    sinking 125
Bangkok Bank x, 91, 93, 110, 117-8,
    131, 141-3
Bangkok Glass 124
Bangkok Post xii
Bangpa-In Paper Mill 114
Bank Asia Finance One 115

Bank of Ayudhya 92
Bank of Thailand 77, 109, 112, 114-6
Bankruptcy 117
Bata 124
Battambang 153
Beijing University 90
Belgium 140, 143
Bhai Kao 169
Bhichai Rattakul xiii, 42, 48, 84,
    121
Bhisadej Rajani, Prince 60
Bhumiphol Adulyadej, King ix,
    xiii, xv-xxiv, 3, 11, 29, 32, 36,
    47, 53-63, 110, 121, 139, 170,
    179, 185-6
    and 1991 coup 8, 184-5
    as god xix, 176
    as monk 101
    finances 54-5
    health 63
    music xviii
    rural development projects xx,
    55-60, 156
Bhuping Palace 8, 57
Black September hijack (1972) 9
Bodirak, Phra xiii, 104
Boonchu Rojanasathien 15, 44, 91,
    117-8, 141
Boonsanong Punyodyana 29
Boonsong Chalethorn 41
Brahmanism 97-8
Brando, Marlon 43, 126
Brazil 111
Breweries 140
Bristol University 117
Britain 73, 102, 115, 117, 151-3,
    160, 167, 170, 172, 175-6, 178,
    180-1
British Telecom 39, 115, 140
Brunei 144, 159
Brynner, Yul xix
Buddhism 5, 33, 49-50, 66-8, 70-1,
    80, 87-8, 97-106, 160, 165, 178

    and economy 108, 112, 117
    and family planning 127
    and farming 132
    missionaries 102
    monks 49, 99-102
    in development 102, 105-6
    in politics 49, 104
    women 78, 103-4
    Supreme Patriarch 8, 101, 104
Buffaloes 133
Bumble Bee Seafoods 136
Bunchoog Ciamwirija 50
Bunnags 42
Bureaucracy 46-7
Burma 4-5, 9, 25, 32, 44, 72, 74,
    84, 107, 117, 122, 149-51, 153,
    156-9, 161, 164, 167-8, 176, 178,
    180
Businessmen 47-8

Cabbages and Condoms 127
Cairo 9
Calcium carbonate 84
Cambodia 41, 53, 99, 117, 122, 149-
    60, 165, 176, 178-80
Cambridge University 171
Canada 144
Canton 103
Cantonese 85, 87
Capital Finance and Securities 91
Carroll, Lewis 65
Cement 84, 143
Center to Promote Knowledge of De-
    mocracy 29
Chai-Anan Samudavanija xiii, 15,
    93
Chalerm Yubamrung ix, xiii, 17,
    21, 34-35
Chali Sophonpanich 91, 142
Chamlong Srimuang ix, xi, xiii, 16-
    17, 38, 44, 50, 54, 90, 104, 110,
    123, 183-5
Chao Phrya River 121, 149

Chaovalit Yongchaiyudh ix, 12, 14-
15, 17, 19, 23, 36, 44-46, 123,
135, 158, 164, 185
Charit Tingsabadh xiii
Charles, Prince xx
Charn Sophonpanich xiii, 91
Charoen Pokphand group xi, 39,
119, 131, 137-40, 143, 164
Chart Thai xi, 9, 13, 24, 31, 39, 42-
3, 116, 144
Chatichai Choonhavan ix, xi xxii, 4,
7-10, 13, 15-17, 19-21, 23-24, 35,
37, 42-3, 46, 54, 71, 98, 111, 116-
7, 119, 144, 157-8, 160, 163, 165-
6, 171-2, 180, 183
Chatri Sophonpanich 91, 118
Chatsiri Sophonpanich 91
Chayachoke Chulasiriwongs xiii
Chen Lufan 164
Chen Yi 163
Cheshire cat 65
Chearavanont family 138
Chia Ek Chaw 137-8
Chia Seaw Whooy 138
Chiang Mai 7-8, 38, 70, 98, 151,
177
Chicago Art Institute 169
Chickens 131, 135-6, 138
Childers' *English-Pali Dictionary* 74
Children 32
Chin Sophonpanich 91, 118, 122
China 5, 13, 30, 41, 44, 66, 72, 86,
93, 107, 111, 125, 137-8, 140,
153-7, 160, 163-5, 167, 172, 180-1
Thais' origin in 83, 149, 164
trade 135
Chinese immigrants 4, 83-95, 104,
126, 138, 160, 163, 178, 181
assimilation 88-9, 93-4, 165
Christians 87, 92
complexion 73, 87
discrimination against 89-90
double identity 89
education 86-7
in business 13, 46, 86, 90-2
in politics 90
names 88
New Year ritual 83
newspapers 87
visit China 93
Chirayu Issarangkun na Ayuthaya
xiii, 55
Chitralada Palace xv, xxi
Chodchoy Sophonpanich 91, 122
Choedchu Sophonpanich 91
Chongsarit Dhanasobhon xiii
Chote Sophonpanich xiii, 91, 93,
118
Chow Kwanyun 88, 90-1
Christianity 87, 100, 102, 150
Chudhawatchara 62
Chula, Prince 72-3
Chulabhorn, Princess 62-3, 128
Chulachomklao Military Academy
23-4, 43
Chulalongkorn, King ix, xv, xvii,
xix, 54, 78, 151, 168
Chulalongkorn University 19, 29-
30, 48, 72, 126, 159
Chupong Kanchanalak xiii
Churchill, Winston 127
Cigarettes 111, 170
Clausewitz, Carl von 15
Coconuts 102
Cohen, Yvan xiii
Cold War 152-4
Commission on Counter-Corruption
37
Communist party 11, 30-31, 41, 60,
99, 106, 161, 163, 169
Condoms 127, 178
Confucianism 66, 93
Contract farming 139
Cornell University 31
Corruption 17, 36-39, 50
Costume 74

Coup of 1991   xxii-xxiii, 3, 7-11,
    54, 140, 146, 183
Coups   27
Cremation   88
Crimes passionelles   69
Crown Properties Bureau   54-5
Cuisine   70-1
Curry   71

Dalai Lama   105, 164
Damrong Krishnamara   118
Debt   117
Democrat Party   29, 38, 42, 48, 84
Democratic Soldiers   14, 23-24, 44,
    113
Democracy   xvi, 32-40
Deng Xiaoping   164
Denmark   115
Dependency theory   113
Dhammakaya   xi, 105
Dhammic socialism   105
Dhanin Chearavanont   ix, xiii, 87,
    137-41, 147
Dharma   xi
Direk Patmasiriwat   xiii
Divorce   77
Dollar   xii
Domino   154, 164, 179
Dow Chemical   143
Drugs   157, 183
Dumri Konuntakiat   136
Dusit Thani group   77

Eastern Seaboard   125, 141, 143
Economist, The   181
Education   124
Elections   27, 33, 186
Electricity   124, 156
Electricity Generating Authority of
    Thailand   119, 157
Electronics   144
Elizabeth, Queen   xxii

Embree, John   76
Emerald Buddha   8, 99, 169
Engineering   142
Erawan Hotel   114
Ethics   80-1
Eton   171
Eucalyptus   136-7
European Community   135, 144, 172
Extraterritoriality   151, 169

Face   34-6, 60, 67-8, 71, 78, 81, 185
Face of Thai Feudalism, The   28
Family   76-7, 81
    planning   126-7, 134
Farang   xi
Fast foods   74, 138
Festivals   70
Fine Arts Department   100
First World War   151
Fish   55, 121
    tuna   136
Foreign investment   114
Forests   122, 136-7
France   30, 151-2, 172, 176, 180-1
Free Thai Movement   152
Friendship Highway   141
Fujitsu   144
Fukuda Takeo   98
Fukuoka Masanobu   132
Fun   69-70

Gandhi, Mahatma   74
General Agreement on Trade and
    Tariffs (GATT)   4, 111
Georgia   115
Germany   74, 136, 143, 147, 177
Glass   143-4
Gleneagles   43
Goddard, Paulette   145
Godfathers   34
Golden Triangle   57, 157
Golkar   15

Good Samaritan 66
Goodman, Benny xvi, xviii
Gorky, Maxim 31
Grand Hyatt Erawan Hotel 97, 114
Greater East Asia Co-prosperity
    Sphere 152
Greece 170
"Green Revolution" 133, 135
Gross Domestic Product xii
GSS Electronics 115, 144
Guardian, The 3
Gulf War 108, 110, 147

Hainan island 84, 92
Hakkas 84, 92
Hanoi 158
Harvard University xviii, 66, 90
Hats 6, 50, 66
Health 124, 126-9
Heinecke, Bill 74
Heineken 140
Heroin 45
Hierarchy 76
Hilltribes 56-7, 102, 153, 156, 179
Hilton Hotel 77
Hirohito, Emperor xxiii
Hmong 57, 59
Ho Chi Minh 29, 113
Ho Chi Minh City 158
Holland 176, 181
Hollywood xix, 76
Homosexuality 21, 23, 44, 67, 79-80
Honda 140
Hong Kong 42, 91, 103, 109, 111,
    114-5, 117, 124, 135, 138, 141,
    144-5, 155
Hu, Jack 142
Human rights 32

IBM 144
Inchcape 87
India xxiii, 5, 33, 51, 74, 97, 102,
    108, 135, 142, 150, 152, 178

Indians 92
Individualism 68-9, 76, 81, 146
Indochina xii, 4, 157-8, 160, 172,
    180
Indonesia 4-5, 15, 25, 48, 51, 87,
    94, 107, 138, 140, 149, 159, 172,
    176, 180-1
Industrial policy 141-5
Industrial safety 146
Inflation 116
Infrastructure 119
Intellectual property rights 111
International Court of Justice 53
Irrigation 56
Isarn xi, 12, 156
Islam 87, 160
Italy 102

Jalaprathan Cement 143
Japan 5, 27, 48, 51, 56, 62, 66-7,
    86, 94, 98, 111-2, 134, 141, 145,
    156, 163, 165-7, 170, 172, 180-1
    aid 166
    in Pacific War 152, 165, 169
    investment 114-6, 144-7
    joint maneuvers 160
Jazz xviii
Jaturporn Pronpan 185
Jensen, Peter 61
Jiang Qing 31
Jit Pumisak 28
Johnson, Lyndon 171
Joint Public-Private Consultative
    Committee on Economic Prob-
    lems 113-4
Journalism 48
Juan Carlos, King xxiii
Jutaba, Roy 142

Kanala Sukhabanji-Khantaprab 19
Karens 72
Karma xi, 33, 97, 105
Karnow, Stanley 65

Kasem Kasemsri xiii
Kaset Ronjanil 185
Kasetsart University 57, 110, 166
Kenya 142
Khao Phra Viharn temple 154
Khien Theeravit xiii
Khmer Rouge 154-5, 165
Khmers 72, 149
King and Agriculture in Thailand, The 58
King and I, The xix, 6, 167
Kissing 6, 66, 79
Klongs 122, 125
Korea 9, 25, 51, 109, 111, 114, 134, 141-2, 145, 177-8
Korn Dabaransi 160
Kosal Sindhavananda 143
Kra Canal Scheme 91
Kraisak Choonhavan 22
Kriangsak Chomanan ix, 23, 31, 38, 41, 44, 46, 54, 67, 157, 164
Krirkkiat Phipatseritham xiii, 142
Kukrit Pramoj ix, xiii, 17, 29, 36, 38, 43-4, 67, 72-3, 83, 134, 163
Kunming 164

Labor 145-7
Laem Chabang 119
Lamsam 92
Land sharing 124
Landon, Kenneth 92
Language 76, 87, 159
Laos 29, 41, 44, 72, 105, 117, 149-54, 156-8, 164-5, 178-80
Law, David 69
League of Nations 151-2
Lee Kuan Yew 31, 88
Leopheiratana brothers 143
Lersak Sombatsiri 77
Lèse-majesté 60-1
Letters from Thailand 84, 88-9
Likhit Dhiravegin 123

Lincoln, Abraham 167
Literacy 124
Loi Krathong 70
London School of Economics (LSE) 77, 135
"Loose structure" 76, 80-1
Louvre 169
Lyman, David xiii

Ma, Johnny 88
Mabtaphut 119, 143
Malays 72, 179
Malaysia xxiii, 5, 87, 94, 102, 108, 138, 151, 159-61, 166-9, 178-9, 181
Male chauvinism 77, 104
Manoon Rupkachorn ix, 22-3
Mao Zedong 163-4
Marcos, Imelda 108
Marijuana 73
Marxism 23, 41, 53, 113, 152-3, 168
Massachusetts Institute of Technology (MIT) 61, 90
Masturbation 78
Matichon 48, 168
Maugham, Somerset 147
McDonald's 102
McNamara, Robert 77
Mechai Viravaidhya ix, xiii, 10, 72-3, 79, 126-8
Meditation 105-6, 147
Mekhong Whisky 99
Mekong River 149, 152-3, 156-7
Mercedes 105-6
Middle-class 81
Milk 57
Millfield School 62
Ministry of Commerce 106
Ministry of Education 102
Mitsubishi Motors 144
Mitsui 115
Mixed marriages 72-3

Moerman, Michael 133-4
Monarchy 47, 50-1, 53-63, 84, 157, 178
Mongkul Kanjanapas 145
Mongkut, King ix, xv-xvii, xix-xx, 6, 49, 101-2, 108, 134, 150-1, 167-8, 176
Monopolies 143
Mons 72, 149
Montri Pongpanich 44
More, Thomas 31
Mormons 100, 103
Motorcycles 140
Mountbatten, Lord Louis 152
Muang Thai 75
Mukdahan 156
Multi-Fibre Agreement 170
Murder rate 69

Nam Choan dam 122
Nam prick 70
Nan Suntasilo, Abbott 105-6
Napoleon Bonaparte 169
Narathiwat 160
Naresuan, King 150
Narong Wongwan 45, 183
Nart Tuntawiroon 125
Nation, The 10, 39, 45
National Assembly 53
National Convention xvi, 29
National Economic and Social Development Board 114
National Economic and Social Development Plan 108
National Paramilitary Club 15, 61
National Petrochemical Corporation 143
Natural gas 143
Navapol 29
Ne Win 153, 157
Neurosis 69
New Aspiration Party 18, 24, 43-4
New York University 92

New Yorker 100
Newland, Tobias xiii
Newly Industrialized Economy (NIE) xii, 2 108-9, 111-2, 123-4, 141, 145, 147, 171
Nigeria 144
Nissan 144
Ng Yuk Long 92
Nong Wah 131
Nongkhai 157
Northeast 58, 61, 124-5, 156
Nuclear physics 61
Nuensaensut 131, 139

Ogan, Billy 73
Oil 43, 118-9
Opium 57, 59, 98, 153
Opium War 151
Oriental Hotel 74, 145, 147
Orwell, George 31
Oxford University xvii, 42-3, 66

Pakistan 153
Palang Dharma xi, 16, 38, 44, 104
Pali 74
Palm trees 102
Pan Bunnag 80
Paribatra, Prince 37
Patpong Road 84, 90
Paris 112
Pathet Lao 153
Pattani 160
Pattaya 9
Patya Saihoo xiii
Pearl Buck Foundation 73
Petrochemicals 140, 142
Pey Osathanagrah 92
Phaendin Nee Kong Krai 166
Phao Siyanond 13, 42
Pharmaceuticals 92
Phaulkon, Constantine 170
Philippines 33, 67, 73, 108, 153, 159
Phillips, Herbert 76, 97

Phin Choonhavan 13, 23, 42
Phisit Pakkasem 114
Phitsanulok 99
Phnom Rung 169
Phra xi
Phra Buddhadhasa 68, 105
Phra Dhammachayo 105
Phra Kittivudho 106
Phra Lokanat 102
Phra Phuttha Chinnarat 99
Phra Siam Thevathiraj 8
Phrakru Sakorn 101
Phuket 119, 122
Phibul Songkram ix, 5, 22, 27, 36,
48, 50, 55, 66, 70, 85-6, 90-1,
107, 126, 152, 158, 163, 169
Pigs 57, 131, 156
Pitpreecha Prasertkul 30-1
Plan to Destroy Buddhism, The 103
Pol Pot 154
Polarization of incomes 123
Pollution 121
Polygamy 77, 88
Pongsak 48, 168
Poon Pat 84, 90
Poon Pisamai Diskul, Princess 78
Population and Community Develop-
ment Association 126
Population growth 2, 126, 129
Pork 84, 88
Portugal 138
Pote Sarasin 92
Prachakorn Thai 42
Prajadhipok, King x, xvii, 37
Pramarn Adireksarn 42
Pramual Sabhavasu 108, 116
Praphas Charusathien x, 13, 19, 28,
53, 99
Prasert Sapsunthorn x, 11, 23
Prasit Tansuvan xiii
Prasong Soonsiri 18
Pratheep Ungsongthon 68

Praves Wasi 79, 128, 132
Prayoon Chanyawongse 79
Prem Tinsulanond x, 3, 15, 18-21,
23, 31, 35, 38, 43, 47, 54, 67,
113, 115, 117, 127, 144
Press 48
Price Waterhouse 142
Pridi Panomyong x, 48, 90, 112-3,
152
Prisoners of war 67
Private enterprise 107-8, 141
Privatization 114
Prok Amranand xiii
Pronouns 76
Prostitution 78-9
Prostration xix
Psychology of Thai People 34
Puang Chon Chao Thai 15, 44
Puey Ungpakorn x, 13, 93, 110, 126

Quality Control Circles 147
Queen Sirikit National Convention
Center 147

R and D 142-3
Race 72-4, 168-9
Rainmaking 55
Rama II, King 83
Ramkhamhaeng, King 108
Ramkhamhaeng University 18, 49
Rassadorn Party 16, 44
Ratanarak 92
Rawee Wanpen 23
Reagan, Ronald 35
Red Gaurs 29, 42
Refugees 32, 153-5
Regional Container Lines 115
Reincarnation 88, 99
Rice 13, 84, 106, 111, 132, 134-5,
157
Rolls Royce 105, 112
Rome 102

Royal barges 150
Royal Development Study Centers 57
Royal Hilltribe Development Project 57
Royal Rain-making Research and Development Project 55
Russia 72-3, 135, 172, 180-1

Sabah 159
Saeksan Prasertkul xiii, 30, 48
Saen Kampolkrang 137
Saha Union Co. 115
Sahaviraya 143
Saisuree Chutikul 77
Salyaveth Lekagul 142
Samak Sundaravej 42, 90
Samakkee Temple 105
Samakkee Tham xi, 24, 44-5, 183, 185
Sangha xi, 8, 49, 99, 101, 104
Santi Asoke xi, 16, 104
Sanuk xi, 69-70, 76
Saowabha, Queen 78
Sapha Patiwat 24
Sapin Luang Presbyterian Chinese Church 87
Sarasin family 92, 102
Sarawak 159
Sarit Thanarat x, 13, 28, 36, 53, 78, 86, 91, 107, 156
Savannakhet 156
Savitri Sophonpanich 91
Science 142
Scotland 72, 126
Seaford 62
Second World War 152, 176
Seiko 145
Seni Pramoj x, xiii, 29, 40, 42, 83, 152, 157
Sex 78-80, 126-8, 147, 178
Shanghai 140
Shans 149, 157

Shantou 91, 137-8
Shell 115
Shenzhen 140
"Siam" 75
Siam Cement Co. 54, 143-4, 147
Siam City Cement 143
Siam Commercial Bank 54
Siam Motors 77
Siam Rath 43
Siddhi Savetsila 44, 73, 166
Siem Reap 153
Sihanouk, Prince 99, 154-5, 178
Silk 100, 145-6
Singapore 31, 51, 88, 102, 109, 111, 114-5, 117, 124, 138, 141, 144-5, 155, 159, 181
Sino-Thai xii, 42, 73, 85, 87-94, 103, 112, 164-5, 177
Sirikit, Queen x, xviii, xx, 56, 61
Sirilak Patanakorn 77
Sirindhorn, Princess x, xxi, 56, 62-3, 78
Sithi-Amnuai, Paul 135
Smile 65, 69, 81-2
Smutara Mekchaidee 140
Snoh Unakul xiii, 110, 112, 114, 117
Soamsawali Kittiyakra 62
Social Action Party 29, 36, 43-4, 98
"Social capitalism" 124
Social security 123
Socialism 112-3
Sodomy 99
Solidarity 44
Solvay 140, 143
Somporn Surarith 124
Somsak T. 81
Somsakdi Xuto xiii, 29, 145
Somtow S. P. 171
Song 105
Songham Panyadee 45
Songkhla 119

Songkran 70
Sophonpanich family x, 91-2, 117
Sophonpanich, Robin 91
Southeast Asia xii
Southeast Asia Treaty Organization
    (SEATO) 11, 92, 153-4, 160,
    164, 169
Southern seaboard 125
Spices 70-1
Spontaneity 69
Spoons 70
Squatters 124
Sri Mariamme Hindu Temple 102
Sriracha 135, 139
Srirat Satapanavat 166
Stanford University 90
Steel 142-3
Stelux 145
Stickles, Gary 144
Stock exchange 77, 99, 116
Strikes 146
Student massacre of 1976 30, 69
Student uprising of 1973 28-29
Students 48-9
Suan Mokh xi, 105
Suchaat Kosonkittiwong 88, 99
Suchinda Kraprayoon x, xvi, xxiii,
    7-8, 10, 18-19, 21-2, 24, 36, 44-5,
    48, 50, 54, 183-5
Suchit Bunbongkorn xiii
Sudsai Hasdin 42
Sukhumbhand Paribatra xiii, 37
Sulak Sivaraksa x, xiii, xix, 32-33,
    61, 74, 87, 110
Sumitomo 143
Sumitr Pitiphat xiii, 109
Summary justice 28
Suntaree Komin 34
Sunthorn Kongsompong x, xvi,
    xxii, 7-8, 19, 22, 77, 183
Suparb Yossandara 77
Suphat Wibulseth 139

Sura Chansrichawla 92
Surnames 5, 88
Suthee Arkasruerk 37
Suthep 77
Suthichai Yoon 10, 45
Suwannaphum 158-9
Switzerland 9, 55, 63

Tai 72
Taiwan 104, 109, 111, 114, 116,
    138, 141-2, 145, 177
Taksin, King 84
Tan Piak Chin 91
Tantalum 122
Tapioca 135
Tarrant, David xiii
Tawat Yip In Isoi 157
Tawee Kanthong 133
Teh clan 84
Telecommunications 39, 119, 140-1
Telephone Organization of Thailand
    11
Television 144
Temples 88
Teochew 84, 87
Textiles 145-6
Thai Airways International 11, 102,
    114
Thai Environmental and Community
    Development Association 122
Thai Farmers Bank 92
Thai Military Bank 12
Thai Petrochemical Industry 143
Thai Red Cross 61
"Thailand" 75
Thailand Business 123
Thailand Development Research In-
    stitute 121, 123
Thaiviet Invexim 157
Thaksin Shinawatra 144
Thammasat University 16, 28-31,
    41, 69, 79, 109, 123, 142, 169

Thanat Khoman xiii, 154
Thanin Kraivixien x, 31, 73, 79, 98
Thanom Kittikachorn x, 13, 28-30,
53, 126, 134
Thatcherism 42
Thawin Rawangphai 103, 135
Theh Chongkhadikij xiii
Thiam Chokwatana 92
Thibaw, King 178
Thienchai Sirisamphan 16, 44
Thirayuth Boonmee xiii, 30, 48, 60
Thompson, Jim 100, 145-6
Tibet 164
Tien Hee 92
Tilapia 55-7
Tom yam 70
Tongbai Tongpao 32
Tongroj Onchan xiii, 110
Tonkin, Derek xiii
Toshiba 77
Tourism 79, 127, 147
Trade 118
Trade unions 76, 146
Turkey 138
Typewriters 99

U Nu 150, 153
Ubol Ratana, Princess 61
Ugly American, The 43, 126
UN Convention on the Rights of the
Child 32
UN Economic and Social Commis-
sion for Asia and the Pacific
(ESCAP) 149
UNESCO 149
UN Food and Agriculture Organiza-
tion (FAO) 55, 58, 149
UN Security Council 86
Uncle Go 73
Ungphakorn, Peter Mytri xiii
Unicord 115, 135

United States xvii, 5, 13, 45, 73, 94,
115, 142, 151-5, 160, 169-72, 180-1
aid 10, 107, 141, 152, 169
bases 153-4, 169-70
GIs 73, 79, 170
investment 114-5
Thai immigrants in 171
trade 111, 136, 144, 170
Universal suffrage 27
University of California 76, 133
Utis Narksavat 99

Vajiralongkorn, Crown Prince x,
xxi, 9, 30, 56, 61-2, 77-8
Vajiravudh, King x, xvii, 5, 54, 79-
80, 85
Vasectomy 127
Vattana, King 178
Versailles Peace Conference 151
Vichit Supanit xiii, 117
Vichit Suraphongchai xiii
Victoria, Queen 98, 167
Vientiane 156-7
Vietnam xxiii, 30, 32, 41, 44, 53,
72, 101-2, 105, 107, 117, 135,
149, 151-2, 154-61, 163, 165,
168, 172, 176, 178-80
Vietnam War 153-4
Violence 69, 86, 179, 184-5
Vitoon Osathanonah 142
Volvo 124
Voromai Kabilsingh 104

Wachtveitl, Kurt 147
Wallace, Bob xiii
Wallop Tarnvanichkul 88
Wan, Prince 74
Washington Post 65
Wat Borvornnives 101
Watcharee Chanmansin 73
Watches 145
Water-splashing 70

Wats   xi, 100
Wattana Iambamroong   76
Westernization   5, 50, 66, 81, 93, 168
*Whence Came the Thai Race?—An
    Inquiry*   164
White elephants   xv-xvii
Wibul Khemchalerm   132-3
Wild Tigers   85
Women   27, 77-9
Wong Chiming   145
World Bank   77, 107, 117, 123, 141-
    2, 147
World Competitiveness Report   147
World Fellowship of Buddhists   78
World Health Organization   142

Yala   160
Yamada Nagamasa   170
Yoshida Shigeru   166
Young Turks   23, 35, 113
Yunnan   9

Zhou Enlai   31, 43, 165